Essays on the Behavioral Study of Politics

 **ESSAYS ON THE**

UNIVERSITY OF ILLINOIS PRESS, URBANA, 1962

BEHAVIORAL STUDY OF POLITICS

EDITED FOR THE INTERNATIONAL POLITICAL SCIENCE ASSOCIATION BY

Austin Ranney

Foreword

Having as its assigned chief objective "to promote the advancement of political science throughout the world," especially by "facilitating the spread of information about significant developments in political science," the International Political Science Association was bound to concern itself with the discussion between "behaviorists" and "nonbehaviorists" which for several years has enlivened professional journals and conferences, especially in the United States.

Could this discussion be considered a private affair of American political science in which the International Association need not appear? The conspicuously sudden vogue of "behavioral studies," given a position of high prestige by the foundations, undoubtedly caused the tendency of certain eminent scholars outside the United States to confuse, reprovingly, the "political behavior school" with all of American political science; and their skepticism about the tendencies toward "scientism" was sometimes justified. In the United States, a certain failure to recognize work done in other countries, due in part to linguistic difficulties, but also, in some cases, to an exclusive interest in American problems, could for some years lend credence to the idea that "behavioral studies" were characteristic only of the United States.

In reality, as the variety of papers assembled in the present volume well shows, it is undoubtedly normal in many countries that progress in methods of inquiry and contact with the other sciences of man—psychology, sociology, economics, anthropology—should have given rise in some scholars to new concerns about the precision of basis data and the formulation of explanatory hypotheses.

This twofold aspiration for precision of the data (and for their measurement, when they are measurable, and sometimes when they are not) and for a more rigorous theoretical formulation, certainly seems to characterize the political scientists who rally under the banner of "political behavior." In the presentation of their hopes, and especially of their criticisms, the political behaviorists have certainly committed some injustices; the results of studies they have conducted with exemplary methodology may sometimes be trivial; their hypotheses are sometimes very banal—all this is quite true and regrettable and should be severely criticized. It is equally true that despite their inadequacies and their excesses, the behavioral studies have enriched the corpus of political science, and their contribution continues to gain in importance in proportion as the behaviorists discover the interest of historical comparisons, the necessity of going beyond national limitations, and the importance of problems raised by political philosophers.

The round table convened by the International Political Science Association at the University of Michigan in September, 1960, and splendidly organized by Professor V. O. Key, who has done so much for the rigorous and balanced development of behavioral studies, marked a stage in the discussion, not its end. The usefulness of this first international convocation on recent developments in the behavioral study of politics seemed so obvious to the Executive Committee of the International Political Science Association that they deemed it desirable to continue and expand the discussion. Accordingly, they placed on the agenda of the Fifth World Congress of the Association, convened at Paris in September, 1961, a topic on "The Contribution of Studies of Political Behavior." Professor Austin Ranney, whom I wish to thank for having undertaken the difficult task of revising the papers presented at Ann Arbor for the preparation of the present volume, was designated rapporteur-general for the topic. Aided by Professor Warren E. Miller as associate rapporteur-general, he was able to invite new papers and preside over the discussion, which showed the interest scholars all over the world have in studies of political behavior as well as the richness and the convergence of leading studies conducted in a large number of countries in recent years.

It was thanks to the generous assistance of the American Political Science Association, and the University of Michigan, to both of whom I wish to express our deep gratitude, that the Ann Arbor

Round Table was held. Particular thanks are due to our host, Professor James K. Pollock, Chairman of the Department of Political Science at the University of Michigan and one of the leading spirits of the International Political Science Association, of which he was President from 1955 to 1958. He showed once again a measure of energy, efficiency, and cordiality which counted for much in the success of the meeting. It remains, finally, to thank, in addition to Professor Key, who planned the program, and Professor Ranney, who prepared the present volume, all the authors and all the participants in the round table. The quality of their contribution has well justified the choice of the topic and the efforts of the organizers.

JACQUES CHAPSAL
Administrator of the *Fondation Nationale des Sciences Politiques,* and
President of the International Political Science Association

Preface

"The unexamined life," said Socrates, "is not worth the living." However deficient may be the professional lives of political scientists in other respects, they have long deserved high marks on at least this score. From its origins in the nineteenth-century fragmentation of history, political economy, and jurisprudence to the present, political science has often been as concerned with methodological questions of *how* to study politics as with substantive questions of *what* political reality is like.

The most recent and perhaps most intense eruption of this perennial self-scrutiny has come in the years since World War II, a period which has produced more—and, in the present writer's opinion, better—analyses of the methodology of political science than any comparable period in the past.[1]

Although these analyses have dealt with many different controversies, the most prominent has been that concerning something called "political behavior." One noteworthy feature of this particular dispute has been the inability of the antagonists to agree on just what they disagree about. Some have seen "political behavior" as merely the study of voting. Others have regarded it as any and all efforts to emphasize the "science" in "political science." Still others have seen it as a proposal to abandon institutions and ideol-

---

[1] A representative though by no means exhaustive list includes: D. Easton, *The Political System* (New York: Alfred A. Knopf, 1953); E. Voegelin, *The New Science of Politics* (Chicago: University of Chicago Press, 1952); C. S. Hyneman, *The Study of Politics* (Urbana: University of Illinois Press, 1959); R. Young, ed., *Approaches to the Study of Politics* (Evanston, Ill.: Northwestern University Press, 1958); and V. Van Dyke, *Political Science: A Philosophical Analysis* (Stanford, Calif.: Stanford University Press, 1960).

ogies as objects of study and units of analysis and to concentrate instead on the psychology of individuals in political situations. This disagreement about the meaning of "political behavior," however, has not noticeably dampened the vigor of the debate about whether it is a good thing.

The roots of today's behavioral movement in political science lie in the works of such distinguished European scholars as Max Weber, Graham Wallas, Andre Siegfried, and Herbert Tingsten. Its post-1945 development, however, has been primarily the work of Americans. In recent years it has drawn increasing attention and comment, by no means all laudatory, from political scientists in other parts of the world.[2] Thus, in planning the program for an international round table conference to be held at the University of Michigan, September 12-15, 1960, the Executive Committee of the International Political Science Association planned "a consideration of the study of political behavior as practiced by American political scientists." They invited one of its most distinguished practitioners, Professor V. O. Key, Jr., of Harvard University, to serve as rapporteur-general and the present writer to serve as his associate.

In executing the Executive Committee's charge, Professor Key and I took the view that "political behavior" is most usefully conceived as an *approach* to the study of *all* political phenomena rather than as the study of any particular area or subdivision of those phenomena. We further took the view that the nature, achievements, and problems of the behavioral approach are better identified and evaluated in the course of considering the findings of substantive behavioral research than in disputations about method isolated from substance.

Accordingly, we invited papers from behaviorally oriented scholars in several subdivisions of American political science in the hope that our sample, while hardly random, might indicate the variety of problems to which the behavioral approach has been applied as well as some of the ramifications of the approach itself. We gained added dimensions for the program from a number of papers by scholars from other nations.

When the Ann Arbor conference adjourned, the president of the International Political Science Association, M. Jacques Chapsal,

---

[2] Cf. B. Crick, *The American Science of Politics, Its Origins and Conditions* (Berkeley and Los Angeles: University of California Press, 1959); and D. E. Butler, *The Study of Political Behaviour* (London: Hutchinson, 1958).

suggested that a volume be prepared comparable to the one which grew out of the round table conference on pressure groups held at the University of Pittsburgh in 1957.[3] The undersigned agreed to serve as editor, and the present volume is the result.

With one exception, the papers presented here were all written for the Ann Arbor conference and have been revised by their authors for publication. The exception is Evron M. Kirkpatrick's opening paper on "The Impact of the Behavioral Approach on Traditional Political Science." This paper, which provides a proper prelude for the many-themed fugue which follows, was initially prepared for another occasion. The editor was able to levy on an old friendship to persuade its author to revise it for inclusion here.

A number of persons have helped to make the preparation of this volume notably less dull and wearisome than such chores usually are. The authors have taken time from their busy lives to make careful revisions of their original papers, and have been both cheerful and forebearing in dealing with the editor's importunings. M. Chapsal and the efficient and considerate secretary-general of the International Political Science Association, M. Serge Hurtig, have frequently given needed moral support. Above all, however, the editor wishes to absolve Professor V. O. Key, Jr., from whatever outrages this volume perpetrates on the Ann Arbor program. The editor also wishes to make the public claim that his year of admiringly following Professor Key up the intellectual heights, through the organizational swamps, and sometimes down the psychological depths of arranging an international scholarly convocation has qualified him for membership in a distinguished and fortunate body: the students of V. O. Key.

AUSTIN RANNEY

Urbana
September 1, 1961

---

[3] H. W. Ehrmann, ed., *Interest Groups on Four Continents* (Pittsburgh: University of Pittsburgh Press, 1958).

Contents

The Impact of the Behavioral Approach on Traditional Political Science

Evron M. Kirkpatrick

AMERICAN POLITICAL SCIENCE ASSOCIATION

My major purpose in this essay is to discuss the impact of the behavioral approach on traditional political science. Like all purposes, this one imposes limits, and I want to discuss briefly these limitations. I do not intend to deal with government or politics *per se* but with political scientists and with what they do; I do not intend to deal with political scientists from Plato to the present but with political scientists and their activities in recent years.

Further, my general emphasis is on the methodology of political science, and this emphasis suggests a further limitation. The term methodology is an ambiguous one, and I want to clarify my understanding and use of the term. Methodology does not mean to me a discussion of methods or techniques only; it may include techniques, but it is more than that. I agree with Lazarsfeld and Rosenberg that "The methodologist is a scholar who is above all *analytical* in his approach to his subject matter. He tells other scholars what they have done, or might do, rather than what they should do. He tells them what order of finding has emerged from their research, not what kind of result is or is not preferable." [1] He, the methodologist, is concerned above all with the assumptions, procedures, the modes of explication and description, and the character of the findings

---

[1] P. F. Lazarsfeld and M. Rosenberg, eds., *The Language of Social Research* (Glencoe, Ill.: The Free Press, 1955), p. 4. This volume, subtitled "A Reader in the Methodology of Social Research," provides an excellent introduction to methodological problems in the social sciences. Even a brief examination of the volume will indicate the variety, complexity, and difficulty of new techniques that have been developed in recent years.

that characterize a given body of scholarship. It follows from this that my main emphasis will be on the analysis of political science by political scientists, with a view to clarifying the assumptions, procedures, and status of the findings of the characteristic work of political scientists today.

I also am keenly aware that to attempt to characterize the large body of literature important to the subject at hand in a single short essay is dangerous, perhaps foolhardy. The space available is by no means adequate to enumerate the multiplicity of values, factors, problems, approaches, and results involved. It is sufficient, however, to raise a number of problems which, when not treated fully, may lead to misunderstanding. Communication among strangers on even simple matters is difficult, and the subject of this essay is not a simple matter. I cannot attempt to cover the subject exhaustively; I can deal only with the major tendencies, give my own brief evaluation, and provide some bibliographic guidance to more comprehensive information and argument.

Finally, in addition to the above limits on what I may hope to accomplish, there are my own deficiencies. There can be little doubt that political science is intrinsically an extremely complex field of study. There are great difficulties in the scientific analysis of its subject matter, and these are complicated by the diversity of views about the assumptions, conditions, procedures, modes of explication, and character of the findings involved in its systematic study. No one man can conceivably be a specialist in all fields of political science and certainly I am not. Therefore, for reasons of the nature and complexity of the subject, the space I have, and my own competence, I will necessarily over-simplify, omitting many of the niceties, modifications, qualifications, exceptions, and examples required for comprehensive examination and strict accuracy.

I want to begin with the proposition that political science aims at being a science. It is necessary, however, to note at the outset the existence of disagreement about the definition of science, and therefore about precisely what it is political science aims at being.[2]

---

[2] See M. R. Cohen, *Reason and Nature: An Essay in the Meaning of the Scientific Method* (New York: Harcourt, Brace and Company, 1931); M. R. Cohen and E. Nagel, *An Introduction to Logic and the Scientific Method* (New York: Harcourt, Brace and Company, 1934). See also C. J. Friedrich, "Political Philosophy and the Science of Politics," in R. Young, ed., *Approches to the Study of Politics* (Evanston, Ill.: Northwestern University Press, 1958), pp. 172-89; H. Feigl and M. Brodbeck, eds., *Readings in the Philosophy of*

Nevertheless, if I may ignore the slang usage which equates science with natural science and take the historical and, I think, correct meaning of science as a body of systematic and orderly thinking about a determinate subject matter, most political scientists would agree upon this minimal definition of the profession's goal. In a less self-conscious age, scholars would probably have accepted this or some similar definition and got on with the business of advising princes, analyzing laws, or collecting constitutions. The twentieth century, however, has been variously described as an age of anxiety and an age of analysis. Both characterizations are correct, and they are complementary. Many political scientists in our own time have, with no small anxiety, analyzed their work and that of their colleagues in the effort to identify the assumptions, procedures, standards, and results of traditional political science. That is to say, they have functioned as methodologists of the discipline.[3]

In many, probably most, instances, however, this collective introspection has not stopped with an analysis of work done in the name of political science, but also has included speculation on the changes in focus and procedure required for the advancement of the discipline. In other words, the methodologists of political science have generally gone beyond telling their colleagues what they have done to telling them what they should do, have gone beyond telling them "what order of finding has emerged from their research" to

Science (New York: Appleton-Century-Crofts, 1953), esp. section VII, "Philosophy of the Social Sciences"; and M. Natanson, "A Study in Philosophy and the Social Sciences," *Social Research*, Vol. 25 (1958), pp. 158-72.

[3] See, for example, D. Easton, *The Political System* (New York: Alfred A. Knopf, 1953); Young, *op. cit.;* H. Eulau, S. J. Eldersveld, and M. Janowitz, *Political Behavior: A Reader in Theory and Research* (Glencoe, Ill.: The Free Press, 1956); S. K. Bailey *et al., Research Frontiers in Politics and Government* (Washington, D. C.: The Brookings Institution, 1955); A. Haddow, *Political Science in American Colleges and Universities, 1636-1900* (New York: D. Appleton-Century Company, 1939); *Goals for Political Science* (New York: published for the American Political Science Association by William Sloane Associates, Inc., 1951); C. S. Hyneman, *The Study of Politics: The Present State of American Political Science* (Urbana: University of Illinois Press, 1959). Hyneman has included a valuable bibliography of books and articles that examine the state of political science as a discipline and a profession, pp. 211-25. See also V. Van Dyke, *Political Science: A Philosophical Analysis* (Stanford, Calif.: Stanford University Press, 1960); Arnold Brecht, *Political Theory: The Foundations of Twentieth Century Political Thought* (Princeton, N.J.: Princeton University Press, 1959). Further evidence of the soul searching that has been going on is to be found in many articles in the *American Political Science Review* and in reports of committees of the American Political Science Association and the Social Science Reseach Council.

arguing the merits of particular orders of findings. This self-scrutiny has, of course, been endemic in all the social sciences in the last decade, partly because the great progress of the natural sciences has produced discontent with the far more modest progress of the social sciences, and partly because of the complexity of the basic subject matter of the social sciences. The study of man in society permits and even encourages broad disagreement among intelligent men.

Recent thought about the proper concern of political science has involved examination of the subject matter, procedures, and goals appropriate to a science of politics and the position of political science in a general social science. It has been variously urged that the individual or the group or a process or a set of relations should replace the state as the focal concern of political scientists, that the requirements of scientific rigor can be more adequately met by greater use of history as a source of data on comparative institutions, by less "historical" data because it is impressionistic and incomplete, by greater efforts toward quantification of data and findings, by greater utilization of laboratory techniques for the study of small groups, by more intensive utilization of political philosophy as a source of concepts and experience, and by greater concentration on the construction and application of mathematical models; it has been argued that political scientists should aspire to the construction of *a* theory of politics valid everywhere and for all time; that political science is "culture bound" and should not dissipate its energies in pursuit of such a will of the wisp; that political science, like all social sciences, is ideographic and cannot fruitfully adopt the goals, methods, or techniques of nomothetic natural sciences; that political science is pre-eminently a policy science and, in this time of trouble, should concentrate on policy oriented problems, research, and so forth.

I do not intend to examine or even enumerate the multiplicity of views on the nature of a political science properly conceived. I will examine, however, in a cursory fashion those views or tendencies which command most attention and adherence from the best qualified members of the profession. This I shall attempt to do with full knowledge that my exposition will not fully satisfy the adherents or proponents of any of the various approaches to political science today; some colleagues will dispute my judgment of what in fact are the dominant tendencies within the discipline, some will dispute the adequacy of my exposition of these tendencies, and still others will disagree with my personal convictions and commitments concerning the most fruitful approach to the field.

As I look at the work of political scientists in the twentieth century, I am most impressed first, with the absence of any unifying definition, unifying method, or unifying theory agreed upon by the profession or reflected in their research, and second, with the endemic dissatisfaction produced by this diversity ever since political science was formally recognized as a discrete discipline by the academic ritual of making it a separate "department" within universities.[4]

There are important grounds for this dissatisfaction. The collective introspection which it has produced is necessary, I think, and fruitful because the questions which political scientists raise about their field are by no means trivial, their answers by no means obvious. There are things men can do without understanding what they are about. Some they do with their bodies, like walking, digesting food, and breathing. Some they do with their minds, like recognizing a friend or a tune. But when they begin to think, to seek knowledge about phenomena through the use of reason, if they are to be effective, they must understand what they are trying to do; and, if a number of people are jointly involved in an enterprise, like the study of politics or government, the minimal level of understanding and agreement among them on what they are about is crucial to the advancement of their purpose.

The extent and intensity with which political scientists have examined the question "What are we about?" is itself evidence of inadequate agreement on goals, procedures, and standards within the profession.

The course offerings in political science at almost any large university or the doctoral dissertations produced in any given year illustrate the diversity of subject matter and approach that characterize the discipline. Choosing a university at random, I note that its catalogue lists the following courses, among others: The History of Political Theory, Public Personnel Administration, Local Govern-

---

[4] This began with the creation of a separate chair for Francis Lieber at Columbia University in 1857, proceeded slowly during the last half of the nineteenth century, and has moved rapidly ahead since the founding of the American Political Science Association and the Social Science Research Council.

ment, Conduct of American Foreign Relations, Political Parties, Public Opinion, Constitutional Law, International Relations, Legislation, Social Security, Public Finance, Constitutional History, Political Problems of Africa, Contemporary Public Affairs, Government and Business, and Communism and Democracy. If we ask ourselves what these courses have in common besides the fact that they are all labeled political science, the answer, I think, is that they all somehow relate to what we vaguely conceive as legal government. And I think it is accurate to say that, whatever it ought to be, traditional political science has been a discipline the primary purpose of which has been the accumulation of facts about the history, agencies, processes, structure, functions, composition, rationale, successes, and failures of legal governments.

Specialists in political philosophy examine the thoughts of philosophers relating to the state and the government of men; specialists in comparative government generally examine the form and functioning of the political institutions of different countries; specialists in international affairs examine the relations among governments; those in constitutional law examine the basic, enduring "constitutional" aspects of the laws of a nation; specialists in political parties and pressure groups examine the influence and interaction of these para-governmental institutions on government; those in public opinion examine the formation, communication, and influences of people's opinons about the affairs of government and so forth.

Traditional political science has been institutional in focus and eclectic approach. Most of the work that has been done by political scientists falls into one of four categories which we may term historical, analytic, prescriptive and descriptive-taxonomic.

By an historical approach I refer not to the use of historical data but to the way it is used. The historical approach involves tracing a given phenomenon through time. Instead of analyzing a subject and dealing with its abstract elements, it is genetic in character. The nineteenth century was pre-eminently concerned with the historical approach, and the historical school of jurisprudence founded by Eichorn and Savigny had great influence on studies in politics. Much of the work of political scientists from the beginnings of political science was historical, and much historical work still goes on. Political scientists study the history of constitutions, of constitutional law, of particular institutions like the presidency, the courts, and political parties, and of international relations, and almost all textbooks and courses devote considerable space and time to the historical aspects of the subject. When it is good, and much of it is, this historical work follows the methods of all sound historical scholarship; it is, nonetheless, history, not political science.

By an analytical approach I mean an approach whose chief aim and method is the analysis of a body of data, a system of concepts, or a policy with a view to clarifying terms, identifying component elements, and exploring logical relations. Traditionally, political scientists employing an analytical approach have tended to concentrate on the analysis of such concepts as the state, law, sovereignty, authority, rights, justice, and the like. Much of the best work in political philosophy falls in this field. One only need recall Socrates' efforts to clarify the meanings of important terms in current usage in his day and the long and distinguished list of his successors. Today one might call attention to a book, T. D. Weldon's *The Vocabulary of Politics*[5] or to R. G. Collingwood's *The New Leviathan.*[6] Also, in this category I would place the analyses of law and of constitutions; in the field of constitutional law, American political scientists have done an extraordinarily good analytical job.

By the prescriptive approach I refer to that part of the literature which is normative in character. This would include books arguing the merits of a particular reform or a particular policy; they may argue for proportional representation, increase of foreign economic aid, "peaceful co-existence," or that representative government is most conducive to the good life. In this category would fall all of the utopias, from Plato's *Republic* to the present day. This approach would include books like W. Y. Elliott's *The Need for Constitutional Reform,*[7] Woodrow Wilson's *Congressional Government,*[8] and Charles A. Beard's *The Open Door at Home: A Trial Philosophy of National Interest.*[9] A distinction should be made between this type of literature, which argues for particular reforms or policies

[5] T. D. Weldon, *The Vocabulary of Politics* (London: Penguin Books, 1953).

[6] R. G. Collingwood, *The New Leviathan* (Oxford: at the Clarendon Press, 1942).

[7] W. Y. Elliott, *The Need for Constitutional Reform: A Program for National Security* (New York: McGraw-Hill Book Company, Inc., 1935).

[8] W. Wilson, *Congressional Government* (New York: Houghton Mifflin, 1885).

[9] C. A. Beard, *The Open Door at Home: A Trial Philosophy of the National Interest* (New York: The Macmillan Company, 1934).

or the maximization of particular values, and the type of literature which attempts to clarify policy alternatives or which outlines the preconditions for the maximization of given values; these latter I would call analytical.

The approaches I have discussed so far are to be found in the literature of political science from Plato and Aristotle down to the present day, and they have made significant contributions to our knowledge about government and politics. For the most part, however, they are approaches that call for work in the library or study, rather than the market place of politics. Also, they provided less description of actual governments and political institutions than seemed desirable to the political scientists who were most active around the turn of this century when the American Political Science Association was founded. Already James Bryce had written *The American Commonwealth* (the first edition was published in 1888) and had said that his purpose was "to paint the institutions and people of America as they are . . . to avoid temptations of the deductive method and to present simply the facts of the case. . . ." [10] And elsewhere he said, "It is facts that are needed; Facts, Facts, Facts." [11] Also, American political science was influenced by the significant developments in the natural sciences with their enormous amount of information about the natural world. The political scientists who formed the American Political Science Association in 1903, therefore, turned their attention to collecting facts about governmental institutions. The articles and books they wrote after the turn of the century are testimony to their assiduous efforts at collecting, organizing, and classifying information about political institutions.

This should already make clear what I mean by the descriptive-taxonomic approach. It is the serious effort at gathering facts, classifying the facts, and describing political institutions and processes. A large part of the work done by political scientists in this century falls in this category. As my colleague Charles Hyneman has put it, this literature describes the organizational structure, the processes of decision-making and action, the politics of control, the policies and actions, and the human environment of legal gov-

---

[10] J. Bryce, *The American Commonwealth* (New York: The Macmillan Company, 1926 ed.), Vol. 1, p. 12.

[11] J. Bryce, *Modern Democracies* (New York: The Macmillan Company, 1924 ed.), Vol. 1, p. 21.

ernment.[12] I do not need to mention specific studies; there are many of them, and every reader of this essay is familiar with the things they include.

I assume, of course, that it is hardly necessary to say that these approaches are not mutually exclusive. Also, while the last of these has been developed predominantly in the past seventy-five years, it is also clear that good works in this field are not limited to that period. After all, Aristotle was collecting constitutions and describing governments over two thousand years ago.

While the categories I have discussed describe the broad tendencies within traditional political science, it should be noted that there are important differences of orientation and emphasis in work falling within each category. The category we have termed descriptive-taxonomic, for example, includes studies of the formal structure of institutions, studies that emphasize function and process, and studies that depict the interaction of structure, function, and process. Similarly, the analytic approach includes studies which emphasize the analysis of concepts, policies, theories, structure, values, and relations. It is broad enough to include books like T. D. Weldon's *Vocabulary of Politics*,[13] and Robert Osgood's *Limited War*.[14] It also should be noted that between the time the first chair in political science was established at Columbia in 1857, and today, significant changes have occurred in the orientation of scholars doing descriptive-taxonomic work on political institutions. Early emphasis on formal and juridical structures gave way to functionally oriented research; this dynamic and functional research in turn pointed up the importance of the activities of nongovernmental organizations and groups for the activities of government. The scope of attention was then broadened to include the relations of these organizations to legal government.[15]

Among recent developments in the field, this increased emphasis on research on systems-in-action, on the operational as well as the formal sources and consequences of government, deserves important mention. These relatively new emphases produced new data, new

---

[12] Hyneman, *op. cit.*, chap. 3.

[13] Weldon, *op. cit.*

[14] R. Osgood, *Limited War* (Chicago: University of Chicago Press, 1957).

[15] Two books that illustrate a modified traditional approach with great effectiveness are: V. O. Key, Jr., *Southern Politics in State and Nation* (New York: Alfred A. Knopf, 1949); and D. B. Truman, *The Governmental Process* (New York: Alfred A. Knopf, 1951).

generalizations, and a sharpened understanding of the operations of governments. They also led to dissatisfaction with the existing conceptual and technical equipment of political science and precipitated a wide scale search for a conceptual framework and technical devices more suited to study the dynamics of government.

Substantial accomplishment resulted and still results from these "traditional" approaches to the study of political institutions. By the middle of this century political scientists knew far more about the institutions of government in this country and in the world than they had known previously. They knew more about the loci of power in society and the operations of that power in and on governments; they knew more about the cultural determinants of government, the organization of government, the electoral process, the elements of policy-making, the character and types of political leadership, the variant relations of ideology to leadership, and so forth.

If the above discussion is accurately descriptive of the mainstream of traditional political science—and I think it is—it ignores an important tendency that has had articulate and persuasive proponents since early in this century. Influenced by developments in the natural sciences, the other social sciences, and perhaps even more by students of the scientific method like Morris Cohen, methodologists within and without the profession found reason for dissatisfaction with what was being done and with the order of findings that resulted. They called attention to the lack of recognition on the part of political scientists of the developments in the other sciences of man, particularly psychology, sociology, anthropology, and psychiatry; they were unhappy about the bulging inventory of facts that had no relation to a comprehensive theory; they noted the extent to which untenable assumptions and premises influenced and distorted findings; they criticized the failure to make better use of statistics and the statistical method; they called attention to the amount of so-called political science that served no function except to bolster the value preferences of the author; they made explicit the low level of generalization of findings; they pointed to the incomparability of much of the data collected; they made clear the difficulty of using the data of political science as it existed for accurate prediction. In brief, many of them accused the profession of dignifying sloppy, impressionistic, crudely empirical, and prejudiced research and writing with the name of science. Dissatisfaction produced ferment, and ferment, change. The challenge to traditional political science resulting from this dissatisfaction probably deserves to be ranked as the most important single recent development in political science.

The chief outgrowth of this ferment—calling for new units of analysis, new methods, new techniques, new data, and development of systematic theory—has been designated by the name "political behavior," which we may term a fifth approach to the study of political science.

Because I am going to over-simplify, it is important to make some general observations at the outset. Between World War II and the mid-fifties, the term political behavior represented both an approach and a challenge, an orientation and a reform movement, a type of research and a rallying cry, a "hurrah" term and a "boo" term. Debate about behavioral techniques and methods was often accompanied by vituperation; discussions were more often aimed at vanquishing adversaries than at clarifying issues. From advocates of the behavioral approach there was often more promise than performance. Heinz Eulau characterized this phase of development in the following terms: "Self appraisal and self differentiation from others is characteristic of the earlier stages of intellectual developments. New approaches are untried and insecure, and new modes of analysis tend to make for preoccupation with methodology. Pay off in the field of research findings is promised, but the promised land is still far away." [16]

The term political behavior was general enough to comprehend a variety of people, propensities, and activities; ambiguous enough that its proponents and representatives disagree about its definition; specific enough to inspire articulate opposition from some proponents of "traditional" political science. Published studies and discussions among political scientists made it clear that several different, and even contradictory, sets of assumptions, methods, techniques, and data were identified with the political behavior movement. One got the impression that the term served as a sort of umbrella, capacious enough to provide temporary shelter for a heterogeneous group united only by dissatisfaction with traditional political science and comprised of persons who would probably move out in

---

[16] H. Eulau, *Recent Developments in the Behavioral Study of Politics* (Stanford, 1961), p. 4. This pamphlet is an excellent short review and evaluation of recent developments in behavioral political research.

quite different directions once the storm of protest against innovation was passed. The situation was so unsatisfactory that the editor of a journal of behavioral tendency defined "political behavior" simply as "political science as some of us would like it to be," [17] and suggested that the term be abandoned entirely as both ambiguous and divisive. Without denying either the ambiguity or divisiveness, I think that the term was and is sufficiently definite and its referents sufficiently constant that it is possible to identify the cluster of assumptions, procedures, techniques, and goals that characterize this approach to the study of political life.

The orientation to the study of political science that I identify by the term political behavior (1) rejects political institutions as the basic unit for research and identifies the behavior of individuals in political situations as the basic unit of analysis, (2) identifies the "social sciences" as "behavioral sciences," and emphasizes the unity of political science with the social sciences, so defined, (3) advocates the utilization and development of more precise techniques for observing, classifying, and measuring data and urges the use of statistical or quantitative formulations wherever possible, and (4) defines the construction of systematic, empirical theory as the goal of political science.

The term political behavior has had a short life, but the tendency has a long history. Its focus on the psychological aspect of political activity was advocated by Graham Wallas as early as 1908, when he attributed the "curiously unsatisfactory" condition of political science in his time to the persistence of an outdated, mistaken psychology and commented that "nearly all students of politics analyze institutions and avoid the analysis of man." [18] In a book published in the same year, Arthur Bentley argued for concentration on the study of human behavior in various types of situations and on functional relations and group processes as the proper focus of a science of politics. Urging that "measure conquers chaos," Bentley further asserted that "If a statement of social facts which lends itself better to measurement is offered, that characteristic entitles it to attention." [19] As early as 1923 a committee of the American Political

---

[17] *PROD*, Vol. 1 (1958), p. 42.

[18] G. Wallas, *Human Nature in Politics*, 3rd ed. (New York: Houghton Mifflin, 1915; 1st ed., 1908), pp. 1, 14.

[19] A. F. Bentley, *The Process of Government* (Bloomington, Ind.: The Principia Press, 1949; 1st ed., 1908), pp. 200-201. It is interesting to note that a sociologist, E. A. Ross, wrote the first book bearing the title *Social Psychology* in 1908, the same year that the Wallas and Bentley books first appeared.

Science Association, headed by Charles E. Merriam, reported that the fourth phase of political science, then beginning, was characterized by the psychological treatment of politics.[20] At the same time that Merriam, father of the influential "Chicago school" of political science, taught, advocated, and predicted greater attention to the psychological dimension of the political process, he served as purveyor and reporter of the other main tenets of the behavioral approach to politics. In 1921, in an article on "The Present State of the Study of Politics," he urged that more attention be given the methods and findings of sociology, social psychology, geography, ethnology, biology, and statistics,[21] and his important book of 1925, *New Aspects of Politics*,[22] proved him intellectual godfather of the behavioral approach by explicating and advocating most of the characteristic goals, methods, procedures, and emphases of political behavior. It is interesting to note that, in the above-mentioned committee report, Merriam listed a tendency toward quantification of data and findings as one of the ten most important trends in political science, and three years later Stuart Rice published his *Quantitative Methods in Politics*.[23] Harold Lasswell, brilliant and precocious student of Merriam's whose prodigious work has been matched by prodigious influence, early emphasized and illustrated the use of psychological categories in the study of politics, the unity of the social sciences, and the utility and possibility of quantifying the data of political science.[24]

A somewhat less obvious, but important antecedent of the behavioral approach is the early work of George Catlin, who, like Lasswell, urged power relations as the core concern of a science of politics.[25]

---

[20] *American Political Science Review*, Vol. 17 (1923), p. 286.

[21] C. E. Merriam, "The Present State of the Study of Politics," *American Political Science Review*, Vol. 15 (1921), pp. 173-85.

[22] C. E. Merriam, *New Aspects of Politics* (Chicago: University of Chicago Press, 1925).

[23] S. Rice, *Quantitative Methods in Politics* (New York: Alfred A. Knopf, 1928).

[24] See, for example, H. D. Lasswell, *Psychopathology and Politics* (1930), reprinted in *The Political Writings of Harold D. Lasswell* (Glencoe, Ill.: The Free Press, 1951), *World Politics and Personal Insecurity* (New York: McGraw-Hill Book Company, Inc., 1935), *Politics: Who Gets What, When, How* (New York: McGraw-Hill Book Company, Inc., 1936), and *Power and Personality* (New York: W. W. Norton and Co., 1948); H. D. Lasswell and A. Kaplan, *Power and Society* (New Haven, Conn.: Yale University Press, 1950).

[25] G. E. G. Catlin, *The Science and Method of Politics* (London: Kegal Paul, Trench, Trubner, and Co., Ltd., 1927), and *A Study of the Principles of Politics* (New York: The Macmillan Company, 1930).

The men I have mentioned thus far—Wallas, Bentley, Merriam, Lasswell, and Catlin—have undoubtedly had a more direct influence on contemporary political science than scholars in the neighboring social science disciplines. Also, all of them may be said to have influenced the development of the social sciences broadly—the contribution of Lasswell to social psychology and anthropology is of fundamental importance in those fields. But, at the same time, they fathered some of the recent developments in the social sciences, generally, part of their influence on political science was to call attention to relevant developments in the other social sciences— particularly sociology, psychiatry, social psychology, and anthropology, and the political behavior approach must be considered part and parcel of a larger movement within the social sciences. It is the political dimension of what has been termed the "revolution in the behavioral sciences." The entire movement is a result of the impact of the natural sciences on the social sciences. It assumes a qualitative continuity of knowledge between the natural and social sciences, its basic postulate being that the concepts and theory of the social sciences can and ought to be made identical with those of the natural sciences. In the words of Ernest Nagel, this means that "in its method of articulating its concepts and evaluating its evidence," the social sciences will be "continuous with the theories of the natural sciences."[26] The belief in qualitative continuity of knowledge and in a single, universally applicable scientific method prompted wholesale examination and adaptation by social scientists of the methods and techniques of the natural sciences. Many, if not most, of the specific techniques of political behavior were borrowed from the other social sciences which borrowed them from the natural sciences in the effort to be more "scientific" and in the hope that similar methods would lead to similar successes.

Where, you may ask, does the political behavior approach take us? What are the consequences of taking the individual as the basic unit for research and theory? What types of data that are relevant to the study of political institutions and situations permit quantification? Which of the categories and techniques of the social sci-

---

[26] E. Nagel, "Problems of Concept and Theory Formation in the Social Sciences," *Science, Language, and Human Rights* (Philadelphia: American Philosophical Association, 1952), p. 63.

ences are useful to the political scientists? What are the consequences of increased theoretical emphasis?

Starting from the premise that a complete description of governmental structure in action "can be supplied only by systematic observations of actual behavior, not by pure speculation or by the
exegesis of texts," [27] research in political behavior has emphasized
the attitudes and motivations of individuals in the effort to discover the effects of personality on behavior in political situations
and the effects of political situations—their structure, rules of procedure, etc.—on personality. Emphasis on the individual's attitudes,
motivations, and perceptions has, of course, resulted in greatly
increased use of interviews as a source of data; as a result, much
work has been devoted to the study of interview techniques not
only with "fixed alternative" questionnaires but also with open-
ended questions. Since responses to the latter are difficult to quantify and since there has been a desire to quantify "whenever and
wherever possible," much attention has been given to the techniques of content analysis which make the employment of statistical techniques possible. [28]

The greatly increased use of survey techniques and interviews as
a source of data and a method of verification has turned the attention of many political scientists to problems of attitude measurement, scale construction, tests of validity and reliability, problems
of "representativeness" of sample and "rapport" in interview situations, evaluation of the relative merits of different types of questionnaires for different types of research problems, and the construction
of "panels" for tracing attitude changes over time—in short, it has
turned the attention of political scientists to a whole range of problems which has occupied sociologists and psychologists for two
decades. Not surprisingly, both the focus and the techniques resulted first in a proliferation of studies in the fields of voting behavior. [29] So great was the early concentration of political behavior-

---

[27] D. B. Truman, "The Implications of Political Behavior Research," *Items*,
Vol. 5 (1951), p. 38.

[28] For discussions of many of the problems of theory and method involved,
see G. Lindzey, *Handbook of Social Psychology* (Cambridge, Mass.: Addison-
Wesley, 1954), 2 vols.; see also Lazarsfeld and Rosenberg, *op. cit.*

[29] For a collection of materials drawn from behaviorally oriented research
up to 1956, see Eulau, Eldersveld, and Janowitz, *op. cit.* As Eulau has subsequently pointed out in his *Recent Developments in the Behavioral Study of
Politics*, p. 5, "To appreciate the changes that have occurred in the last five
years one need only look at what was included in *Political Behavior* and what

alists on voting behavior that it was necessary for those sympathetic with the behavioral approach to take pains to point out that the term "political behavior" should be considerably more inclusive.[30]

Since 1955, this situation has been radically altered, until today, it is accurate to say that the behavioral approach has been incorporated into the mainstream of American political science. An institutional reflection of the speed with which the behavioral approach was assimilated by scholars working in all the major fields of political science is found in the programs of the national meetings of the American Political Science Association. In 1956, the Association formally recognized the interest of a substantial number of its members in behavioral studies by including in its annual meeting program a series of panel discussions devoted to "political behavior." By 1959, however, studies utilizing the behavioral approach had begun to appear in most of the traditional fields of research in politics, and the Association abandoned special panels on the subject; the results of behavioral studies were reported and discussed in regular panels on Political Parties, Legislation, International Relations, Public Administration, and so forth.

For obvious reasons, electoral research has remained a special field of interest for many proponents of the behavioral approach, and, since 1955, studies of the social, psychological, and institutional determinants and consequences of voting behavior have appeared at a rapidly accelerating rate. There have been studies concerned with assessing the influence—if any—of such social factors as religion, age, economic class, family, race, ethnic background, and occupation on voting behavior.[31] There have been motivational

---

was left out. What was left out was not due to the editors' oversight, but because there simply was no adequate empirical material available for inclusion. And in some fields inclusion often involved the only material available. There was no dearth of studies in voting behavior, but there was little else."

[30] Truman, "The Implications of Political Behavior Research," p. 37.

[31] For a review of work produced up to 1955, see S. M. Lipset, "Political Sociology: 1945-1955," in H. Zetterberg, ed., *Sociology in the United States of America* (Paris: UNESCO, 1956); S. M. Lipset et al., "The Psychology of Voting," in Lindzey, *op. cit.*; P. H. Rossi, "Four Landmarks in Voting Research," in E. Burdick and A. J. Brodbeck, eds., *American Voting Behavior* (Glencoe, Ill.: The Free Press, 1949). For an excellent review of studies after 1955, see Eulau, *Recent Developments in the Behavioral Study of Politics*, pp. 15-22, esp. p. 19 for studies of the type mentioned at this point in the text. See also the articles in Burdick and Brodbeck, *op. cit.* Examples of the kinds of studies referred to at this point in the text include: L. H. Fuchs, *The Political Behavior of American Jews* (Glencoe, Ill.: The Free Press, 1956); J. H.

studies which attempted, with varying success, to analyze the psychological determinants of the influence of social factors on voting behavior by focusing attention on voter perceptions rather than on objective social affiliations. These studies are almost invariably more complex and their findings more refined than those concerned simply with the relation between objective social situations and voting behavior.[32] At their best, the findings (1) demonstrate the influence of various social factors on voting, (2) isolate the psychological variables which determine the influence of social situations on voting behavior, and (3) identify and assess the importance of all factors which influence voter perceptions and the contexts which affect the relative influence of different factors on voter perceptions. The behavioral approach also has stimulated increased work on other types of election studies, including analyses of the causes and consequences of straight and split ticket voting, interparty competition, party cohesiveness, and increased interest in the development of election typologies.[33]

Fenton, *The Catholic Vote* (New Orleans: The Hauser Press, 1960); H. D. Price, *The Negro and Southern Politics* (New York: New York University Press, 1957); D. E. Stokes, *Voting Research and the Businessman in Politics* (Foundation for Research in Human Behavior, 1960); R. C. Wood, *Suburbia: Its People and Their Politics* (Boston: Houghton Mifflin, 1959); F. A. Pinner, Paul Jacobs, and Philip Selznick, *Old Age and Political Behavior* (Berkeley: University of California Press, 1960). For an interesting study of the impact of local party activity on the electorate, see D. Katz and S. J. Eldersveld, "The Impact of Local Party Activity on the Electorate," *Public Opinion Quarterly*, Vol. 25 (1961), pp. 1-24.

[32] See Eulau, *op. cit.*, p. 19. Examples include: M. B. Levin, *The Alienated Voter: Politics in Boston* (New York: Holt, Rinehart and Winston, 1960); R. E. Agger, "Independents and Party Identifiers: Characteristics and Behavior in 1952," in Burdick and Brodbeck, *op. cit.*, pp. 308-29; H. Eulau, "Identification with Class and Political Perspective," *Journal of Politics*, Vol. 18 (1956), pp. 232-53; and H. McClosky and H. E. Dahlgren, "Primary Group Influences on Party Loyalty," *American Political Science Review*, Vol. 53 (1959), pp. 757-76.

[33] See Eulau, *Recent Developments in the Behavioral Study of Politics*, pp. 20-22. Examples include: D. M. Ogden, "A Voting Behavior Approach to Split-Ticket Voting," *Western Political Quarterly*, Vol. 11 (1959), pp. 481-93; W. A. Glaser, "Intention and Voting Turnout," *American Political Science Review*, Vol. 52 (1958), pp. 1030-40; V. O. Key, Jr., *American State Politics* (New York: Alfred A. Knopf, 1956); L. D. Epstein, *Politics in Wisconsin* (Madison: University of Wisconsin Press, 1958); J. H. Fenton, *Politics in the Border States* (New Orleans: The Hauser Press, 1957); D. Lockard, *New England State Politics* (Princeton, N.J.: Princeton University Press, 1959); and some of the studies in Burdick and Brodbeck, *op. cit.* See also A. Campbell, "Surge and Decline: A Study of Electoral Change," *Public Opinion Quarterly*, Vol. 24 (1960), pp. 397-418. Two interesting recent reports that indicate im-

nomena will result in more realistic and accurate conceptions of the relations between politics and personality than has the work of scholars from neighboring disciplines.[41]

The proliferation of studies on voting behavior and the work on politics and personality are probably the most striking products of the behavioral approach. The true measure of the influence and importance of this new tendency in American political science, however, is the speed and extent to which it has spread among scholars working in other subfields of discipline. Already published are numerous studies of the legislative process in which traditional and behavioral techniques are successfully integrated. These studies typically blend the traditional institutional description with sta-

---

[41] For an excellent statement on the relation of psychology and politics, see Herbert Hyman's "Psychological Perspectives in Politics," in his *Political Socialization* (Glencoe, Ill.: The Free Press, 1959), chap. 1. Hyman's book provides an excellent inventory of relevant work up to 1959; a large part of the work done to date, as noted above, has been done by psychologists and sociologists. Political scientists, however, are making a steadily increasing number of contributions. Robert E. Lane of Yale University has been doing significant work in this field: R. E. Lane, "Political Character and Political Analysis," *Psychiatry*, Vol. 16 (1953), pp. 387-98; "Depth Interviews on the Personal Meaning of Politics," *PROD*, Vol. 1 (1957), pp. 10-13; "The Fear of Equality," *American Political Science Review*, Vol. 53 (1959), pp. 36-51; *Political Life* (Glencoe, Ill.: The Free Press, 1959). Alexander and Juliette George have done an excellent study of the relation of Colonel House and Woodrow Wilson: A. L. and J. L. George, *Woodrow Wilson and Colonel House: A Personality Study* (New York: John Day, 1956). Herbert McClosky has been using propositions from classical political theory and personality inventories and scales derived from personality theory to study political personality: see his "Conservatism and Personality," *American Political Science Review*, Vol. 52 (1959), pp. 27-45. David Easton, Harold Guetzkow, David Greenstein, and a number of others are now working on one or another aspect of political socialization. See R. D. Hess and D. Easton, "The Child's Changing Image of the Presidency," *Public Opinion Quarterly*, Vol. 24 (1960), pp. 632-44; F. L. Greenstein, "The Benevolent Leader: Children's Images of Political Authority," *American Political Science Review*, Vol. 54 (1960), pp. 934-43; and G. Almond and J. S. Coleman, eds., *The Politics of Developing Areas* (Princeton, N.J.: Princeton University Press, 1960), which discusses political socialization as one of the functions of the political system and uses it as one of the categories for analyzing the countries studied in the book. Here again, as with many other aspects of the behavioral orientation, there are significant antecedents of the work being done. Classical political theory was well aware of the problems, and Charles Merriam emphasized the importance of work on this aspect of politics in *The Making of Citizens* (Chicago: University of Chicago Press, 1931) and *Civic Education in the United States* (New York: Charles Scribner's Sons, 1934). In *The Making of Citizens* Merriam was concerned with a number of countries and examined the parts played by schools, political parties, language and literature, the press, movies, political personalities, symbolism, and the like.

tistical, sociometric, and psychometric analysis, in the effort to cut through formal groups and hierarchies to the functional structures and processes through which laws are made.[42] In the field of constitutional law the behavioral approach is evident in the increasing number of studies which investigate the influence of individual and informal factors on the development of law, including the biographies of judges, the influence of procedure, the corporate interests of the courts, and the political contexts of decisions; and game theory and quantitative analysis are used to supplement legal and historical analysis in an increasing number of studies.[43] In comparative government,[44] local government,[45] public administration,[46]

[42] See J. C. Wahlke and H. Eulau, eds., *Legislative Behavior: A Reader in Theory and Research* (Glencoe, Ill.: The Free Press, 1959). Eulau, *Recent Developments in the Behavioral Study of Politics*, pp. 22-27, categorizes and cites many of the recent studies. One of the most important recent books is D. B. Truman, *The Congressional Party* (New York: John Wiley & Sons, Inc., 1959), which is an intensive study of the operations of the party system in a single Congress. Mention should also be made of D. M. Mathews, *U.S. Senators and Their World* (Chapel Hill: University of North Carolina Press, 1960).

[43] See C. H. Pritchett, *The Roosevelt Court: A Study in Judicial Politics and Values, 1937-1947* (New York: The Macmillan Company, 1948); J. W. Peltason, *Federal Courts in the Political Process* (Garden City, N.Y.: Doubleday and Co., 1955); G. A. Schubert, *Quantitative Analysis of Judicial Behavior* (Glencoe, Ill.: The Free Press, 1959), and *Constitutional Politics* (New York: Holt, Rinehart, and Winston, 1960); C. Vose, *Caucasians Only: The Supreme Court, the NAACP, and the Restrictive Covenant Cases* (Berkeley and Los Angeles: University of California Press, 1959). Mention should also be made of the excellent little book by A. F. Westin, *The Anatomy of a Constitutional Law Case* (New York: The Macmillan Company, 1958). It should be noted that the legal realists, as exemplified by Jerome Frank, had already pointed the way to a more careful consideration of the role of the judge as influenced by his personal character, values, and experience.

[44] Much excellent work is being done in the field of comparative government, particularly on non-Western countries. See, for example, W. H. Wriggins, *Ceylon: Dilemmas of a New Nation* (Princeton, N.J.: Princeton University Press, 1960); D. E. Apter, *The Gold Coast in Transition* (Princeton, N.J.: Princeton University Press, 1955); J. S. Coleman, *Nigeria: Background to Nationalism* (Berkeley and Los Angeles: University of California Press, 1958); and Almond and Coleman, *op. cit.* There are, of course, a very large number of excellent studies on the Soviet Union and a number on western Europe. For an interesting example on France, see N. Leites, *On the Game of Politics in France* (Stanford, Calif.: Stanford University Press, 1959).

The introductory essay by Gabriel Almond on "A Functional Approach to Political Science" in Almond and Coleman, *op. cit.*, pp. 3-64, is especially worth noting. Almond picks up and develops much more adequately the functional approach suggested over half a century ago by Frank J. Goodnow in his *Politics and Administration* (New York: The Macmillan Company, 1900). Harold Lasswell has also made significant contributions to this approach: see *The Decision Process: Seven Categories of Functional Analysis* (College Park,

international politics, and foreign policy,[47] traditional approaches
are being supplemented by typically behavioral techniques; conventional categories are giving way to new conceptual schemes
capable of integrating new types of data and new orders of findings.

Too often, the behavioral approach to political science, as to

---

Md.: Bureau of Governmental Research, University of Maryland, 1956). Turning away from the usual structural approach and asking functional questions,
Almond focuses attention on many matters that have been quite neglected by
political scientists. The chapters in the book applying the type of analysis suggested to the politics of Southeast Asia, South Asia, sub-Saharan Africa, the
Near East, and Latin America will, I feel sure, be the forerunners of a new
kind of literature in comparative government.

[45] In the field of local government, increasing concern with rapid urbanization and with the development of great metropolitan areas has turned the
attention of some who have a behavioral orientation to this field. The studies
of Robert A. Dahl in New Haven and of Robert Agger and his co-workers
should produce valuable new data for formulating and testing hypotheses.
The book by Wallace Sayre and Herbert Kaufman, *Governing New York City:
Politics in the Metropolis* (New York: Russell Sage Foundation, 1960) is an
important one and sets forth a new framework for the analysis of local government. A number of studies have been done by sociologists who have been
concerned with the power structure and other aspects of the local community:
see, for example, F. A. Hunter, *Community Power Structure* (Chapel Hill:
University of North Carolina Press, 1953). Much of this latter work, however,
shows considerable lack of knowledge of political science.

[46] In the field of administrative behavior the work of Herbert A. Simon and
James G. March is well known. Vincent Ostrom, Fred W. Riggs, R. V. Pres-
thus, and others have been doing important empirical and theoretical work
following up Simon's important book *Administrative Behavior* (New York:
The Macmillan Company, 1947). Simon's book, of course, owes much to the
work of a businessman, Chester Barnard, whose book *The Functions of the
Executive* (Cambridge, Mass.: Harvard University Press, 1938), had a major
influence on Simon and others. In their book *Organizations* (New York: John
Wiley & Sons, Inc., 1958), done with the collaboration of Harold Guetzkow,
March and Simon provide a valuable summary and analysis of work done to
date. The bibliography, at pp. 213-48, is especially valuable.

[47] In the field of international affairs and foreign policy a great deal of excellent work has been done. The people working in these fields and their work
is generally well known and need not be cited. It is worthwhile to note, however, the excellent bibliographical quarterly *Current Thought on Peace and
War: A Quarterly Digest of Literature and Research in Progress on the Problems of World Order and Conflict* (published in Durham, North Carolina).
Also, the excellent bibliography in R. C. Snyder and J. A. Robinson, *National
and International Decision Making* (New York: Institute for International
Order, 1961) is of great value; the text of the Snyder–Robinson volume is a
very imaginative and suggestive discussion of needed research. For an important attempt at constructing a theory of international politics, see M. A. Kaplan, *System and Process in International Politics* (New York: John Wiley &
Sons, Inc., 1957).

social science generally, is conceived as involving techniques only. To preclude the possibility that this essay convey such an impression, let me deal with this point directly. Technical innovations there are to be sure—test instruments, survey methods, statistical analysis,[48] content analysis,[49] experiments with small groups in social science laboratories,[50] mathematical models [51]—all have been associated with the behavioral approach. But to equate them with the behavioral approach is to confuse ends with means. These technical innovations have not occurred in a conceptual vacuum; they followed on a new conception of political process and political system and are necessary tools for analyzing the new types of data required by the new conception of politics. The first consequence of conceiving institutions as men acting in specified areas is to define as relevant to the study of politics types of data to which little attention has been given previously. Technical innovation followed in response to needs for tools, techniques, or instruments by which such data could be accumulated and analyzed. The development of the new tools and techniques itself had consequences; subjects previously accessible only to speculation and conjecture were made accessible to systematic investigation. The accumulation of new data led to the development of additional techniques,

---

[48] The publication of V. O. Key, Jr., *A Primer of Statistics for Political Scientists* (New York: Thomas Y. Crowell Company, 1954) gave considerable impetus to the study of statistics by political scientists.

[49] See H. D. Lasswell, N. Leites, and associates, *Language of Politics: Studies in Quantitative Semantics* (New York: George W. Stewart, 1949). For a recent analysis of the relevance of propaganda analysis for the study of politics and for an analysis of methods, see A. L. George, *Propaganda Analysis: A Study of Inferences Made from Nazi Propaganda in World War II* (Evanston, Ill.: Row, Peterson and Co., 1959). A great deal of excellent work has been done by sociologists and psychologists in the whole field of communications research: See, for example, B. R. Berelson and M. Janowitz, *Reader in Public Opinion and Communication* (Glencoe, Ill.: The Free Press, 1950 and 1953). See also B. R. Berelson, *Content Analysis in Communications Research* (Glencoe, Ill.: The Free Press, 1952).

[50] See the recent examination of the relevance of small group research for political science by Sidney Verba, *Small Groups and Political Behavior* (Princeton, N.J.: Princeton University Press, 1960).

[51] See P. F. Lazarsfeld, *Mathematical Thinking in the Social Sciences* (Glencoe, Ill.: The Free Press, 1954). For a valuable discussion of the construction of social science models, see the essay by Herbert Simon, "Some Strategic Considerations in the Construction of Social Science Models" in *ibid.*, pp. 388-415. For an interesting attempt to use a model in the development of democratic theory, see A. Downs, *An Economic Theory of Democracy* (New York: Harper and Brothers, 1957).

new methods of analysis, and new theory. Attitudes, feelings, perceptions, values, and motivations of individuals, for example, had long been traditional subjects of speculation. The development of the new science of statistics and of the sample survey, for the first time, affords the opportunity to take such matters out of the realm of speculation and make them accessible to investigation through scientific sampling and judicious interviewing. In the same fashion psychoanalytic techniques, content analysis, and other methods of research have made objective analysis possible where only subjective impressions could be obtained before.

It is possible, of course, that concern with techniques will pre-empt the attention of the behaviorally oriented political—or social—scientist, and where this happens unfortunate results follow. However, just as behaviorally oriented researchers must guard against permitting technical preoccupations to overshadow substantive goals, the rest of us should not permit disagreement with one or more techniques to dominate our evaluation of the behavioral approach.

The amount of behaviorally oriented research in politics is growing at a rapid pace, as the above brief summary demonstrates, and I, like most other political scientists, have views about the behavioral approach to the study of politics, about its promise for the future, and about its effects on the profession as a whole. On balance, as I have already made clear, I think the ferment it has produced within the discipline has been and is a very good thing. It should result in general progress toward the common goal of all political scientists which is, as I have stated at the outset, the accumulation of a systematic and orderly body of knowledge about the political universe—a universe whose importance can hardly be overstated in this period when governments will determine nothing less than the continued existence of human life. I welcome the efforts of behaviorists to increase the reliability of our findings by making them more precise, more rigorous, and less impressionistic, and I welcome the development and utilization of any and all techniques for accomplishing this purpose. I think the methodological preoccupation of behaviorists has had the salutary effect of making all political scientists more self-conscious about their goals, procedures, and findings. I am convinced that the interdisciplinary focus of the behaviorists has awakened political scientists in general to the range of alternative approaches, orientations, goals, and methods open to those concerned with the study of man in society, has widely disseminated the available knowledge about the behavior of men and groups in a wide range of activities related to politics, and has created greater awareness of the kinds of technical devices available for the study of social—or political—activities. Furthermore, I am convinced that the theoretical emphasis of the behaviorists has led to a more concerted search for regularities and uniformities by most political scientists. In other words, I think the behaviorists have contributed and are contributing to an effort to shift the study of political science to the theoretical level, and I believe that it is desirable to make the effort to develop systematic theory if we are to achieve the most useful knowledge of government and politics.[52]

I seriously doubt, however, that the political behavior approach is going to pre-empt the field of political science in the foreseeable future, nor would I be happy to see this happen. The behavioral sciences, generally have yet to prove their claim to be able to construct a science of man, to discover the laws of human behavior which can serve as a basis for accurate prediction and control. The millions of dollars poured into behavioral research have produced refinements of concept and method, vast quantities of new data, interesting hypotheses, some theoretical advances, and a good many fortunes for the entrepreneurs of market research. But so far, they have not produced a "science" of human behavior, in the sense in which science is understood in the natural sciences. The tentative, partial nature of the findings of behavioral research are most heavily emphasized by the behavioralists themselves who, as one observer has noted, "make everything sound like a prolegomena to the real thing."[53] Behaviorally oriented political scientists are sometimes disposed to imagine that the lack of a reliable theory of political behavior can be attributed to the extent to which political science is uniquely retrograde among the social sciences. But it is interesting and, I think significant, to note that the editor of the *Handbook of Social Psychology* asked himself: "Are the major empirical advances summarized in the second volume (of this Handbook) in reality a legitimate by-product of theoretical con-

---

[52] See D. B. Truman, "The Impact on Political Science of the Revolution in the Behavioral Sciences," in *Research Frontiers in Politics and Government*, pp. 202-31, particularly 230-31.

[53] R. B. Weaver, *The Ethics of Rhetoric* (Chicago: Henry Regnery Company, 1953), p. 192.

ceptions and sophisticated method?" and answered, "No," commenting that "In fairness to science in action (as opposed to science on the books) . . . social psychology has made its advances largely on the shoulders of random empiricists and naive realists." [54]

At the same time, it would be a mistake to be unduly dismayed by the failure of the behavioral sciences to have completed so great a task so recently undertaken. But it would be unduly sanguine and, if you will, unscientific to take on faith the claims of ability to construct a social—or political science—whose theory is as reliable a guide to prediction and control as that of the natural sciences. On the face of it, there are important differences between the data of the natural and social sciences. The latter are more complex, and as Morris Cohen commented, "With the greater complexity of social facts are connected (1) their less repeatable character, (2) their less direct observability, (3) their greater variability and lesser uniformity, and (4) the greater difficulty of isolating one factor at a time." [55] Their units do not admit of simple addition since a man behaves differently when alone than in a small group and still differently when in a crowd. Man's behavior is purposive, or if you prefer, intentional; at the same time, man is capable of dissimulation and of willfully or consciously distorting his attitudes and motives. Furthermore, these difficulties, which are intrinsic to the study of man in society, are compounded for political science by the commitment of political scientists to the study of vast aggregates of men—that is, of political institutions. These aggregates are still less directly observable, and controllable (for purposes of experiment) than are small groups. They are more complex and pose more complex problems for isolating and identifying determinate variables. It may well be that the study of politics can progress from an historical to a theoretical science. But this will only happen, first, if sufficient numbers of political scientists apply themselves to the effort, and second, if they rigorously refuse the tempting belief that a science of politics can be constructed out of a hodgepodge of technical gimmicks and a borrowed vocabulary. The basic postulate of the behavioral sciences and political behavior is that "the concepts of the social sciences, as well as the theoretical matrix for those concepts, are identical or ought to be made identical with

---

[54] Lindzey, op. cit., Vol. 1, p. viii.
[55] M. R. Cohen, Reason and Nature, p. 351.

those of the natural sciences." [56] Evidence and prudence alike argue that this assumption, claim, and goal be viewed as a fascinating, tantalizing hypothesis, itself subject to verification.

Whether political science is fundamentally "basic" or "applied," its subject matter is complex, difficult, and of the first order of importance in the lives of men. Who governs, how they gain power, how they exercise power, why men obey it, how they are controlled, to what ends they use power, and how its use relates to the values, aspirations, hopes, and fears of those who live under it are surely the central questions of any science of politics. Their answer requires knowledge about men *and* institutions. A *both . . . and* approach to whether the basic unit of research and theory should be individuals, groups, or institutions is apt to prove more fruitful than an *either . . . or* approach—at least for the foreseeable future.

That traditional and behavioral approaches to the study of politics are not mutually exclusive has already been demonstrated by their integration in the large number of studies cited above. In his excellent lecture at Brookings Institution several years ago, David Truman warned:

> There are and will continue to be various levels of research in political science, the more basic abstracting from a greater variety of temporal and spatial particularities, but the continuing institutional focus of political science remains at all levels the defining, and in a sense limiting, factor. This point, it seems to me, is the fundamental one. . . . Unless the point is kept clearly in mind, it seems to me, the political scientist runs the danger, first, of failing to be what he pretends to be, a student of political institutions, second, of becoming ensnared in futile and myopic preoccupations with technique and third, of misusing the materials of behavioral science.[57]

The warning was both apt and timely; the danger with which it is concerned is, I think, already passed. American political scientists have not abandoned institutional analysis in favor of psychologizing and are self-conscious about this pitfall. The "war" between behavioralists and "traditionalists" was short-lived, and although a degree of mutual distrust lingers, the growing number of political scientists—particularly younger members of the profession—who

---

[56] M. Natanson, "A Study in Philosophy and the Social Sciences," *Social Research,* Vol. 25 (1958), p. 161.

[57] Truman, "The Impact on Political Science of the Revolution in the Behavioral Sciences," p. 225; this essay is a particularly valuable review of the impact of the behavioral sciences on political science.

insist on remaining neutral while borrowing from both sides, insures that the "war" will not recur.[58]

There is good reason for the speed with which the behavioral approach has been absorbed into the mainstream of American political science: namely, it represents no sharp break with the past. Examination of the history of political science makes clear, I think, that the discontinuities are less real than apparent. Some of the techniques associated with behavioral research are radically new and utilize radically new inventions, such as high speed computers, but it could be argued—successfully I think—that computers and other behavioral instruments make possible or accomplish more efficiently and more reliably types of analysis with which some political scientists have been experimenting since early in the twentieth century.[59]

Finally, I should like to comment briefly on the notion that the behavioral tendency in social science is somehow anti-democratic. This position has been most recently resurrected in the ill-informed and ill-tempered book by Bernard Crick.[60] The only possible grounds I am able to discern for this fear is one which applies to

---

[58] Avery Leiserson in his recent excellent book *Parties and Politics: An Institutional and Behavioral Approach* (New York: Alfred A. Knopf, 1958) makes this clear both in his title and his text. On pages 370-71, commenting on the behavioral and institutional approaches, he says, ". . . it is increasingly becoming evident that the institutional and behavioral approaches are complementary and necessary to each other. The weakness of the institutionalists lies in their inability to identify and measure the factors which produce the variations in personal and mass behavior from the formal requirements and expectations of the political system; hence their emphasis on coercion, moral values, ideologies, and the importance they ascribe to an x-factor of political skill and judgment in supporting their institutional description and prescription. The weakness of the behavioralists lies in an over-emphasis upon methods of data collection and quantitative analysis of miniscular problems of questionable relevance to the sweeping institutional complexes of politics. But both the macro-analysis of legal, structural, traditional and multi-group institutions and processes of government, and the micro-analysis of the variables affecting *individual* political attitudes and behavior, are essential components of political knowledge."

[59] While there has been a greatly increased use of both descriptive and analytical statistics under the influence of the behavioral approach, Stuart A. Rice published his *Quantitative Methods in Politics* in 1928 (New York: Alfred A. Knopf, 1928). It should also be kept in mind that the science of statistics is a recent creation, namely of the twentieth century.

[60] B. Crick, *The American Science of Politics* (Berkeley and Los Angeles: University of California Press, 1959). For a much sounder, though still critical, appraisal by another British political scientist, see D. E. Butler, *The Study of Political Behaviour* (London: Hutchinson, 1959).

any increase in man's ability to control his natural or social environment. Any such knowledge may conceivably be monopolized and manipulated by a hypothetical tyrant to achieve selfish ends. Weather control might be made to cause drouths, but to eschew research into weather because it could be put to damaging uses and thereby leave the world at the mercy of uncontrolled climatic extremes is not only to prefer present known evils to hypothetical ones, it is also to withdraw from science, which, if it has any single goal, is the extension of the influence of reason in life.[61]

It seems to me, therefore, that representatives of all schools of political science would be well advised, as it seems to me they are now doing, to disdain internecine struggles in favor of an open-minded eclecticism—which, in fact, has produced our best work to date. Considering how to advance the science of politics, we can do well to keep constantly in mind the comment of Gaetano Salvemini: "The scientist is not one who, wishing to open a door, must once and for all choose from among a bunch of keys the one key which alone is good. Scientific research is a series of successive approaches to the truth, comparable to an exploration in an unknown land. Each explorer checks and adds to the findings of his predecessors, and facilitates for his successors the attainment of the goal they all have in common." [62]

---

[61] See G. A. Lundberg, *Can Science Save Us?* (New York: Longmans, Green, and Co., 1961) for a discussion of the importance of the application of the scientific method in the social sciences.

[62] Gaetano Salvemini, *Historians and Scientists* (Cambridge, Mass.: Harvard University Press, 1939), pp. 112-13.

Recent Developments
in Survey Studies of Political Behavior

Angus Campbell
UNIVERSITY OF MICHIGAN

The application of survey techniques to the study of political behavior followed on a very substantial history of aggregative studies of the vote, and it was greatly influenced by the character of these early studies. Since aggregative analysis was limited
either to variables that could be associated with political subdivisions or to data about the voter that were part of the voting
record, the demographic and social characteristics of the voters
naturally became the focus of aggregative analysis. Thus, we find
Professor Tingsten's well-known study of political behavior [1] principally concerned with the voting of men and women, people of
different age, different occupations, different social classes, different
points of residence—rural and urban—and the like. When survey
methodologies reached the point of development that they could
be applied to the study of the vote, the studies which were done
tended to emphasize these same variables. The first intensive survey study of the vote in the United States went so far as to conclude that social characteristics of the kind we have mentioned
"determine political preference." [2]

While there is always a great deal of interest in how various
segments of the population vote—farmers, labor union members,
women, youth, ethnic and religious groups, and the like—the heavy
emphasis on social structural variables in the early survey studies
of voting led to considerable dissatisfaction on the part of political

---

[1] H. Tingsten, *Political Behavior* (London: P. S. King, 1937).
[2] P. F. Lazarsfeld, B. R. Berelson, and H. Gaudet, *The People's Choice*
(New York: Columbia University Press, 1948).

scientists who viewed the functioning of the political system in a broader framework of thought. One prominent spokesman of this profession complained that surveys threatened to take politics out of the study of electoral behavior.[3] It is my belief that this early fixation on social structure as the basis of political behavior was a natural development from earlier emphasis in research on voting, but that the survey technique is by no means limited to such a narrow approach to the study of politics and that there are now developing several new lines of survey research which may prove much more interesting to the political scientist than the early studies.

Three such developments seem to me to have particular interest, and I should like to discuss them in turn. The first of these is the use of surveys to study the influence of political institutions on political behavior; second is the use of surveys for the interpretation of mass behavior; and third is the use of surveys for the analysis of the interaction of different levels of the political system.

I

Survey analysts have typically paid little attention to the institutional structure within which political behavior occurs. That is to say, they have seemed to assume that political institutions were the same for everyone and could therefore be ignored. It is not difficult to demonstrate that this assumption is quite improper; not only do the political institutions of a heterogeneous country like the United States vary greatly for different segments of the electorate, but the same institutions may be shown to have quite different effects on the individual citizens who live within them.

A simple example may illustrate my point, an example taken from a Survey Research Center study of straight and split ticket voting.[4] As you know, the American electoral system permits the voter to divide his vote between the candidates for president and vice-president of one party and the candidates for the lesser offices of the other party. However, the different states differ in the procedures a voter must go through in voting a straight ticket or a split

---

[3] V. O. Key, Jr., and F. Munger, "Social Determinism and Electoral Decision: The Case of Indiana," in E. Burdick and A. J. Brodbeck, eds., *American Voting Behavior* (Glencoe, Ill.: The Free Press, 1959), pp. 281-99.

[4] A. Campbell and W. E. Miller, "The Motivational Basis of Straight and Split Ticket Voting," *American Political Science Review*, Vol. 51 (1957), pp. 293-312.

ticket. In about half the states, the ballot form permits him to re-solve the entire series of decisions for all offices by the simple pro-cedure of marking a party circle or pulling a party lever. In the other states, it is generally necessary for the voter to go through the ballot, choosing one candidate from the list for each office. Since all candidates are identified with their party label, it is thus possible for him to vote a straight ticket by selecting all of the candidates of his party. This simple difference in the rules govern-ing the marking of the ballot has a substantial effect on the way the voter casts his vote. We find, in the states which make it rela-tively easy for the voter to mark a straight ticket, that the number of straight tickets marked is some 20 per cent higher than in those states where the ballot requires a series of separate decisions among the candidates for each of the various offices. There is very little doubt that the sheer form of the ballot influences the number of straight and split tickets that are cast.

We find results of even greater interest when we undertake to show which members of the electorate were influenced by this aspect of the electoral machinery and which were not. We find that the form of the ballot had no influence whatever on those voters who had a strong personal attachment to one of the major parties. Strongly identified Republicans or Democrats were as likely to vote a straight ticket with one form of the ballot as with the other. With those voters whose party attachment was weak, however, the ballot form which facilitated the marking of a straight ticket increased the proportion of straight ticket voting by some 25 per cent and among those voters with no party affiliation—people who called themselves Independents—the effect amounted to 60 per cent. In other words, the ballot form has its greatest influence on those voters whose motivation to vote a straight ticket was least intense. Those voters who were strongly party-oriented were not distracted by the necessity of selecting their party's candidates all the way down the ticket. The independent voters, less likely to vote a straight ticket under any circumstances, were even less likely to vote a straight ticket if the ballot form made it difficult to do so.

By introducing this simple institutional variable into our survey analysis we have achieved a better explanation of an important as-pect of American voting, we can predict how the vote would be affected by a change in this institutional form, and we know in what strata of the electorate such a change would be most influential. These are significant additions to the information a conventional survey analysis would have given us.

It is not only such simple institutional forms as type of ballot that can be exploited as survey variables. We have recently undertaken a study of the influence on voting turnout of the various restrictions which the separate states of this country place on voting.[5] The different states differ a great deal in the obstacles they create for the would-be voter. Regulations differ in regard to the required length of naturalized American citizenship, the residence requirements in the voting district, the presence of illiteracy tests for voting, and, in some cases, the payment of a poll tax. By combining these various regulations into a rough scale, it is possible to classify the states as restrictive or permissive in their institutional requirements regarding the franchise.

One might assume that voting turnout would vary directly according to the severity of these requirements; the facts are not so simple, however. In the northern states there is no difference in turnout among the states which differ in the permissiveness of their election laws. In the South there is a difference in the expected direction. Negro voting is quite clearly associated with the restrictiveness of the suffrage in both the North and South. These findings do not depend on survey data; they might have been obtained from a careful study of precinct voting records in the various states. However, when we add the kind of information that can be obtained only through interview surveys, we reach an insight about these data that no study of voting records could have provided. We find that it is not just Negroes who are inhibited from voting by institutional restrictions on the suffrage; more basically, it is people whose general political motivation is low. Negroes are undoubtedly subject to many especially devised impediments to the vote, especially in those southern areas where they make up a substantial proportion of the population, but they are not the only ones affected by the various restrictive regulations on the vote. People whose political motivation is high, according to our measurement, are likely to vote, whatever obstacles the suffrage laws may place in their path. People whose political motivation is low, and this includes most Negroes, are much more easily discouraged from the

---

[5] A. Campbell, P. E. Converse, W. E. Miller, and D. E. Stokes, *The American Voter* (New York: John Wiley & Sons, Inc., 1960).

use of the franchise. We find again that political institutions do not have the same psychological reality for the entire society and that it is possible to learn something of the conditions under which they have or do not have effects on behavior.

Perhaps the most important of the institutions which influence political behavior are the political parties themselves. There are many instructive descriptions of party organizations throughout the world; [6] we may consider ourselves well-informed regarding the formal structure of the parties, the characteristics of their leadership, the content of their policy statements, and the nature of their activities. We know a great deal less about the way these activities are translated into political attitudes and behavior at the level of the general electorate.

What can survey research tell us about the impact of these party activities? It can certainly tell us who responds to the party's appeals for financial contributions or volunteer work, who goes to party rallies, who listens to the party appeals and can remember the party slogans and candidates, and who is not reached at all.[7] These are important descriptive facts, giving us a realistic appraisal of the extent to which the electorate actually participates in the electoral process.

We can go further than this, however, and inquire into the psychological mechanisms which underlie public response to the party's activities. This has led us to the concept of party identification, the sense of attachment most citizens feel toward the party of their choice. We find that this sense of party-belonging can be reliably measured, that it is (in this country at least) remarkably durable, and most important, that it exerts a powerful influence on what the individual perceives in the political world around him, how he evaluates what he sees, and how he reacts to it.[8] The relationship between the party organizations and the electorate is largely mediated through this basic partisan orientation. The parties labor diligently to create and foster this sense of loyalty, and their success

---

[6] For example, M. Duverger, *Political Parties* (London: Methuen, 1954), or S. Neumann, ed., *Modern Political Parties* (Chicago: University of Chicago Press, 1956).

[7] See, for example, J. Westerståhl and B. Särlvik, *The Swedish Election Campaign of 1954, Non-voting and Media Studies,* Progress Report II (mimeo.).

[8] See Campbell *et al., op. cit.,* chap. 6.

in this effort determines in large part their capacity to influence the attitudes and behavior of the electorate.

One additional step in the study of the parties suggests itself. How much would our data concerning party impact in the United States differ if the American party system were different? It is not easy to bring the party system into a research design as an independent variable since party systems are typically national, and variation would require cross-national comparisons. We need not dwell on the problems of gathering directly comparable survey data in different countries; the difficulties are apparent.

Nevertheless, beginnings are being made. One such study is a comparison of the multi-party system of Norway with the two-party system of the United States.[9] National surveys specifically intended to produce comparable data have been carried out in these two countries. The basic assumption underlying this analysis is that the phenomenon of party identification is essentially the same in the two countries, but because of the group-related character of the Norwegian parties and the strong emphasis on party ideologies, the adherents of the different parties in that country will be more distinctive both in their demographic characteristics and in their attitudes regarding national policies than the adherents of the American parties. Preliminary analysis indicates that these expectations are supported. So far as we can judge from a comparison of only two countries, the multi-party system seems to be associated with social and ideological cleavages within the electorate greater than one is likely to find in a two-party system of the American kind.[10]

These examples offer a suggestion of what may be achieved by the inclusion of institutional variables in survey analysis. By examining the impact of these institutions on the members of our samples we learn something new about the character of the institutions themselves. By including the institutions as one attribute of a motivational model, we find it possible to explore generalities regarding the relation of motivation and behavior that might otherwise have escaped us.

---

[9] A. Campbell and H. Valen, "Party Identification in Norway and the United States," *Public Opinion Quarterly*, Vol. 25 (1961), pp. 505-25.

[10] A comparison of voting behavior in France and the United States which will make it possible to extend these observations is being carried out by Professor Georges Dupeux of the University of Bordeaux and Professor Philip E. Converse of the University of Michigan.

II

The use of survey data for the interpretation of mass behavior offers important possibilities going far beyond what can ordinarily be done with aggregative statistics.

Political scientists in many countries have at hand very voluminous records of the voting behavior of their electorate. In some cases these records have been kept over a long period of time and with great care. Each new election adds a new chapter to this archive of voting statistics. There is no doubt that aggregative statistics have analytical strengths that survey data do not have. Very important, for example, is the fact that, being full reports of the vote, they permit analysis of the smallest political unit. Surveys which are broad enough to represent the national population are never capable of reliably representing political units as small as the state. Surveys which are capable of representing small units, such as towns or counties, are never large enough in scope to represent the state or the nation. Secondly, the fact that aggregative data have commonly been systematically reported over a period of many years makes possible the analysis of trends and regularities in voting behavior at the various local and national levels over time. There is no reason why survey research may not eventually acquire the same regularity of report that more traditional aggregative series have, but at the moment only the beginnings of such series exist. Finally, we may usually assume that aggregative statistics are less subject to errors of one kind or another than are survey data. It is apparent, for one thing, that a complete count is not subject to the errors of sampling which are implicit in any attempt to represent a total population by the selection of a small segment. It is also undoubtedly true that the voting machine and the ballot give a more nearly valid report of whether and how people have voted than the report which these persons give a survey interviewer. Voting statistics are certainly not free of error, as various recounts of the vote have shown, but in general we may properly assume that the total error is rather small.

With all their advantages, aggregative data are often very difficult to interpret. It may be apparent that the turnout or the partisanship of the vote has altered sharply from one election to the next or that such variations may follow visible patterns over the years. But it may be very difficult to know what has given rise to these changes or what these systematic fluctuations mean.

Perhaps the most striking example of the ambiguities of interpretation that arise from the analysis of aggregative voting statistics is the confusion of voices that is heard after each national election in this country. It is commonplace to hear the voting results described as expressing a public demand for movement to the left or to the right, for greater economy or for more generous expenditures, for governmental action or inaction, for maintenance of the status quo, or for a movement backward or forward. Even scholarly interpretations of the public mandate as expressed in the vote are contradictory and unconvincing. By themselves the aggregative totals of the vote are too bare to tell us what the electorate intended in the exercise of its franchise.

We now find that a great deal can be learned about the meaning of the vote from the sensitive use of the survey technique. We can find, for example, to what extent the electorate structures its view of the party contest along an ideological dimension, that is, to what extent it conceptualizes political action in terms of conservative or liberal. The results make it apparent that most commentators on the political scene greatly overstate the political sophistication of the voters. We may also discern in some detail the extent to which the supporters of the different parties or candidates differ in their positions on specific policy issues. Here again we find in the American two-party situation impressively little difference between the adherents of the two parties. Inquiring further, we discover that a large proportion of the voters who make the electoral decisions are unable to distinguish where the two parties stand on the major issues.

These specific inquiries dramatize the failure of the electorate to conceptualize political choices in quite the manner some theorists have thought they should. In order to achieve a positive description of the motivating forces which do underlie the mass vote, it is necessary to broaden our view and our interviewing methods to permit the voter himself to tell us what concerns him about the parties and candidates between which he is being asked to make a choice. It is possible, for example, to obtain from the voter a representation of his image of the candidates for the major offices. We may find this to be highly elaborate or very impoverished, positive or negative, strong or weak. In any case, these images become part of the political background which underlies the voting decision. Similarly we may record the voter's concern with matters of policy

—both foreign and domestic. This may be vague, lacking in ideological structure, and hardly more than a sense of frustration. But it may be intense. Finally, we find that the image of parties plays an important role in the voter's motivation. If the party in office has come under serious criticism and is associated with corruption or ineptitude, it may well suffer in the public image. If the party has historically been associated in the public mind with particular segments of the population, this may contribute in a positive or negative way to the voter's decision between the parties.

We find it possible, then, to describe the elements of the political environment which are important for the electorate at the time of the vote. We are able to assess the relative importance the voters as a whole give to these elements, and we can compare the pattern which these elements assume in one election with another. We find, for example, substantial differences in the motives which impelled the voters in the presidential elections in 1952 and 1956 in the United States.[11] In 1952 three major elements were important in the public mind—a growing lack of confidence in the integrity of the federal government in Washington, a profound impatience with the course of international affairs, especially the Korean War, and a great admiration for the person of General Eisenhower. Needless to say, all of these factors worked to the disadvantage of the Democratic party. While the vote for President Eisenhower in 1956 did not differ greatly from the proportion reached in the previous election, it was based on a very different perception of the political environment. The image of the Democratic party as a party of corruption and personal politics virtually disappeared during the first four years of that party's banishment from the White House. The memory of Korea had also faded and international affairs seemed much less pressing. The one element which increased in strength was the popular image of the President, and this was structured, even more than it had been four years earlier, in terms of his attractive personal qualities rather than in terms of his association with specific federal programs or policies.

It is our belief that these survey methods have brought us much closer to a valid understanding of the mandate implied by the presidential vote than we have ever been before. We are not only able to measure the political elements which are important for the elec-

[11] D. E. Stokes, A. Campbell, and W. E. Miller, "Components of Electoral Decision," *American Political Science Review*, Vol. 52 (1958), pp. 367-87.

torate at the time of their decision, we may also compare the major components of the electorate which contribute importantly to the total vote. Thus, it is possible to compare the pattern of motives which underlies the vote of labor union members, for example, to that of the business and professional class, to the metropolitan voter and the rural voter, and to the voters of different races, religions, and regions. Most important, perhaps, we can compare the political motives of those people in the electorate who are most active and vocal with those whose role is more passive.

It would be foolish, of course, to imply that we are now able to know all that is important to know about the public mandate. There is reason to feel encouraged, however, that survey research has reached a point of technical development at which it can reveal at least some of the mysteries which lie behind the bare aggregative totals which election statistics provide.

We have noted that as aggregative election statistics accumulate over time they make possible the identification of regularities in the vote. Many such regularities are well known to political scientists. But political scientists are frequently at a loss to know how to interpret the voting fluctuations which they see in the aggregative records. We find an interesting example of this situation in the almost invariable loss which the party holding the White House in American elections suffers in the off-year election which follows. In every off-year congressional election since 1860, with the single exception of 1934, the party which had won the preceding presidential election has lost seats in the House of Representatives. There have been numerous explanations as to why this occurs, most of them based on the presumed coattail effect which the winning presidential candidate exerts on the vote of his congressional compatriots. Since it is impossible to make an accurate estimate of this coattail influence from the aggregative vote, it has never been possible to confirm or reject these explanations.

We now find, however, that properly designed survey research can tell us with considerable accuracy what the actual relationship between a presidential vote and a congressional vote is.[12] We have recently interviewed a sample of the American electorate at the time of a presidential election, and we have interviewed the same people again two years later at the time of the off-year congres-

---

[12] A. Campbell, "Surge and Decline: A Study of Electoral Change," *Public Opinion Quarterly*, Vol. 24 (1960), pp. 397-418.

sional elections. We find what we regard as a systematic relationship between the character of the vote in a high-turnout "surge" election and in a low turnout election preceding or following. The presidential party loses votes in the congressional elections which follow because of two movements within the total vote: (1) many voters who turn out to support the winning candidate in the presidential election are not sufficiently motivated to go to the polls in the congressional election, and (2) many voters who leave their customary party position to vote for the winning presidential candidate return to their party in the election which follows. These movements, both damaging to the presidential party, will inevitably occur in greater or less degree unless the underlying party commitments of the electorate undergo a basic realignment. A fundamental change of this character did occur in the American electorate during the early 1930's, and it was responsible for the one reversal (in 1934) of this highly dependable relationship between presidential and congressional votes.

It is our belief that this explanation of the presidential-congressional vote shift can be integrated as a special case into a broader theory of electoral change which comprehends such additional regularities of the vote as the invariable increase in turnout in presidential elections from the preceding congressional elections, the greater fluctuation in the partisanship of the presidential votes as compared to the congressional vote, and the unidirectional quality of partisan shift associated with large upsurges in turnout in presidential elections.

To what extent survey techniques may eventually prove useful in the illumination of historical regularities we do not know. It is obvious that our ability to analyze changes in the vote will increase as we accumulate survey data over time. There is particular promise in the further development of reinterview studies which cover successive political events, since the accumulation of data for the same individuals over time offers much greater possibility for the detection of the causes of change than we have in successive samples which are unrelated.

III

While it is generally true that survey studies of political behavior have been primarily concerned with voters, this again is largely an historical accident growing out of the earlier period of aggregative studies. Survey techniques are as adaptable to the study of small populations as they are to that of large, and we are now beginning to see the possibilities available to interview studies of small but important segments of the political system. The recent study of four state legislatures by Buchanan, Eulau, Ferguson, and Wahlke [13] illustrates very well the type of research approach that can be made to formally constituted political bodies. Professor Eldersveld's study of the delegates to the 1952 and 1956 national nominating conventions in this country provides an example of systematic inquiry at another important political level.[14] A number of studies of local political leadership are currently in progress in the United States and elsewhere (Cutright and Rossi,[15] Katz and Eldersveld,[16] Nixon and Marvick,[17] Rokkan and Valen [18]). Such studies can be done without the heavy resources of personnel and money which the large-scale national studies imply. And for this reason among others I think we will see a considerable development of such research among political scientists.

Of course it is apparent that interview studies of political leadership are subject to special problems which are not so pressing in studies of the general population. There are undoubtedly many areas of inquiry which would have great fascination for the student of political affairs but high-placed political figures would regard them as too sensitive or too incriminating to discuss. Survey researchers have learned a good deal about how to develop and conduct an interview, but they do not have any psychological truth serum, and they recognize that there are limits beyond which further pressing brings no results. It is not always clear what these limits are, however, until they have been tested, and, in any case, there is much to be learned about the political process which does not require the revelation of confidential information.

---

[13] H. Eulau, W. Buchanan, L. Ferguson, and J. C. Wahlke, "The Political Socialization of American State Legislators," *Midwest Journal of Political Science,* Vol. 3 (1959), pp. 188-206.

[14] Professor Samuel Eldersveld's report on his studies of the American nominating convention is in preparation.

[15] P. Cutright and P. H. Rossi, "Grass Roots Politicians and the Vote," *American Sociological Review,* Vol. 23 (1958), pp. 171-79.

[16] D. Katz and S. Eldersveld, "The Impact of Local Party Activity on the Electorate," *Public Opinion Quarterly,* Vol. 25 (1961), pp. 1-24.

[17] C. R. Nixon and D. Marvick, "Active Campaign Workers: A Study of Self-recruited Elites," a paper presented to the American Political Science Association Convention, September, 1956 (mimeo.).

[18] S. Rokkan and H. Valen, "A Survey of the 1957 Norwegian Elections" (to appear).

While survey techniques have generally been used to study a single segment of the political system, recent studies have undertaken to bring together survey information from different levels of the political system with the purpose of analyzing the manner in which these different levels interact. A particularly interesting example of this type of study is currently being prepared for publication by Professors Samuel Eldersveld and Daniel Katz of the University of Michigan. The general purpose of their study was to illuminate the functioning of the party organizations in a large metropolitan community. They took as their unit of analysis the precinct, the smallest political subdivision in urban politics, and undertook to analyze the character of the interaction between the precinct leaders of the two parties and the electorate in their precincts. Their sample of precinct chairmen made it possible to describe in some detail the characteristics of these volunteer workers who comprise the first level of party organization in metropolitan politics. The concern of Eldersveld and Katz is not so much with the usual demographic characteristics as with the manner in which these people were recruited, their orientations toward their work, their concepts of their role, and their methods of operation. More important, however, the authors hope to be able to demonstrate the manner and the extent to which the precinct chairmen influence political attitudes and behavior in their precincts and, in turn, how the characteristics and style of action of the precinct chairman are determined by the characteristics of the precinct which he leads. This study, based on detailed interviews with precinct chairmen and with samples of the electorate in their precincts, should provide us for the first time with a systematic description of the way in which politics operates at the precinct level. There have been numerous impressionistic, personal history kinds of report on urban politics, and they undoubtedly have their value. This study, however, has a comprehension and rigor of design and technique which will make possible a quite different type of analysis.

A second example of a survey study intended to bridge different levels of the political system is currently being carried out by Professors Warren Miller and Donald Stokes at the University of Michigan.[19] This ambitious project brings together interview in-

---

[19] A preliminary statement of the design of this study may be found in W. E. Miller's "The Party and the Representative Process," a paper presented to the American Political Science Association Convention, September, 1959 (mimeo.).

formation from a sample of candidates to the House of Representatives with information from the constituents of the districts in which they sought office. Here again, descriptive information will be made available regarding an important stratum of the American political structure—the candidates to the lower house of Congress. More important, however, the study is designed to make possible a comparison of the candidates with the electorate from which they seek election. One of the central concerns of the authors is the problem of representation, the extent to which the policy positions taken by the candidates coincide with or digress from the positions held by the people who vote for or against them. Since nearly half of the candidates are incumbent members of Congress, it is possible to add to the information which the interviews make available the actual votes of the Congressmen on important issues during their preceding term of office. The study is not predicated on any normative assumptions as to how closely a congressman's attitudes or votes should conform to those of his constituents, but it should tell us something of the political conditions which predispose to this type of conformity and of those which do not.

This study, like the Eldersveld-Katz study, is basically concerned with the problem of political communication. On the one side it is investigating the extent to which the electorate are aware of the policy positions being taken by the candidates between whom they are choosing, and on the other side it seeks to find the extent to which the candidates are informed about the policy attitudes held by the people whose votes they seek. Preliminary analysis makes it apparent that in the American elections communication between the candidates and their constituents is in many cases very poor, that voters typically do not know the positions of the candidates they are voting for, and candidates typically misconceive the attitudes held by the voters in their districts. This analysis should ultimately suggest some general principles as to how political information travels between these strata of the political system and under what conditions it is received or rejected.

CONCLUSION

Political scientists have sometimes been critical of survey studies of politics, feeling that the authors in some cases were more interested in the methodologies they were using than in the problems they were applying them to. No doubt there is some justice in this view, but it should not be pressed too intemperately. It is probably inevitable that during the period when the techniques of sampling, interviewing, and statistical analysis were developing so rapidly, questions of methodology should have had a peculiar fascination for those people who were using and developing them. It is important to recognize, however, that the period of preoccupation with methodology is now passing, and we are at present in a phase of consolidation and refinement. Although new and important methodological discoveries will undoubtedly come, the basic procedures of survey research are now quite well standardized and are in use all over the world.

It has also been said that the survey approach to the study of politics has been more productive of descriptive data than it has of data which have proved useful in the development of theory. It would be surprising if this were not true in the early stages of exploration of new areas of information. As we gain experience, we may expect that the development of theory and the collection of data may gradually achieve a relationship more closely resembling symbiosis than has generally been true in the past. It is often said that good theory leads to the discovery of new data, but it is probably no less valid to say that good data lead to the development of new theory.

It may be remarked in passing that the problem of achieving a productive relationship between data and theory is not unique to survey research or to the study of political behavior. It is a general problem throughout the social sciences. It results in part, no doubt, from a failure of empirical researchers to exploit the resources of theory which are available to them. It is due in no small part, however, to the fact that much theory in the social sciences is virtually impervious to empirical test. Such theory cannot be very helpful to the development of a discipline which aspires to call itself a science.

The significance of the advances which have been made in the study of political behavior in the last twenty years should neither be exaggerated nor depreciated. It is certainly not true that we now know how to submit to empirical test all of the important questions which have interested students of politics for the past 2000 years. Many of these questions may lie outside our competence for a very long time to come. We will always be handicapped by our inability to manipulate the major variables which underlie political action. We do not control political events, and we cannot arrange experimental designs to fit our scientific curiosities. Our attempts to exploit so-called "experiments of nature" are likely to lead us into cross-national comparisons, with all of their peculiar hazards. The restraints of confidentiality which surround much political information will continue to be frustrating. We may continue to make rather slow progress in the study of high-level decision-making, partly because this partakes as much of clinical psychology as it does of politics.

On the other hand, it is apparent that these new methodological inventions have made possible stimulating contributions to the study of political behavior and that they give promise of much greater achievements in the future. It is not likely that survey studies of political behavior will displace other more familiar methods of studying the political process. There are many areas of research on politics to which other methods are very much better adapted than survey methods are. They do, however, increase the strength of our total research armamentarium and bring into our purview much new, interesting, and valuable information.

The recent developments which have been briefly reviewed here do not by any means comprise a complete inventory of the present status of survey studies on political behavior. They were chosen specifically to demonstrate the diversity with which this approach is moving. They may be sufficient to make the point that survey research is a versatile instrument of inquiry and that it is increasingly being brought to bear on broader and more important problems of the functioning of the political system.

The Comparative Study of Political Participation: Notes Toward A Perspective on Current Research*

Stein Rokkan

THE CHRISTIAN MICHELSEN INSTITUTE

THE EMERGENCE OF MICROPOLITICS

However academic, the discipline of politics has not escaped the impact of changes in the conditions and contexts of governmental decision-making. New tasks for inquiry and interpretation have come to the fore as new developments have brought about new inflows of data.

In the first phases of the growth of nation-states the emphasis was on the analysis of data produced at the upper levels of each hierarchy and at the centers of decision-making: the outputs of commands, regulations, and laws from monarchs, cabinets, courts, administrative agencies, parliaments, and councils, and the records of deliberations and bargains within and between such bodies as well as within parties, clubs, and associations of notables and other prominent power holders.

With the gradual extension of the suffrage and the growth of mass parties in the Western polities during the nineteenth and

* This paper is a product of work I undertook during 1959-60 as a Fellow of the Center for Advanced Study in the Behavioral Sciences at Stanford, California. I am greatly indebted to the director and staff of the center for all aid and assistance in my work. I also wish to acknowledge my intellectual debts for ideas gleaned in stimulating discussions with Reinhard Bendix, Angus Campbell, James Coleman, Samuel Eldersveld, Heinz Eulau, Daniel Katz, Herbert Kaufman, V. O. Key, Jr., Seymour Martin Lipset, Robert McKenzie, Robert Merton, Talcott Parsons, Peter Rossi, and Carl Schorske.

twentieth centuries the conditions for scholarly work on politics underwent change; the entry into politics of the underprivileged strata of the national communities and the organization of standardized "one citizen, one vote" elections not only set new tasks for research but also called for new approaches and new techniques of study. The expansion of the representative bases of each regime and the mobilization of all accountable citizens into direct confrontation with the issues of politics brought about an extraordinary increase and diversification in the data for research: not just statistics on turnout and party support but also information on the memberships of the parties, the attendance at their meetings and demonstrations, the circulation of their newspapers and their campaign literature, the growth of support from voluntary associations, and the results of canvasses and polls. These data did not easily lend themselves to treatment by the traditional methods of historiography nor could it be dealt with through the established procedures of institutional description; it could only be systematically exploited through the use of techniques of statistical analysis, and it could only be meaningfully interpreted within the broader framework of the concepts and models of the generalizing sciences of society.

It took some time before the potentialities of these new bodies of data were fully realized by Western students of politics, but from the 'thirties onward there was unmistakable evidence of academic recognition of statistical studies of parties, popular movements, and mass reactions to politics. The spectacular expansion of empirical research in the social sciences stimulated the development of new techniques and new approaches to the study of what came to be called "micropolitics"—the analysis of the individual citizens' reactions to the political events and alternatives in their communities.

Three fundamental technical and methodological developments accelerated the growth of this branch of politics: first, the development of statistical machinery for the handling of the often overwhelming masses of individual or aggregated data; second, the development of probabilistic procedures for sampling in the handling of existing data as well as in the collection of new data; and third, the establishment in one country after another of organizations for the conduct of interview surveys of mass reactions to politics.

THE CHALLENGE OF COMPARATIVE MICROANALYSIS

Vast bodies of data on micropolitical behaviors have been accumulated in the democracies of the West over recent decades, and increasing numbers of studies have been undertaken to establish distributions, to trace trends, and to account for differences in such data. The bulk of these studies have limited themselves to one national setting. They may have compared data for different local communities, constituencies, and regions, but they have stayed within the over-all structure of the national political system. Very few studies have ventured beyond the one national setting and sought to account for constituencies and differences across several systems.

The early comparative studies of turnout and party vote hardly went beyond the collation of parallel series of aggregate figures. Herbert Tingsten was the first to see the potentialities of comparative microanalysis in the exploration of general propositions about factors in political behavior. He was particularly concerned with the reactions of the newest entrants into the national mass electorates, the workers and the women, and he assembled statistics for a variety of elections and referenda in the countries of the West to test hypotheses about conditions likely to affect their actions in this new institutional setting.[1]

With the growth of organized interview research in the countries of the West after World War II came a scattering of attempts at comparisons of data on voters and the background and motivation of their decisions, but only a handful of these studies went beyond the collation of independently produced tabulations toward a detailed consideration of the system contexts of the reactions reported on in the interviews.[2] There is much to be mined from the rap-

---

[1] H. Tingsten, *Political Behavior* (London: P. S. King, 1937).

[2] Large numbers of tables for the social and religious backgrounds of voting in western Europe have been assembled in J. J. deJong, *Overheid en onderdaan* (Wageningen, Netherlands: Zomer & Keunings, 1956) and in M. P. Fogarty, *Christian Democracy in Western Europe* (Notre Dame, Ind.: University of Notre Dame Press, 1957), chap. 22. Matti Dogan has compared western European survey data on the electoral behavior of women in "Le comportement politique des femmes dans les pays de l'Europe occidentale," *La Condition Sociale de la Femme* (Brussels: Institut de Sociologie Solvay, 1956), pp. 147-86, and on the party allegiances of workers in "Le vote ouvrier en Europe occidentale," *Revue Française de Sociologie*, Vol. 1 (1960), pp. 25-54. S. M. Lipset has assembled an extensive file of tabulations and IBM cards

idly growing archives of the private, academic, and governmental survey organizations in the different countries.[3] Much the same questions about socio-economic origins and current status have been asked in extensive series of election surveys for each country, and some of these surveys have gone far beyond the obvious questions about turnout and party choice and inquired into motivations for the vote, party images, exposure to party campaign efforts, interest and level of information, participation in politics and community life. The collation of comparative tables from independently designed and organized surveys will invariably prove tricky and the interpretation of findings from such "secondary analysis" will often be fraught with hazards, but this is clearly an essential step in the development of systematic research on the dynamics of mass reactions to politics in systems of differing structure.[4] So far, we have records of only half a dozen attempts to go further in the direction of designing and carrying out cross-nationally co-ordinated survey operations in a series of countries to ensure a basis for systematic comparisons; the most extensive program of this kind is probably the one currently under way at Princeton and Yale universities under the direction of Gabriel Almond.[5] Such programs of

---

from a wide variety of surveys of a number of Western countries and has reported some of his findings in *Political Man* (Garden City, N.Y.: Doubleday and Co., 1960), especially chaps. 6 and 7.

[3] On the possibility of developing an international archive of raw data from interview surveys, see a report to the Ford Foundation by York Lucci and Stein Rokkan, *A Library Center of Survey Research Data* (New York: Columbia University School of Library Service, 1957). The Roper Public Opinion Center at Williams College has now built up a substantial archive of IBM cards and other records of surveys not only from the United States, but also from a number of other countries. The files of the center have been open to qualified scholars, but the center itself does not undertake comparative evaluations or analyses of the data assembled.

[4] On the problem of "levels" in comparative studies see H. C. J. Duijker and S. Rokkan, "Organizational Aspects of Cross-National Social Research," *Journal of Social Issues,* Vol. 10 (1954), pp. 8-24; and S. Rokkan, "Current Sociological Research: A Note on Trends toward International Comparability," *Transactions of the Third World Congress of Sociology,* Vol. 7 (1956), pp. 51-60.

[5] Earlier attempts include: the nine-nation UNESCO survey of national stereotypes, only peripherally concerned with political behavior, W. Buchanan and H. Cantril, *How Nations See Each Other* (Urbana: University of Illinois Press, 1953); the surveys carried out by the Organization for Comparative Social Research of teachers' politics in seven countries of western Europe, S. Rokkan, "Party Preferences and Opinion Patterns in Western Europe: A Comparative Analysis," *International Social Science Bulletin,* Vol. 7 (1955), pp. 575-96; the Columbia University surveys of opinions in six Middle Eastern

co-ordinated cross-national research are costly and confront social scientists with complex but challenging problems of design and organization. Not only does it become possible to ensure better coverage of items and variables across the countries to be compared, but it also becomes possible to standardize field procedures, question sequences, and response classifications; to evaluate with greater precision the comparability of the data; and, what is crucial in this line of analysis, to explore, in much more detail than through secondary analysis of independently conducted surveys, the structural contexts of the individual reaction to politics.

In analyses of one-nation records of elections and other consultations of the general citizenry, the structural contexts of such microbehaviors are regularly overlooked or deliberately disregarded. The electoral codes are assumed to be uniformly enforced throughout the system, the alternatives facing the citizen are taken to be roughly equivalent in all communities, and the instituted procedures for registering and aggregating the citizen's decisions are assumed to make the data comparable across the entire nation-state. Such analyses, consequently, will focus on the variations in the individual reactions to these uniform sets of stimuli, not on the possible effects of variations in the local settings of the electoral decisions. Such assumptions will generally prove justifiable in analyses of citizen reactions in referenda and plebiscites within unitary nation-states, but will rarely hold for analyses of sequences of elections between parties. Even in highly centralized systems, there will be marked local differences in the range and character of the alternatives presented to the citizens on polling day, not just because of the variations in the group appeals of the party candidates but even more because of the variations in the extent of local resistance to partisan conflict. Even highly disciplined national party organizations are not able to present the same alternatives to the citizens in all constituencies, let alone at elections at all levels of government. Such variations in the range and character of the alternatives facing the citizen, whether from one national

countries, D. Lerner, *The Passing of Traditional Society* (Glencoe, Ill.: The Free Press, 1958); the comparative "élite" interviews conducted in Britain, France, and West Germany under the direction of Daniel Lerner and currently under analysis at the Center for International Studies at M.I.T.; the studies conducted in a number of countries by the Institute for International Social Research on "protest voting," H. Cantril, *The Politics of Despair* (New York: Basic Books, 1958), and on the foreign policy views of legislators, L. A. Free, *Six Allies and a Neutral* (Glencoe, Ill.: The Free Press, 1959).

election to another or from one level of government to another, are bound to affect in various ways not only his behaviors on successive polling days but also his basic sense of identification with one contesting party rather than another. In our ecological analysis of commune data for turnout in Norway, we have found telling evidence of the importance of variations between national and local elections: if *fewer* parties present themselves at local than at national elections in the given commune, turnout will be *low* also at the national elections, but if the *same* range of party alternatives is presented at local as at national elections, turnout will be *average or high*. This raises intriguing problems of "macro-micro" analysis of the sequences of steps in the electoral decision-making process. The national party organizations set alternatives for the actual or potential leaders in each constituency, the constituency parties set alternatives for the actual or potential party officials in each unit of local administration, and only the local party organizations are in a position to ensure that the same broad alternatives of choice are put before the general citizenry in every election.[6] The behavior of the citizen at the polls represents his decisions between institutionally set alternatives and reflects in one way or another his experiences flowing from decisions among alternatives in earlier elections. Even in a system of completely "nationalized" politics, therefore, any analysis of electoral behavior will be incomplete as long as it has not traced the effects of differences between communities and changes over time in the ranges and characteristics of the alternatives presented to the electorate.

This goes *a fortiori* for analyses within federations of states differing not only in their party systems but in their electoral provisions and procedures. Within the United States, V. O. Key, Jr., has urged the importance of comparative community studies for an understanding of the "macro contexts" of individual political decisions; such studies "might shed light on the questions of the relation between the extent and nature of citizen participation and

---

[6] For details of the Norwegian program, see S. Rokkan and H. Valen, "Parties, Elections, and Political Behaviour in the Northern Countries: A Review of Recent Research," O. Stammer, ed., *Politische Forschung* (Köln-Opladen, Germany: Westdeutscher Verlag, 1960), pp. 120-25, with bibliography at pp. 237-49. An analysis of the effects of differences in the degree of "politicization" of local elections is given in S. Rokkan and H. Valen, "The Mobilization of the Periphery," *Acta Sociologica*, Vol. 6 (1962).

the character of political systems in the large."[7] So far, however, the vast majority of political behavior studies in the United States has either concentrated on single communities or dealt with samples of the entire national electorate. There are indications, however, of a trend toward increasing investments in comparative data gathering across communities differing in the formal and institutional settings of their politics as well as in their party traditions and their leadership. The controversy over methodology and theory in the study of "community power elites" has stimulated a great deal of interest in the comparison of local political systems,[8] but the comparative studies so far undertaken have concentrated on top decision-makers and influential people rather than on the general citizenry and its reactions.[9] The most promising designs for detailed quantitative analysis of the impact of macroforces on microbehaviors, the Rossi-Cutright[10] and Eldersveld-Katz[11] studies of precinct and ward variations in the efficacy of party organizations, have so far been developed within metropolitan and other large urban areas. Similar explorations of the effects of structural contexts on citizen decisions at the polls have been attempted at the county and the state levels. The regional panel surveys organized by the Bureau of Applied Social Research at Columbia University

---

[7] V. O. Key, Jr., *Politics, Parties and Pressure Groups*, 4th ed. (New York: Thomas Y. Crowell Company, 1958), p. 638.

[8] The simple technique of "élite sociometry" used in F. Hunter, *Community Power Structure* (Chapel Hill: University of North Carolina Press, 1953), was taken up in a wide variety of local studies but has lately come under vigorous attack from Robert A. Dahl and his co-workers at Yale University: see Dahl's article, "A Critique of the Ruling Élite Model," *American Political Science Review*, Vol. 52 (1958), pp. 463-69; and the detailed discusison of studies of this type in N. W. Polsby, *Community Power and Political Theory* (unpublished Ph.D. dissertation, Yale University, 1960).

[9] Peter H. Rossi has suggested a typology of local political systems and a set of hypotheses about the socio-cultural bases of community politics which can only be put to a test through such "macro-micro" studies: see "Power and Community Structure," *Midwest Journal of Political Science*, Vol. 4 (1960), pp. 390-401, and "Theory and Method in the Study of Power in the Local Community," a paper delivered at the Conference on Metropolitan Leadership, Northwestern University, April, 1960.

[10] P. Cutright and P. H. Rossi, "Grass Roots Politicians and the Vote," *American Sociological Review*, Vol. 23 (1958), pp. 171-79; cf. Rossi and Cutright, "The Impact of Party Organization in an Industrial Setting," in M. Janowitz, ed., *Community Power Systems* (Glencoe, Ill.: The Free Press, 1961), pp. 81-116.

[11] D. Katz and S. J. Eldersveld, "The Impact of Local Party Activity upon the Electorate," *Public Opinion Quarterly*, Vol. 25 (1961), pp. 1-27.

were motivated by such concerns.[12] The Survey Research Center at the University of Michigan has endeavored to strengthen the tie-in between studies of national cross-sections and studies of local communities and has shown, in the analysis of the nationwide sample data for the 1956 election, that it is possible to find meaningful ways of analyzing within this research design the effects of differences in the "macro" contexts of the electoral act. Angus Campbell and his co-workers have shown how the state-to-state differences in suffrage requirements affect the lifetime frequency of turnout at elections both in the North and the South and have documented the importance of the formal rules of registration as well as of the form of the ballot for the actual voting of citizens differing in the strength of their partisanship and their concern with politics.[13] Warren Miller has gone further to an exploration of the effects of county-to-county differences in the character of the party system [14] on individual political orientations and decisions and has taken an important step toward bridging the "micro-macro" gap through the design of a nationwide study of the interrelations between party candidates for Congress and the citizens in their constituencies.

These developments in the design and organization of cross-community and cross-constituency studies within national systems cannot fail to influence the continuing efforts to advance comparative microanalyses across different nations; they force us to differentiate our comparisons by levels in each system, they alert us to new sources of variations, and they add further perspective in our interpretations of similarities and differences.

With the accumulation of attempts to assemble parallel micro-tabulations across differing political systems has come an increasing concern with the underlying logic of such comparisons and with the "grammar" of cross-national research. So far, no single scholar has ventured a frontal attack on these problems; what we find in the literature are varieties of hints and suggestions but

---

[12] W. McPhee and W. Glazer, *Congressional Voting* (to be published soon by The Free Press of Glencoe, Ill.).

[13] A. Campbell and W. Miller, "The Motivational Basis of Straight and Split Ticket Voting," *American Political Science Review*, Vol. 51 (1957), pp. 273-312. See also A. Campbell, P. E. Converse, W. E. Miller, and D. E. Stokes, *The American Voter* (New York: John Wiley & Sons, Inc., 1960), chap. 11.

[14] W. Miller, "One-Party Politics and the Voter," *American Political Science Review*, Vol. 50 (1956), pp. 707-25.

hardly a single attempt at a systematic treatment. This is true for comparisons in most fields of the social sciences [15] and is eminently true of comparative politics.[16] This is a challenge to all scholars concerned to advance the codification of the procedures of observation, analysis, and inference in the study of politics. What I can do toward this end in this paper is very little; I shall suggest some distinctions I have found important in my current work on electoral and other forms of political behavior, I shall present a chart for the location of major variables in the comparative study of such microdata, and I shall try to formulate and discuss in historical and comparative terms three central problems in the study of citizen participation in public affairs.

PARADIGMS AND MODELS FOR COMPARISONS OF MICRODATA

Comparisons of micropolitical data lead to analyses in two distinct directions: (1) the direction of the structurally set restraints on the decisions recorded—the rules of procedure and the enforcement practices, the number of alternatives and the difference between them, the methods used in aggregating the choices and determining the outcomes, and the probabilities of "pay-off" for choices of each of the given alternatives; and (2) the direction of the personal background of the choice between the given alternatives, the experiences and expectations, the group pressures and the individual motivations prompting the choice for one alternative rather than another.

In the language of David Easton's model of the political proc-

---

[15] Social anthropologists have, for obvious reasons, paid more attention to these problems than other social scientists: cf. J. W. Whiting, "The Cross-cultural Method," in G. Lindzey, ed., *Handbook of Social Psychology* (Cambridge, Mass.: Addison-Wesley, 1954), Vol. 1, pp. 523-31; and O. Lewis, "Comparisons in Social Anthropology," in W. L. Thomas, Jr., ed., *Current Anthropology* (Chicago: University of Chicago Press, 1956), pp. 259-92.

[16] None of the discussions of the methodology of comparative politics published over the last decade deal in any detail with microcomparisons. G. Heckscher's account of the IPSA symposium, *The Study of Comparative Government and Politics* (London: Allen & Unwin, 1957) has hardly more than one page about cross-national analyses of electoral statistics. The most important contribution to theory development and model construction in comparative politics is Gabriel Almond's introduction to G. Almond and J. S. Coleman, eds., *The Politics of Developing Areas* (Princeton, N.J.: Princeton University Press, 1960), pp. 3-64. This, however, is only indirectly concerned with microcomparisons.

ess,[17] the restraints on the microdecisions constitute outputs from the system; they regulate and set conditions for the feedback flow of inputs into the system from the general territorial population. In any such system changes in the outputs will occur whenever the variations in the inputs exceed critical limits. With the rapid changes in the socio-economic bases of politics in the Western systems during the nineteenth and the early twentieth century went a series of crucial changes in the outputs of restraints on microdecisions: political citizenship rights were extended to vast numbers of hitherto unrecognized members of the national community, the formal equality of all citizens was recognized through the institution of "one citizen, one vote" rules, and procedures were introduced to ensure the compulsory anonymity of each vote. Since the end of World War I these basic restraints have been maintained without much change in the majority of Western systems despite marked variations in the outcomes of elections and other consultations. The rules for the aggregation of votes into mandates have proved much less stable and have been modified again and again under the impact of changing constellations of microdecisions. The restraints on the number and the range of alternatives facing the individual citizen will, within flexible limits, vary with the results of successive consultations of the given constituency; this holds true for the "pay-off" probabilities for each of the choices open to him. A party may lose so many votes at time t_1 that it will prove unable to present itself as an alternative at time t_2. Two parties may compete so hard to reach the majority point that they may become indistinguishable in their appeals and their policy commitments and provoke the development of splinter movements presenting new alternatives to the citizens.[18] Changes in the alignments of socio-economic groupings behind the parties in a system may bring about greater dissensus or increasing consensus across party lines and as a result make for changes in the ranges of alternatives open to the citizenry at election time.[19]

---

[17] D. Easton, "An Approach to the Analysis of Political Systems," *World Politics*, Vol. 9 (1957), pp. 383-400. Compare the further development of this model in Almond and Coleman, *op. cit.*, pp. 12-25.

[18] For formalizations of such "micro-macro" interdependencies, see particularly A. Downs, *An Economic Theory of Democracy* (New York: Harper and Brothers, 1957), chap. 8.

[19] The possibility that the realignment of voters brought about by continued economic growth will push further toward between-party consensus is discussed

These "macro-micro" interdependencies have been recognized again and again in analyses of electoral and other political behavior data, but the implications have nowhere been spelled out in any detail in a comparative framework.

The studies we find in the literature may roughly be grouped in four classes according to the direction of the analysis: (1) "micro-micro" studies focusing on relationships between individual background characteristics, roles, cognitions, and motivations on the one hand and political dispositions and decisions on the other; (2) "macro-micro" studies exploring the effects of variations and changes in structural contexts on the rates of given political decisions and on the strength and direction of "micro-micro" relationships; (3) "micro-macro" studies concerned with the effects of the attitudes and decisions of the general citizenry on the policies, strategies, and tactics of the parties and on the operation of the established systems of structural restraints on decision-making; and finally, (4) "macro-macro" studies concerned with the functions of given structural restraints in the maintenance, legitimation, and stabilization of the over-all political system.

A conscientious classification of all the categories of variables taken into account in studies of each of these types would require a great deal of space. It is enough here to point to a series of distinctions of possible "orders of comparison" in the exploration of "micro-micro" and "macro-micro" propositions; this is done in Table 1.

This typology starts out from direct comparisons of the aggregated rates of given political behaviors within territorial units— comparisons of such familiar statistics as those for relative turnout and party strength or those of less accessible data such as the proportions of dues-paying party members, of attendants at party meetings, of subscribers to party journals, of listeners to party broadcasts, and of active "opinion leaders." These are all examples of "dependent" variables. It is the task of comparative analysis to account for variations in such rates through breakdowns at successive levels of the political system. In the schematic typology presented here only four such levels have been distinguished: (1) the level of the roles and statuses of the individual actor in the collectivities and the organizations of which he is part;

---

in S. Rokkan, "National Consensus and Political Participation" (Stanford: Center for Advanced Study in the Behavioral Sciences, 1960, mimeo.).

TABLE 1. A TYPOLOGY OF "ORDERS" OF COMPARISONS: Microcomparisons of Lower Complexity

Order	Alternatives set for citizen		Collectivities significant for citizen	Citizen's		Examples of propositions derived and/or derivable from the given order of comparison
	National level (N)	Local level (L)	(C)	Regular Roles (R)	Political Behavior (B)	
First:					*micro*	(1) Turnout rates (B) for national electorates higher in western Europe than in the U. S.
Second: N	*macro*				micro	(2) Turnout rates (B) higher in systems with official registration and short ballots (N) than in systems with voluntary registration and complex ballots.
L		*macro*			micro	(3) Turnout rates (B) for localities increase with the proportions of votes cast for dominant party (L).
C			*macro*		micro	(4) Turnout rates (B) for localities increase with increasing socio-economic or cultural homogeneity (C).
R				*micro*	micro	(5) Turnout rates (B) higher for men and married citizens than for women and single citizens (R).
Third: NL	*macro*	*macro*			micro	(6) Turnout rates (B) for localities increase with one party dominance (L) in PR systems (N), not in plurality systems.

NC	*macro*			micro	(7) Turnout rates (B) for localities more likely to increase with increasing socio-economic homogeneity (C) within markedly status-polarized party systems (N).
NR	*macro*			micro	(8) Educational differential in political participation (R-B) smaller the more marked the status polarization of the national party system (N).
LC	*macro*	*macro*	*micro*		(9) Turnout rates (B) not so likely to increase with increasing socio-economic homogeneity (C) in non-partisan local elections (L).
LR	*macro*	*macro*	*micro*		(10) Educational differential in political participation (R-B) will be more marked the less partisan the politics of the locality (L).
CR	*macro*	*macro*	*micro*	*micro*	(11) Status differential in turnout (R-B) decreases with increasing residential segregation of workers *vs.* others (C).

Sources:

(1) H. Gosnell, *Why Europe Votes* (Chicago: University of Chicago Press, 1930), chap. 8; cf. S. Rokkan and A. Campbell, "Citizen Participation in Political Life: Norway and the United States of America," *International Social Science Journal*, Vol. 12 (1960), pp. 71-72.

(2) Gosnell, *op. cit.*, pp. 185-87.

(3) E. Allardt, *Social struktur och politisk aktivitet* (Helsinki: Söderström, 1956), pp. 30-33. The alternative proposition, that turnout will be highest in closely contested districts was documented by Gosnell, *op. cit.*, Tables II, V, VII, and pp. 199-201. Tabulations for Britain indicate that the highest turnouts will be found either in closely contested constituencies or in heavily labor-dominated ones, cf. H. G. Nicholas, *The British General Election of 1950* (London: Macmillan and Co., 1951), p. 318.

(4) Allardt, *op. cit.*, pp. 56-59.

(5) Tingsten, *op. cit.*; M. Dogan and J. Narbonne, *Les françaises face à la politique* (Paris: Armand Colin, 1955), chap. 6; Allardt, *op. cit.*, pp. 124-30.

(6) Rokkan and Valen, *op. cit.*, pp. 36-37.

(7) Implications of findings in Rokkan and Campbell, *op. cit.*, not documented.

(8) Rokkan and Campbell, *op. cit.*, pp. 84-89 and 93-96.

(9) Not documented.

(10) Not documented; derivable from P. H. Rossi, *op. cit.*, pp. 37-42.

(11) This is Tingsten's "law of the social center of gravity," *op. cit.*, pp. 170-72; cf. E. Allardt and K. Brunn, "Characteristics of the Finnish Non-Voter," *Transactions of the Westermarck Society*, Vol. 3 (1956), pp. 55-76; Lipset, *op. cit.*, pp. 205-07.

(2) the level of the macrocharacteristics of such collectivities or organizations, whether aggregated across their members or determined by their structure, their leadership, or their position in the established conflict alignments in the political system; (3) the structural restraints on microdecisions at the local level, the level of the most immediate unit of elective government in the actor's regular environment; and (4) the structural restraints on microdecisions at the national level, the level of the total territorial system within which the actor is a political subject.

Several further levels could no doubt be distinguished, but these are the ones most likely to prove useful in comparisons across unitary nation-states; federations add further complexity to any scheme of comparison.

Only three orders of comparison are identified and exemplified in the chart; only very few comparisons so far attempted go any further, although this is logically perfectly possible.

The "second order" comparisons most frequently found in the research literature are of the "micro-micro" variety; such comparisons are essentially replications of the same analytical breakdowns within a variety of localities and national systems to test the generality of differences in political behavior between individuals in different roles. Most of Tingsten's analyses were of this order; he studied differences in turnout and "left-right" voting by sex, age, marital status, education, and occupation. His most important analyses, however, went beyond this stage; in these he concerned himself with the broader social settings most likely to bring about such "micro-micro" relationships. He showed for several localities that the socio-economic homogeneity of the residential area affected the differences in turnout between workers and middle class citizens and, what was sociologically of even greater interest, that this curve for "residence-sensitivity" was markedly steeper for women than for men.[20]

The following were clearly "third order" comparisons: localities and areas were ranked on given unit characteristics to determine the effects of the residential environment on the political behaviors of citizens differing in their role positions within the community. This type of comparison has become a major analytical device in political sociology; the much-discussed theories

---

[20] Tingsten, *op. cit.*, pp. 126-27, 170-72. Cf. R. E. Lane, *Political Life* (Glencoe, Ill.: The Free Press, 1959), pp. 262-64.

about the stabilizing impact of increasing cross-class communication and the radicalizing effects of working-class isolation clearly prompt continued application of such third order comparisons.[21] In these comparisons, the structural restraints set by the electoral procedures and the party systems are deliberately disregarded, at least in the first rounds of analysis; the comparisons aim at the establishment across a variety of political systems of generalizations about political reactions in residential environments differing in their socio-cultural homogeneity. The rationale for cross-national studies of this kind is two-fold: by going beyond the one nation, the *number of cases* that can be tested is vastly increased, and the *range of variability* in the cases is extended. The between-community variability within the given nation may be very small and produce only minor variations in the dependent behaviors; to get data on cases farther apart on the given collectivity variable it is essential to go to a number of different national settings. This, of course, goes for any group or collectivity of potential political relevance for the citizen who is part of it—families, work organizations, unions, churches, sects, voluntary associations, or parties. I have myself suggested as a possible task for comparative political research the collection of data on the degree of "status distinctiveness" of the major parties of the West and the testing of hypotheses about the effects of within-party homogeneity vs. heterogeneity on the recruitment of active participants.[22] What is important here is perhaps not so much the establishment of invariant relationships as the identification and analysis of deviant cases; this may give us new cues to the historical study of particular developments and alert us to sources of variations at higher levels within each system. Third order comparisons of the recruitment channels within different parties could in this way lead on to "fourth order" comparisons of the local settings of these processes and to "fifth order" comparisons of the over-all national decision-making structures and the limits they set for the parties and their active participants.

Our tentative typology of comparisons implies a "model" of the

---

[21] S. M. Lipset and J. Linz, *The Social Bases of Political Diversity* (Stanford: Center for Advanced Study in the Behavioral Sciences, 1956), chap. 7; A. Kornhauser, *The Politics of Mass Society* (Glencoe, Ill.: The Free Press, 1959), chap. 12.

[22] S. Rokkan, "Citizen Participation in Political Life: Introduction," *International Social Science Journal*, Vol. 12 (1960), pp. 13-14.

TABLE 2. LOCATION CHART FOR VARIABLES IN ELECTION RESEARCH

Citizen's Life Cycle

				◀MACRO	
				MICRO▶	
State of System	External circumstances; central decision-making; cleavage bases; conflict alignments		Changes	→	Current state
Alternatives for Citizen	Suffrage requirements; electoral procedures, barriers; party organizations, differences on policy *Nationally:* Range of party choice, chances to gain mandates, power *Locally:* Nonpartisan traditions		Changes	→	Current alternatives
Message Flows — Sources	Governmental, official; parties, movements, organizations; publicists, ideologues		Changes in volume content, lines of argumentation	→	Current campaign
Message Flows — Channels	*Mass:* mass media, party literature, rallies *Role:* local party workers, opinion leaders		Changes in channels	→	Current campaign
Message Flows — Exposure	*Mass:* accessibility, nearness to urban centers *Role:* nearness to activists; political divisions within/between role environments		Changes in accessibility	→	Current campaign
Roles in Regular Environments	*Parents' roles/activities* Community; kin, friendship circles; household; work milieu; associations; church, sect	*Own entrance* Socialization; formal education; apprenticeship →	*Mobility* Residential; social; marital; occupational; economic; religious	→	*Current roles/activities* Community; kin, friends; household; work milieu; associations; church, sect

SYSTEM DIMENSION ◄ MICRO

Orientations / Identifications	*Parents' orientations to/identifications with* Own community, kin, ethnicity; paternal authority; economic conditions, prospects; workmates, unions; church, sect; parties	*Own on entering adulthood* Conformity—revolt	Own current orientations/identifications
Perceived Alternatives	*Parents' perceptions/images* Local political alternatives, difference in policies, leaders, support, chances to gain mandates, majority	*Own early perceptions/images* Changes in local context	Own current perceptions/images
	National political alternatives	Changes nationally	
Political Behavior — Private	*Parents' behaviors* Interest in, knowledge of politics; information seeking; articulateness on issues; commitments on issues; party preference	*Own on entering electorate* "Socialization" to political activity/inactivity	Own current level of private participation
Political Behavior — Public	*Parents' behaviors* Open advocacy of policies; activity in policy-influencing organizations; party membership, subscriptions	*Own on entering electorate* Recruitment to active participation	Own current public/organizational activity
	Elections { Active campaign work / Turnout / Party vote }	First votes	Own current turnout; current party vote

TIME DIMENSION ►

complex processes leading to individual political decisions. The typology singles out as crucially important in the flow of influences on the given political act the roles the individual has in his life environments, the collectivities he identifies with, the choices open to him within his immediate local community, and the choices open to him as a subject of a national political system. These have been the basic categories of variables in research on electoral statistics since the early pioneers, and they are still the ones that account for the greatest number of tabulations in the literature. The development of survey research has made it possible to go much further in the differentiation of variables within each of these categories and, what is even more important, to enrich the analysis through the addition of information on other phases in the process —on the exposure to influences from the mass media and the immediate role environment; on reactions to conditions within these environments; on identifications with politically relevant collectivities; on images of ideologies, parties, and alternatives for action; on the interest manifested in political affairs; and on the manifold forms of private or public participation in conflicts over policies and between parties. This extraordinary wealth and diversity of data cannot easily be fitted into a coherent theory of the processes at work in such differing structural contexts. In planning our program of electoral studies in Norway we did not attempt to construct anything like a "conceptual model" for such research, but we did find it helpful to work out in some detail a "location chart" for the principal variables to be taken into account either in the design of the actual data-gathering instruments or in the analyses and interpretations of the information assembled. In comparing our Norwegian data with evidence from studies in other countries we have found this a useful framework for the discussion of similarities and differences; it is therefore reproduced here, after some revision, as Table 2.

   This chart represents essentially an attempt at a codification, within the limits of a two-dimensional schema, of the designs of data gathering and analysis now in use in research on elections and other forms of mass participation in politics. The "locations of politically relevant variability" are ordered along two axes: a "macromicro" axis running from the conditions in the total political system down through the influences on the citizen in his everyday roles to his actual decisions during the campaign and on polling day, and a time axis running from the situation in the citizen's family of origin through the changes in his environments during the formative years of early adulthood to his current situation.

In its basic structure this two-dimensional schema will be seen to be closely akin to the notion of a "funnel of causality" so suggestively set out by Angus Campbell and his co-workers in their discussion of strategies of research in their volume on the 1956 presidential election.[23] The focus is on the terminal acts of choice at the election under study, in our chart these are located in the lower right corner; in the funnel model they are at the end of the narrowing stem. In both models time is a central ordering dimension; the final political act is traced back to conditions and events in the life history of the citizens and the system that he is part of. In the Michigan model the conditions at each cross-section in time are ordered from a central core of politically relevant and personally experienced events toward a periphery of politically irrelevant events beyond the actor's ken. In the chart we used in designing our Norwegian studies, we focused on what we considered to be the analytically relevant conditions at each cross-section in time and ordered these by levels in the political system: at the first level, nearest to the terminal acts under study, the citizen's behaviors in other political contexts, his privately expressed concerns with public issues, and his public participation in policy-influencing organizations or in political parties; at the second level, his images and judgments of the political alternatives open to him; at the third, his orientations and attitudes to critical issues in his regular environments and his identifications with collectivities engaged on one side or the other in given conflicts; at the fourth, his roles and activities in his regular environments, the collectivities he spends the bulk of his time in; at the fifth, his exposure to political influences in these environments, through majority pressure, through active opinion leaders, and through the mass media; at the sixth, and this is the first "macro" level, the messages, the information, the arguments, and the appeals sent to him from the organizations and the corporate units active in the contests for support within the system; at the seventh, the actual alternatives set by the system for the ordinary citizen, locally as well as nationally; and finally, the eighth level, the given state of the system, the external pressures on it, the cleavages within it, and the alignments of forces

---

[23] Campbell *et al., op. cit.,* pp. 24-32.

among the full-time decision-makers, whether political, administrative, economic, or cultural.

A chart such as this is not a substitute for a rigorous design; it simply serves as a guide to remind us of sources of variation to be taken into account whether data on the sources can be assembled or not. What is important here is that it underscores the need to take contexts into account in comparing data on political behavior, whether within one national system or across several systems.

CONTRASTING CONTEXTS OF CITIZEN PARTICIPATION IN DECISION-MAKING: THE ELECTORAL VS. THE TRADITIONAL AND THE ORGANIZATIONAL

The lines of influence set out in our chart converge on the terminal acts of choice on election day: the choice between turning out and staying home, the choice between the n lists or the n candidates.

These acts constitute inputs into the process of decision-making for the territorial community, but they make up only one of the great variety of categories of such inputs. Individual acts of disobedience or resistance, spontaneous demonstrations, public articulations of opinion, mass media campaigns, demands, appeals, and threats from organized movements and interest groups, offers and counteroffers in bargains between corporate units, and reactions and suggestions flowing back from administrative agencies are examples of inputs to be taken into account in any analysis of the processes of decision-making in the nation-state. How do the electoral inputs fit into this broader framework of articulations of demands and aggregations of pressure? [24] This is a problem of central importance in the integration of approaches to the study of political processes: important in the analysis of the functional unity of systems and important in the study of the motivations and manifestations of individual participation in the affairs of the community and the nation.

This problem has a crucial historical dimension. The processes of centralization and democratization during the nineteenth and the early twentieth century brought about a more and more marked

---

[24] The concepts of "interest articulation" and "interest aggregation" are discussed in detail in Almond and Coleman, *op. cit.*, pp. 33-45.

contrast between the electoral and the other channels of participation in decision-making; the seemingly irresistible trend toward the formal standardization of procedures and enforcement practices gradually sets the electoral mode of aggregation distinctly apart from other modes, both from the traditional influences of locally dominant families and from the emerging influences of functionally differentiated national organizations.

In full-fledged political democracies, electoral acts of participation will differ from other acts on three crucial counts: (1) the universality of access—all accountable adults without severe criminal records are given the vote, however peripheral their concern for politics and public affairs and however dependent and subordinate their roles in their community or their organizations; (2) the equality of influence—each vote cast counts as one anonymous unit of influence and is completely divorced from the person and the roles of the participating citizen; and (3) the privacy and the "irresponsibility" of the participant's act—the vote is given the status of a "privileged communication" to the territorial authorities, there is no feedback to the citizen's other roles in his community, and it is consequently up to each voter to decide whether or not to reveal his act and take responsibility for it in his day-to-day environment.

The history of the movement toward formal democracy in the West could appropriately be written as an analysis of the sequences of decisions that led to the adoption and enforcement of these three institutional solutions to the problem of the legitimacy of representation. What was central in this development was the growing acceptance of the concept of the *unit citizen* of the nation-state acting in abstraction from his particular roles in the organizational and institutional structure of society. It is tempting to see the development of these channels for mass participation in politics as one element in the complex series of processes that led to the growth and integration of territorially defined nation-states. The extension of political citizenship rights to all accountable adults and the equalization of all votes within a standardized system of electoral decision-making were two of the several important facets of an over-all process of political mobilization within the national territory—a process bringing about a steady increase in the proportion of the territorial population standing in direct, unmediated communication with the central authorities.[25] It is not difficult to trace this process in the history of the consolidation and integration of the nation-states in the West in the nineteenth century, and there are important parallels in the current developments in the new states in Africa and Asia.[26] Essentially what we find is a process of institutional innovation leading to the imposition of formally equal obligations and to the granting of formally equal rights to all accountable adults independent of differences in their established influence through roles in the kinship system, the local community, or other corporate bodies. Direct taxation, military conscription, and compulsory education would be major examples of formally universalized obligations to the nation-state, while equality before the courts, social security provisions, and universal suffrage would be the principal examples of national citizen rights.[27] We rarely find any straight progression toward the universalization of all these obligations and all these rights; what we find is a series of temporary compromises in a complex bargaining process between major power groups in each polity.

What needs to be emphasized in this context is that this process of nation-building brought with it almost as a matter of necessity the enfranchisement of vast masses of politically inarticulate citizens and at the same time made it formally possible for them to cut off traditional allegiances to the local communities and their hierarchies of influence. Edmund Burke was probably the first to see the growth of formal equality in this perspective; he denounced

---

[25] For an attempt to develop this concept in detail, see K. Deutsch, *Nationalism and Social Communication* (New York: John Wiley & Sons, Inc., 1953), pp. 100-101. For a fascinating analysis of the role of the mass media in such processes of political mobilization, see Lerner, *op. cit.*

[26] The term "political mobilization" is discussed by D. A. Rustow, *Politics and Westernization in the Near East* (Princeton, N.J.: Center for International Studies, 1956), pp. 16-18. Comparative studies of the impact of mass suffrage in underdeveloped countries are essential for an understanding of factors making for integration or dissensus: cf. W. J. M. Mackenzie and K. Robinson, eds., *Five Elections in Africa* (Oxford: at the Clarendon Press, 1960); and T. E. Smith, *Elections in Developing Countries* (London: Macmillan and Co., Ltd., 1960). A fascinating account of the effects of the introduction of a system of mass elections in a traditional, highly stratified society is J. J. Maquet and M. d'Hertefelt, *Élections en Société féodale: une étude sur l'introduction du vote populaire au Ruanda-Urundi* (Brussels: Académie royale des Sciences coloniales, 1959).

[27] The most remarkable single-nation study of such processes of change is T. H. Marshall, *Citizenship and Social Class* (London: Cambridge University Press, 1950).

the French Revolution for instituting an abstract equality of citizenship in order to insure greater centralization under the national government. Alexis de Tocqueville went further in this analysis of the parallel movements toward national integration and universal suffrage. He saw in the growth of *démocratie* a part-process in the total mobilization of all adult subjects into direct, unmediated relationships to the nation-state. *Démocratie* implied more than an extension of political citizenship rights to the bourgeoisie and the lower classes; it stood for a trend toward the disintegration of all intermediate authorities between the government and the mass of legally equal citizens. In fact, for Tocqueville the leveling of all differences in legal and political status among the subjects of the regime was at the heart of the over-all trend toward a centralization of territorial authority in the nation-states; the demands of the subjects for greater equality strengthened the claims of the centralized state, and the central power holders reinforced these same demands in order to undercut all interference from intermediary powers, whether feudal, local, or associational. Tocqueville prophesied that this dialectical process would be accelerated through the growth of manufacturing industries and the decline of local power based on agriculture—industrialization not only would bring with it changes in the social structure and intensify the demands for equality of status but would also create conflicts that would increase the need for regulations of local affairs by the central government.

How did these projections into the future fit the actual facts of the political developments in the Western nation-states during the hundred years that followed? Tocqueville proved remarkably prophetic at one level—the level of the development of formal political institutions and regulations. The continued growth of the manufacturing industries *did* bring about increased centralization of the national decision-making systems and *did* lead to the equalization of citizenship rights and obligations; by the end of World War I practically all nations of the West had introduced universal manhood suffrage, and a majority of them also extended these rights to women. What Tocqueville was less ready to see was that this development toward formal equalization could proceed *pari passu* with the steady growth of a pluralist network of associations and corporate bodies; the systems of "one citizen, one vote" decision-making were gradually balanced off, so to speak, against systems of bargaining, consultation, and representation among growing numbers of interest organizations, voluntary associations, and public bodies. Tocqueville saw this coming in his description of the political and civil associations in the United States, but somehow these insights did little to change his central vision of the growth of mass democracy. He did not see that the institutionalization of formal equality would not only allow, but sometimes even encourage, the persistence of traditional loyalties to local notables and trusted spokesmen in guilds and associations and, what was to become even more important, set the stage for the growth of new organizations.

THREE CENTRAL PROBLEMS FOR COMPARATIVE RESEARCH ON CITIZEN PARTICIPATION

Gabriel Almond has argued persuasively for the development of "dualistic models" in the comparison of political systems at different stages of growth; a system may be "modern," "universalistic," and "achievement-oriented" at one level and in one of its channels of decison-making and still remain "traditional," "particularistic," and "ascriptive" at other levels and in other channels of decision-making.[28] National political systems are "multistructural"; the growing complexity of the economy may bring about a variety of differentiated rational-legal systems of decision-making, but the traditional local structures will invariably persist in one form or another and decisively affect the actual functioning of the new institutions.

Almond urges the importance of this perspective in functional comparisons of total systems. The perspective is of equal importance in the study of the structural contexts of individual participation in decision-making. Almond's primary example highlights the contrast between the opportunities for formal participation opened up by the extension of the suffrage and the persistence of earlier structures of dependence on local spokesmen; the contrast between the assumptions of equality, anonymity, and individual choice underlying the institutions of mass democracy and the discovery in *The People's Choice* [28a] and a long series of other empirical stud-

---

[28] Almond and Coleman, *op. cit.*, pp. 20-25.

[28a] P. F. Lazarsfeld *et al.*, *The People's Choice* (New York: Duell, Sloan and Pearce, Inc., 1944). Similar findings are reported for Sweden by B. Anderson and C. O. Melen, "Lazarsfeld's Two-Step Hypothesis: Data from Swedish

ies of the importance of face-to-face communication with opinion leaders in the immediate environments of the enfranchised citizen.

Students of political behavior have again and again been struck by this contrast between the "one citizen, one vote" provisions of political democracy and the persistent inequalities in the actual processes of decision-making. Study after study has underscored the contrast between the high proportions of voters and the very low proportions of politically concerned and alert citizens within the mass electorate; on the one hand a large majority of *only-voters*, of citizens who turn up at their polling stations but show very little articulate concern about the issue of politics, only rudimentary knowledge of the alternatives, and no willingness to take an active part in the conflict between the parties, and on the other hand a small minority of active participants in the political system, of articulate and informed citizens motivated to act and to take a stand.

These inequalities have persisted in all mass democracies; they invariably became even more marked with the extension of the suffrage to women. The improvement of educational standards, the spread of the mass media of communication, and the organizational work of the mass parties may have helped to raise the "political literacy" levels in most systems, but the basic inequalities in participation have remained. The persistence of the inequalities raises a series of questions about the implications of the introduction of universal suffrage for the functioning of modern political systems. So far, such questions of functional relationships have mainly been raised in discussions of evidence from single countries.[29] To gain a comparative perspective on such "macro-macro" consequences we shall clearly have to do much more to collate data from countries differing in their characteristic sequences of development toward full-fledged democracy and differing in the political alignments of the masses of citizens enfranchised through these developments.

Surveys," *Acta Sociologica*, Vol. 4 (1959), pp. 20-23. Cf. also L. Himmelstrand, *Social Pressures Attitudes and Democratic Processes* (Stockholm: Almquist & Wiksell, 1960), sect. 2.5.5.

[29] See particularly B. Berelson, "Democratic Theory and Public Opinion," *Public Opinion Quarterly*, Vol. 16 (1952), pp. 313-30; B. Berelson, P. F. Lazarsfeld, and W. N. McPhee, *Voting* (Chicago: University of Chicago Press, 1954), pp. 314-17; R. S. Milne and H. C. Mackenzie, *Marginal Seat* (London: The Hansard Society, 1958), chap. 13; Lane, *op. cit.*, pp. 340-48; Campbell *et al.*, *op. cit.*, chap. 20.

We need *historical* comparisons of the processes of decision-making which led to the expansion of the electorate and the standardization of registration and voting procedures; we need *statistical* comparisons of trends in political reactions of the masses of lower class citizens and of women after their entry into the electorate; and we need *institutional and structural* comparisons of the different ways in which the pressures of the mass electorate, the parties, and the elective bodies are dovetailed into a broader system of decision-making among interest organizations and private and public corporate units.

These are the three sets of problems I consider crucial in any systematic study of the structural contexts of political participation: (1) the series of decisions which *set the formal conditions* for the political mobilization of the masses of inarticulate subjects within each territory, (2) the actual *rates of mobilization* to political activity and the conditions making for higher or lower rates, (3) the conditions for given types of tie-ins between party-political activities and participation in *other policy-influencing groups, collectivities, and organizations.*

This is not the place for a detailed discussion of the current status of research on each of these problems. I shall limit myself to a few suggestions of promising lines of analysis.

The Institutional Settings and the Structural Restraints

Discussing the progress of democracy in the United States, Alexis de Tocqueville pointed to an "invariable rule in the history of society"—once the first step had been taken to reduce the qualifications for the vote, it would be impossible to halt the movement at any point short of universal suffrage.[30] It is extraordinary to see how Tocqueville's projections turned out to fit the actual developments toward full-fledged formal democracy in nation-state after nation-state. The decisions to extend the vote were not uniformly a response to pressures from below; they were as often the results of contests for influence at the top and of deliberate moves to broaden the bases for an integrated national power structure. The French Revolution had sown its plebiscitarian seeds, and the success of Napoleon III had a distinct impact on political minds in

---

[30] A. de Tocqueville, *De la Démocratie en Amérique* (Paris: Gosselin, 1835), Vol. 1, chap. 4.

western Europe.[31] By a much-debated historical coincidence, the two great Conservative leaders, Disraeli and Bismarck, proceeded in 1867 within months of each other to extend the suffrage further than their Liberal antagonists had wanted.[32] In both cases these "leaps in the dark" were motivated by a profound belief that the entry of the working classes into the electorate would strengthen the unity and stability of the nation-state. Disraeli expressed great faith in the working class and saw a major source of strength for the Conservative party in these new entrants into the electorate. In the words of a *Times* obituary sixteen years later, Disraeli discerned the Conservative working man "in the inarticulate mass of the English populace" just as "the sculptor perceived the angel in a block of marble."[33] Bismarck also saw a major ally against the Liberals in the working class and was clearly very much influenced in his decision by his secret conversations with Ferdinand Lassalle —the Junker and the Socialist found a common ground in their belief in the integrating and centralizing impact of the introduction of universal manhood suffrage.[34] The motive for extending the suffrage to the workers was patently not to create a channel for the articulation of the interests of the economically dependent strata; the objective was to strengthen the policies of centralization by enlisting the support of the least articulate classes in German society. Bismarck even toyed with the possibility of introducing a system for ensuring numerical support through the tacit acquiescence of the inarticulate masses; the votes of those who did not turn out were to be counted in favor of the governmental candi-

[31] Cf. particularly H. Gollwitzer, "Der Cäsarismus Napoleons III im Widerhall der öffentlichen Meinung Deutschlands," *Historische Zeitschrift,* Vol. 173 (1952), pp. 23-76.

[32] For the developments leading to the Second Reform Act, see particularly C. Seymour, *Electoral Reform in England and Wales* (New Haven, Conn.: Yale University Press, 1916). For the decision of the North German Federation, see H. Oncken, *Historisch-politische Aufsätze u. Reden* (Munich: Oldenbourg, 1914), Vol. 2, pp. 157-92; and W. Gagel, *Die Wahlrechtsfrage in der Geschichte der deutschen liberalen Parteien* (Düsseldorf: Droste, 1959).

[33] The London *Times,* April 18, 1883, quoted in R. T. McKenzie, *British Political Parties* (London: Macmillan and Co., 1955), p. 147. The most recent discussion of the Conservative belief of "one man, one vote, one value" is in Sir Ivor Jennings, *Party Politics, I: Appeal to the People* (Cambridge: Cambridge University Press, 1960), pp. 18-28.

[34] E. R. Augst, *Bismarcks Stellung zum parlamentarischen Wahlrecht* (Diss. Leipzig, 1916); and G. Mayer, *Bismarck u. Lassalle* (Berlin: Dietz, 1929).

dates.[35] Lassalle developed the idea (he called it his *Zauberre-zepte*)[36] of ensuring results in the same direction by a system of obligatory voting. This idea was not taken up in the debate over the constitution of the North German Federation but was later to become a standard strategy in efforts to ensure an equilibrium of power in mass suffrage systems.[37]

At the heart of the bitter debates over the extension of the suffrage were conflicting expectations concerning the repercussions of the entry of the "politically illiterate" into the arena: conflicting views of the allegiances and probable reactions of these masses once they were enfranchised and conflicting evaluations of the possibilities of controlling and channeling these new forces. Liberals tended to express fear of an irresponsible and disruptive radicalization of politics; Conservative and Christian party leaders were more likely to see in the enfranchisement of the lower classes and of all women a major strategic move in the stabilization of the national system against the attacks from the Socialist Left. An extraordinary variety of institutional compromises were tried out in response to these conflicting pressures. The history of these innovations is not of merely antiquarian interest; these developments set the stage for the organization of mass politics in each country and the particular solutions reached at each stage helped to determine the conditions for the integration of the lower classes into the national community.

In a systematic comparison of the sequences of decisions that led to the introduction of full-fledged formal democracy a great number of dimensions of institutional change would have to be considered. For the present purposes a simplified schematic chart has been prepared (Table 3) to set in relief some of the salient differences between western European countries in the developments that led to the enfranchisement of the politically least articulate strata of each population.[38] This chart takes into account

---

[35] Mayer, *op. cit.*, p. 36; E. Eyck, *Bismarck* (Erlenbach-Zürich: Rentsch, 1945), Vol. 1, p. 601.

[36] Letter to Bismarck, January 13, 1864, in Mayer, *op. cit.*, p. 81.

[37] For a general review of these developments, see K. Braunias, *Das parlamentarische Wahlrecht* (Berlin: de Gruyter, 1932), Vol. 2, pp. 35-45.

[38] For secondary sources see: C. Seymour and D. P. Frary, *How the World Votes* (Springfield, Mass.: Nichols, 1918), 2 vols.; and Braunias, *op. cit.*, Vol. 1.

TABLE 3. COMPARATIVE CHRONOLOGY OF SUFFRAGE EXTENSIONS: Some Contrasts in Western Europe

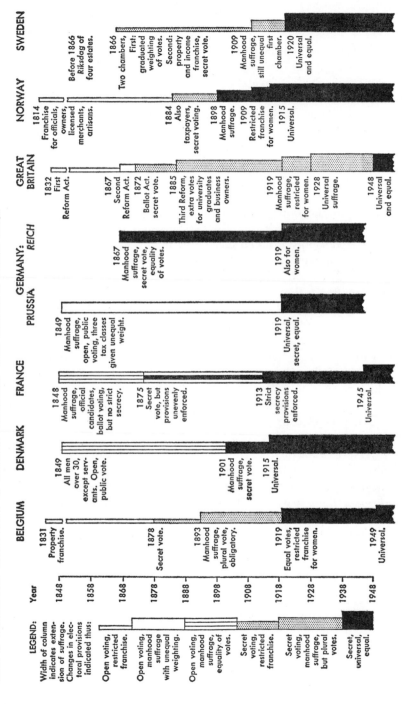

only three dimensions of variation: the steps in the extension of the suffrage, the decisions on the weighting of the votes, and the steps toward the privatization of electoral preferences.

A comparison of these sequences of decisions reveals some marked contrasts both in the number of years and the number of steps it took to reach universal suffrage and in the decisions taken at the point of entry into politics of the hitherto unrecognized strata of the population.

It would be difficult to devise an electoral measure more calculated to alienate the lower classes from the national political system than the one promulgated in Prussia in 1849: all adult men were given the vote, but the workers and the lower middle class were given only a token chance to influence the elections because of the three-class division of the electorate. What is even more remarkable about the Prussian case is that it was possible to maintain for more than two generations a system of universal manhood suffrage with oral voting at public sessions. Of other countries only Denmark kept up provisions for public voting for any length of time after the introduction of near-universal manhood suffrage. In France the provisions for secrecy were largely nominal far into the era of the Third Republic; mayors and other officials had little difficulty in controlling the votes of the less articulate. In most other countries of western Europe provisions for the secrecy of the vote either preceded or were developed *pari passu* with the extension of the suffrage.

The extraordinary contrast between the electoral systems of Prussia and the Reich from 1870 to 1918 has given rise to a great deal of discussion among historians and political theorists. In Prussia there was a system of extremely unequal, open, and indirect elections; in the Reich, a system of equal, secret, and direct voting, which was for a Diet without decisive influence in the affairs of the nation. There is a wealth of evidence to show that this constellation of institutions was highly disfunctional; the extension of the suffrage appeared to encourage the participation of the lower classes, but the contrast between the two systems of elections made for widespread resentment and helped to isolate the workers in permanent opposition to the regime.

Ernst Fraenkel has recently suggested that the introduction of secret voting in the Reich contributed decisively to the isolation

of the urban working class in *eine soziale Ghettopartei*.[39] What he
has in mind is that the deep resentments caused by the Prussian
system of unequal and open voting could find secret and safe expression in votes for the Reichstag without any pressure on the
ordinary voter to articulate his feelings openly in his community.
In the deeply divided German society, the introduction of secret
voting in fact tended to keep the newly enfranchised citizens in
isolation outside the national political system and clearly did not
contribute to the integration of the polity.

Interestingly enough, the evidence for the developments in other
countries, particularly in Britain, suggest the opposite. The Ballot
Act was passed five years after the decisive extension of the suffrage in 1867 and coincided with the great efforts of the Conservative party to organize clubs of workingmen for political action.
The Ballot Act drastically reduced the opportunities for local influence on the worker vote through bribery and chicanery but at
the same time made it possible for the "deferent working man" to
vote with his superiors without making this an issue in his day-to-
day life with his fellow workers. The decisive difference between
the developments in Britain and in Germany after the extension of
the suffrage in 1867 was no doubt due to the action of the parties;
in Britain both the Conservatives and the Liberals developed mass
organizations aimed at the new entrants into the electorate; in
Germany the parties on the right remained *Honoratiorenparteien*
and left it to the Social Democrats to develop a network of political,
social, and cultural organizations for the workers which kept them
clearly apart from the rest of the body politic. The introduction of
secret voting in both countries accentuated these differences in development.

This contrast raises a series of intriguing questions about the
functions for political systems of the introduction of institutions
for the safeguarding of the privacy of the voting act. It is remarkable how little attention has been given in the literature to the
effects of these profound changes in electoral procedures.[40] What

---

[39] E. Fraenkel, "Parlament und öffentliche Meinung," in *Zur Geschichte und
Problematik der Demokratie: Festgabe für H. Herzfeld* (Berlin: Duncker &
Humblot, 1958), p. 178.

[40] The formal history of the Anglo-Saxon systems is well covered in J. H.
Wigmore, *The Australian Ballot System* (Boston: Boston Book Co., 1889);
and E. D. Evans, *A History of the Australian Ballot System in the United
States* (Chicago: University of Chicago Press, 1917). On other systems, see

can be said at this stage will of necessity be based on speculation and only scattered and unsystematic evidence.

Tocqueville would clearly have seen in the provisions for secrecy a further extension of the tendency for the centralizing nation-state to enter into direct communication with each individual subject and to undermine all intermediary powers. The essential effect of the secrecy institution is to accentuate the equality of each voter by isolating him from the hierarchical influences in the local community. Through the secrecy provisions the power of the local aristocracy, the notables, and the clergy is further reduced and, to follow the Tocqueville model, the tendencies toward centralization correspondingly strengthened.

In sociological terms we might say that in the situation of secret voting the individual adult is cut off from all his roles in the subordinate systems of the household, the neighborhood, the work organization, the church, and the civil association and set to act exclusively in the abstract role as a citizen of the over-all political system; there will be no feedback from what he does in this anonymous role to what he does in the other roles and therefore no need for him to take responsibility for the act of voting in his everyday interaction in his regular environment.

The obvious manifest reasons for introducing the secrecy provisions were the numerous public scandals over attempts at intimidation and bribery. The primary motive for the introduction of the ballot system was to make it possible to escape sanctions from superiors; this was the essence of the Chartists' early demands and has also been a basic concern of working-class movements.

What has been less emphasized in histories of electoral institutions is that the provisions for secrecy could cut the voter off from his peers as well as his superiors. It is often overlooked that there are two distinct elements in the secrecy provisions: the first is to make it *possible* for the voter to keep his decision private and avoid sanctions from those he *does not* want to know; the second is to make it *impossible* for the voter to prove how he voted to those he *does* want to know. The very rigorous rules set up in country after country for the invalidation of all irregularly marked ballots was directed to the second point; they were devised to ensure that the citizen could no longer treat his vote as a commodity for sale.

G. Mayer, *Das parlamentarische Wahlrecht* (Berlin: Haering, 1901), pp. 528-65. Also, see Braunias, *op. cit.*, Vol. 2, pp. 168-74.

He might well be bribed, but the price per vote would clearly decrease as soon as it proved impossible to check whether it was actually delivered.[41] The salient point here is that by ensuring the complete anonymity of the ballots it became possible not only to reduce bribery of the economically dependent by their superiors but also to reduce the pressures towards conformity and solidarity within the working class.

The secrecy provisions clearly constituted an important mechanism of escape for the politically inarticulate entrants to the electorate. The actual political effects of making the vote private varied enormously, however, with the organizational environments of these citizens.[42] In Germany the Social Domocratic party was able, at least in the major cities, to create a highly homogeneous working-class environment through the development of a wide variety of secondary organizations; it became what Sigmund Neumann has called *eine integral Partei,* a party that could claim the allegiance of its voters in all their social roles and therefore could isolate them from disturbing cross-pressures. In this case the introduction of secret voting for the Reichstag contributed further to the isolation of this subsystem since it reduced to a minimum the need for community interaction about political differences. In Britain the mass-directed efforts of the Conservative and the Liberal parties subjected the new entrants into the electorate to conflicting pressures; in this situation the institution of secrecy became an important device for the stabilization of the system since it allowed legitimate withdrawal from open political strife, not just by abstaining from the vote, but also by keeping preferences private and without consequence in everyday life. With increasing social mobility and the cross-cutting influences brought about by expanding associations in the community and the nation, more and more workers must have come under conflicting political pressures and must have felt

---

[41] See Seymour, *op. cit.,* pp. 434-35. For details on the effect on the "vote market," see H. J. Hanham, *Elections and Party Management: Politics in the Time of Disraeli and Gladstone* (London: Longmans, Green and Co., 1959), chap. 13.

[42] This, of course, is the theme of Ostrogorski's volumes. For a detailed account of developments in England, Scotland, Wales, and Ireland, see Hanham, *op. cit.* For developments in Germany see particularly G. A. Ritter, *Die Arbeiterbewegung im wilhelminischen Reich* (Berlin: Dahlem, Colloquium, 1959); and T. A. Nipperdey, *Die Organisation der deutschen Parteien vor 1918* (Düsseldorf: Droste, 1961).

the need for such provisions for the privatization of the act of voting.

What is crucial here is that this need for privatization tends to be much more marked among the politically inarticulate than among those who for one reason or another have become motivated to concern themselves with public issues. Under regulations for secret voting there is an important *asymmetry* in the system-voter relationship; the system is pledged to the safeguarding of the secrecy of the vote, but the worker is under no legal obligations to keep his preferences private, however little he can do to provide direct proof of his actual behavior at the poll. The institution of secret voting in this way places every citizen before another set of alternative decisions: should he keep his vote completely to himself, as is his right, or should he make his preference known to others within his primary groups only, to those within the organizations and associations he is part of, or to the general public?

This, in fact, brings about a stratification of the electorate on a "privacy-publicity" dimension: from those who never reveal their vote to anyone to those who publicly take their stand on the alternatives set and openly proclaim how they will or have voted. The active and militant in the political parties clearly cannot make much use of the secrecy provisions which may be important for them in the choice of particular candidates. However, it is part of their community role to commit themselves publicly between the major alternatives.

The Political Mobilization of the Inarticulate Strata

The effects of the secrecy provisions on the behavior of the masses of workers and later of women enfranchised through the final universalization of the suffrage have never been systematically studied. The marked contrasts in the turnout proportions between parallel elections in Prussia and in the Reich have frequently been documented, but no detailed ecological comparisons of results in open elections and results in secret elections have, as far as I have been able to ascertain, ever been attempted. Erik Högh has under way a fascinating analysis of the electoral registers for a sample of Danish constituencies from the period of open elections: here it will be of the greatest interest to analyze the extent of participation and the political preferences of the various categories of manual workers.

Comparative research on the processes of entry into politics is indeed still in its infancy. Tingsten was probably the first to give serious attention to the study of the electoral records for the last to be enfranchised, the workers and the women.[43] His actual analyses, however, did not go beyond the first step in this process, the use of the vote. Statistics on the turnout of the latest entrants into the electorate were available for some countries. Statistics on their further advances into the political arena have generally proved much more difficult to assemble and, what is crucial here, much more difficult to break down by categories of the electorate.

Maurice Duverger assembled an important body of comparative information on party memberships and established trends in the member-voter ratios for mass parties in western Europe.[44] These, however, were all derived from aggregate figures for entire parties, without any breakdowns by the occupation or the sex of the member. Historical statistics on the recruitment of party members from the ranks of the latest entrants into the electorate may still be assembled for the better-documented parties, but the data are often fragmentary and hard to evaluate. The outlook for historical comparisons is markedly better for the ultimate steps in participation in each system, the competitive participation in candidacies and the actual participation in decision-making in formally established elective offices. For such studies there will generally prove to be an abundance of documentary materials available for coding and counting, but so far hardly anything has been done in any country to assemble such statistics for the lower rungs of political systems. There is a growing body of literature on the recruitment of partici-

---

[43] Tingsten's work on the behavior of recently enfranchised groups needs to be completed and systematized on a variety of points. Quite particularly, it would be of great theoretical interest to undertake comparative analyses of the rate of "politicization" in the peripheral areas of each nation-state, the remote, less "modernized" areas of the national territory. This is a central concern in our current studies of electoral participation in Norway, to be reported on in the volume *Valg i Norge*, now in preparation. We find clear evidence that women are least prone to vote in the less accessible, least politicized areas along the coast. It is of interest to note that similar differences in the votes for women appeared in German statistics just after the introduction of female suffrage: cf. Gabriele Bremme, *Die politische Rolle der Frau in Deutschland* (Göttingen, Germany: Vandenhoeck & Ruprecht, 1956), p. 45, but have tended to disappear in postwar elections. This has been interpreted in terms of a process of "mobilization" by E. Paul in E. Paul, ed., *Wahlen und Wähler in Westdeutschland* (Villingen, Germany: Ring-Verlag, 1960), pp. 156-63.

[44] M. Duverger, *Political Parties* (London: Methuen, 1954), chap. 2.

pants in central, national decision-making,[45] but to reach fuller understanding of the "entry-into-politics" process, we shall clearly have to collect data on candidates and officers in samples of local administrative districts.[46]

Data on the socio-economic backgrounds of party members, candidates, and elected officials can to a large extent be assembled from regularly maintained "bookkeeping" records. Sources of this kind will only rarely, however, offer detailed data for analyses of the paths of recruitment and the over-all patterns of participation in community life, in policy-influencing organization, and in the flow of public and private communication about the polity and its affairs. To ensure a basis for such analyses we will normally have to proceed to direct data gathering, either through local inquiries and the use of informants or through personal interviews. Two distinct strategies of data gathering have been developed in such studies: the one starts out from rosters of organizationally visible participants (for example, party members,[47] party officials,[48] candidates, and elected officials); the other is to select cross-sectional samples from the electorate-at-large and to rely on breakdowns by levels of activity within the samples. Each procedure has its drawbacks as well as its advantages; the ideal solution is a design that combines the two.[49] Studies focusing exclusively on the visible participants will only allow very few comparisons with the rest of the electorate. Cross-sectional studies will allow a wide range of direct comparisons but in most cases will have to be prohibitively large to permit analyses of upper-echelon participants.[50] The basic diffi-

---

[45] Cf. H. D. Lasswell *et al.*, *The Comparative Study of Elites* (Stanford: Stanford University Press, 1952); D. Marvick, ed., *Political Decision-Makers: Recruitment and Performance* (Glencoe, Ill.: The Free Press, 1961).

[46] Our Norwegian program of research on parties, elections, and political behavior includes a study of the recruitment to local elective offices, but so far only for elections after World War II: cf. Rokkan and Campbell, *op. cit.*, pp. 81-84.

[47] Two examples are: O. Rantala's work on the membership of the Conservative party in Finland, *Konservatiivinen puolueyhteisö* (Helsinki: Tammi, 1956); and Renate Mayntz's study of the CDU members in a district of Berlin, *Parteiengruppen in der Grossstadt* (Cologne: Westdeutscher Verlag, 1959).

[48] An example is H. Valen and D. Katz, "An Electoral Contest in a Norwegian Community," in M. Janowitz, *op. cit.*, pp. 207-36.

[49] Two attempts in this direction are: Katz and Eldersveld, *op. cit.*; and Valen and Katz, *op. cit.*

[50] This, of course, will vary with the administrative structure and the population density of the country. Figures for Finland and Norway indicate that up

culty, however, lies in the time dimension; in most Western countries it took years after the final extension of the suffrage before adequate survey data started to get accumulated. Any time series that can be established for the recruitment of active participants among the lower strata and among women will be very short indeed. Something can be done through breakdowns by age within the samples, even more through systematic use of recall questions about the activity levels in the family or origin, and through analyses of social and political mobility, but serious gaps in our knowledge of the time sequences in the "entry-into-politics" processes will remain whatever we do in this direction.

However limited the possibilities of historical comparisons, cross-national analyses of survey data are clearly essential in any attempt to reach some understanding of the implications of mass suffrage for the functioning of Western-type political systems. Comparisons of the extent and scope of participation within the lower socio-economic strata can help us to gain insight into the functional importance of the right to vote: What does the suffrage mean for citizens in these strata? Is voting a peripheral activity of little consequence, or does it fit in with a wider range of participant activities in the community, in associations, in politics? Sample surveys can give us data on these wider contexts of participation, and comparisons of such data across communities and across national systems can give us clues to an understanding of the importance of the structural settings and the alternatives in the system for the recruitment of active participants from the lower strata within each society.

Our recent attempt at comparing data on participation from two systems differing as much from each other as Norway and the United States [51] points to a possible line of research in this direction. Our principal concern here was with the extent of political participation within the lower strata of two electorates: the workers as contrasted with the salaried employees, the professional people and the businessmen; the primary-educated as contrasted with the secondary-educated and the college-educated. We found for both countries the usual differences in turnout between the strata, and

---

to 2 per cent of any nationwide sample will be candidates for offices in local elections: see the articles on "Finland" and "Norway and the United States of America" in S. Rokkan, ed., "Citizen Participation in Political Life," *International Social Science Journal*, Vol. 12 (1960), esp. pp. 31-32 and 81-84.

[51] Rokkan and Campbell, *op. cit.*

we found consistent differences in the same direction for the extent of attention to the mass media during the campaign. We dealt with replications of "micro-micro" breakdowns. What changed the character of the analysis was the finding that there were no such uniform differences between the strata for organizational activity in politics. Using a simple index of participation based on party membership, attendance at meetings, and electoral work, we found no consistent differences between strata in the Norwegian sample but a marked and consistent one in the United States. We interpreted this to reflect the contrast between the two regimes in the alternatives set for the citizens, both as voters and potential recruits to party activity: in Norway a markedly class-distinct, "status-polarized" party system, in the United States much less correspondence between the lines of socio-economic cleavage and the lines of political conflict.[52] To explore this further we proceeded to a third-order "macro-micro-micro" comparison (CR-B in the typology suggested in Table 1). We placed the parties in the two systems in order of rank according to the proportions of manual workers among their voters, and we found that the class character of the parties made a decisive difference in the recruitment of active participants in political work. In the Norwegian Labour party we found manual workers more likely to be active than middle class voters. In the more heterogeneous Democratic party in the United States we found a tendency in the opposite direction: the level of participation was slightly lower for workers than for middle class voters. The most marked status differentials in participation were found within the parties with the lowest proportions of working-class voters—the opposition parties in Norway and the Republican parties in the United States. This, of course, cannot be taken to be conclusive evidence; the differences were found within nation-wide cross-sections and will need to be tested by categories of communities. However, the findings do suggest important hypotheses for continued comparative research: they accentuate the importance of assembling data on the character of the political choices confronting the worker, on the opportunities open to him for experience and training in organizational skills, and on the channels of recruitment from class-distinct associations such as unions to membership and activity in political parties.

---

[52] For a general discussion of "status-polarization," see Campbell et al., op. cit., chap. 13.

Perhaps the most important set of factors to be taken into account in any cooperative study of participation bears on the organizational bases for the recruitment of active supporters in party-political work: How open, direct, and stable are the channels of recruitment from the given economic, cultural, or religious organization to the given party? What are the alternative "policy pay-offs" of other affiliations, other modes of influence, or for the given organization? What are the alternative prospects of achievement and advancement for the active participants in the given organization?

Questions along these lines may be raised for any association or organization and for any party. They are of particular importance in comparative studies of the socio-economic bases for party conflict. In pushing further our tentative comparisons between Norway and the United States, these are exactly the questions we shall want to explore in detail: the character of the tie-ins between the different labor unions and the parties, the distinctiveness of the union votes, the extent of recruitment from union activity to political activity, and the relationships between union activity and participation in other organizations and associations in the community and the nation.[53]

Party-Political Activity, Community Influence, and Organizational Power

With these questions we are already at the heart of another important area for comparative research: the study of factors which cause differences between systems and changes within systems in connection with the importance of party politics and elections in the over-all process of decision-making for the territorial population.

In an attempt to clarify issues in the current debate over method and theory in the study of community power structures, Peter Rossi recently suggested a typology and a set of hypotheses of general importance in comparative research on participation.[54]

Rossi's basic concern is with community conditions making for separation between the political elite and the economic elite. In terms of our discussion the focus of his analysis is on conditions

---

[53] A report of a comparison of union-party tie-ins is in progress.

[54] Rossi, "Theory and Method in the Study of Power in the Local Community."

for the development of two distinct channels of decision-making, one based on mass suffrage and party organization, the other based on professional status, managerial position, and the control of wealth.

Rossi specifies three sets of conditions for the development of such separate channels: (1) the *size* of the community—this determines the extent to which local government offices will be full-time roles segregated from any other roles of the incumbents; (2) the strength of *partisan traditions* in local government, the stability and competitive character of the local party system; and (3) the extent of *"political crystallization,"* [55] the extent to which the social structure of the community is reflected in the divisions of the electorate at the polls.

Rossi sees a "natural strain" in community life toward overlap and congruence between the economic and political dominance. This is the normal situation in small communities in the United States, whether run by the Democrats in the South or the Republicans in the North. There is a tendency in the same direction in larger communities with strong traditions of nonpartisan "managerial" governments; such traditions generally tend to strengthen the position of the local economic elite and to prevent the growth of "countervailing powers" deriving their strength from the mass suffrage.

A marked separation between political and economic elites will generally be found in northern cities governed by Democratic politicians deriving their power from socio-economically and ethnically distinct electorates. In such communities the level of status polarization will regularly be found to be as high as in countries with clearly class-divided party systems throughout their territory.[56] If we compared just these United States cities with cities in a country with a major labor party such as Norway we should *not* find differences of the magnitude we reported for nationwide samples. It is important to note that in the United States a high level of status polarization in the division of local votes does not appear to increase appreciably the recruitment of working class

---

[55] This is the term introduced by G. E. Lenski, *American Sociological Review,* Vol. 19 (1954), pp. 405-13; in this context it is synonymous with the term "status polarization" used elsewhere in this paper.

[56] Correlations by precinct between economic/ethnic indices and the Democratic vote have been found to be very high in such cities: see Rossi and Cutright, *op. cit.;* and Katz and Eldersveld, *op. cit.*

citizens to public positions. Comparative evidence from communities differing in the level of status polarization should not be very difficult to assemble, but the scattered local studies at hand are not always easy to compare for rates of recruitment. Reviewing such evidence as is at hand, Rossi finds that the cleavage between the political and the occupational elites will largely tend to be a cleavage within the world of business and the professions; the leaders in the "public" sectors of such communities are most likely to be recruited from the ranks of small businessmen and lawyers at the hearts of extensive networks of local face-to-face acquaintances while the leaders in the "private" economic and professional sectors are more likely to derive their power from positions in large-scale, territory-wide organizations cutting across a variety of localities.[57]

Here we touch on an important theme in the analysis of the implications of mass suffrage for the functioning of pluralist political systems: what changes will occur in the over-all processes of decision-making with the mobilization of the less articulate electorates for political action and with the consequent growth of independent centers of electoral power?

Rossi hypothesizes that the three basic strategies used by economic elites in countering the effects of this growth of electoral power will be these: (1) the promotion of nonpartisan electoral systems and of technically neutral administrative agencies; (2) the intensified proliferation of privately controlled community institutions and voluntary civic associations serving as instruments of influence and pressure in conflicts over local policies; and (3) the development of state-wide or nationwide interest organizations to influence policies beyond the control of the local political elite.

Hypotheses of this kind may be tested either diachronically or synchronically. Several attempts have been made to establish trends toward a withdrawal of the economic elites from local polities in the United States over the last decades,[58] but the factors accounting for such trends are complex and certainly cannot be attributed solely to the growth of independent electoral power centers. Synchronic comparisons of the extent of private policy-

---

[57] This contrast is discussed in some detail by Rossi in a thought-provoking paper recently prepared for the Fund for the Advancement of Education, " 'Public' and 'Private' Leadership in America" (May, 1960, mimeo.).

[58] R. O. Schulze, "The Role of Economic Dominants in Community Power Structure," *American Sociological Review,* Vol. 23 (1958), pp. 3-9; also: "The Bifurcation of Power in a Satellite City" in M. Janowitz, *op. cit.,* pp. 19-80.

influencing activity through community institutions and voluntary associations have, to my knowledge, never been attempted in the United States. Rossi's hypothesis is that such activities would be more extensive when the separation of the economic from the political elite in the community is more marked. The basic task here would be to find some meaningful measure of the "importance" of the private institutions and the voluntary associations in each community; mere statistics on size of memberships and the economic roles of the active participants would not be likely to take us very far in this direction.

Whatever the technical difficulties of testing the hypotheses suggested by Rossi, the underlying reasoning about the processes of decision-making in mass-suffrage systems will clearly prove important in future attempts at cross-national comparisons.

The most straightforward of the tasks to be taken up in comparative research on these wider contexts of participation is the collation of national statistics on the recruitment of members and officers in different categories of voluntary associations. Studies of the linkages between association memberships and political activity have been undertaken in several countries over the last years,[59] and evidence on the character of such linkages can now be assembled for a wide range of structurally different systems. The studies so far undertaken have focused on social activities in the community and in wider organizations as sets of conditioning variables in explaining levels of political partisanship and participation. The simplest way of establishing the linkages have been by direct counts of the total number of nonpolitical memberships and offices held by each respondent and by analyses of the correlations with indices of political activity. In moving toward comparative analyses of channels of influence on community policy making it will clearly be essential to go beyond such crude correlations; voluntary associa-

---

[59] For the United States, see the secondary analyses of NORC data by C. R. Wright and H. H. Hyman, "Voluntary Association Memberships of American Adults," *American Sociological Review*, Vol. 23 (1958), pp. 284-94. For Finland, see: Erik Allardt *et al.*, "On the Cumulative Nature of Leisure-Time Activities," *Acta Sociologica*, Vol. 3 (1958), pp. 165-72. For Germany, see: E. Reigzrotzski, *Soziale Verflechtungen in der Bundesrepublik* (Tübingen, Germany: Mohr, 1956). For Norway, see: S. Rokkan, "Electoral Activity, Party Membership and Organizational Influence," *Acta Sociologica*, Vol. 4 (1959), pp. 25-37. For Sweden, see: H. Zetterberg, "Voluntary Associations and Organized Power," *Industria International* (in press).

tions and private organizations will have to be differentiated not only according to their substantive goals and their membership criteria [60] but also in terms of the socio-economic background and political partisanship of their clientele and their leaders and, what is of particular importance here, in terms of the "pay-off" probabilities of action through parties vs. action directly on policy makers and administrative agencies. Detailed studies along these lines would require the co-ordination of institutional analyses and surveys of samples of community leaders as well as of the rank-and-file electorate. Attempts in this direction have been made in some countries,[61] but research in this area is still at a very early stage of development.

Comparative research along these lines may help us to gain further insight into the implications of the processes of political change in systems undergoing economic growth. With the early phases of industrialization went a variety of tendencies toward both greater integration of the national decision-making machinery and a widening of the representative bases of each regime. The introduction of mass suffrage made it possible to mobilize the lower strata of economically dependent citizens into distinct political parties and set the stage for the development of new channels of influence on the processes of decision at local and national levels. At the same time, and partly in reaction to these developments, most systems of the West witnessed an extraordinary growth in the scope and activity of voluntary associations and interest organizations. With the continued growth and diversification of each national economy, these networks of organizations tended to cut across the earlier party-political divisions and to create cross pressures making for a lowering of the polarization in the system.[62] If Rossi is right in his conjectures, we are faced here with an intriguing process of historical dialectics; the extension of the suffrage increased the chances for a status polarization of national politics, but this very polarization brought about a proliferation of sectional and functional organizations which in turn tended to soften the over-all strains in the

---

[60] Cf. A. M. Rose, *Theory and Method in the Social Sciences* (Minneapolis: University of Minnesota Press, 1954), chap. 3.

[61] Reports are in preparation on the efforts made toward this end within the Norwegian program of research on parties, elections, and political behavior.

[62] This point of view has been developed in further detail for Sweden by H. Zetterberg, *op. cit.*

system and reduce the level of polarization.[63] What we tend to find is an accumulation of forces making for a narrowing of the alternatives for national politics, a fragmentation of the networks of policy-influencing organizations, and a consequent decline in the importance of the decisions of the electorate-at-large. This may tend to lower the level of general political participation and to alienate from politics sizable sections of the once enfranchised citizenry, leaving the basic decisions to a bargaining process between interest organizations, parties, and agencies and departments of the national bureaucracy. We see tendencies in these directions in many countries of the West; the developments toward *Entideologisierung* and "all party governments" are cases in point.[64] We know far too little about the dynamics of these developments, and we need to do much more to facilitate co-operation and coordination in the study of these problems in different countries.

---

[63] N. W. Polsby, *op. cit.*, chap. 7, has suggested such a cyclical pattern for developments in United States cities since the peak inflows of ethnically distinct lower class citizens.

[64] Cf. especially O. Kirchheimer, "The Waning of Opposition in Parliamentary Regimes," *Social Research*, Vol. 24 (1957), pp. 127-56; and A. Vulpius, *Die Allparteienregierung* (Frankfurt a/M: Metzner, 1957).

The Utility and Limitations of Aggregate Data in the Study of Electoral Behavior

Austin Ranney
UNIVERSITY OF ILLINOIS

Scholarly studies of electoral behavior depend mainly upon two types of data for their raw materials. The first type is commonly called "aggregate data" and consists of distributions of whole populations among the categories of various systems of classification without providing information about which category any *particular* unit of any population falls into. A familiar example is provided by official election returns, which gave us such information as the fact that in the 1956 presidential elections the voters of Champaign County, Illinois, were divided 28,190 for Eisenhower and 13,799 for Stevenson. The returns cannot, however, tell us into which category Dean J. W. Doe or Professor D. G. Roe fell. The election laws, indeed, are designed to prevent any such disclosure of information about how specific persons cast their votes.

The second type of data may be called "individual data" and consists of facts specifically and directly known about particular units of populations. One example is provided by a roll of registered voters: not only do we know how many persons are registered in a particular county, but we can readily discover which particular persons are and are not registered. Far more widely used in the study of electoral behavior, however, are "sample survey data," which consist of recorded responses directly obtained from certain individuals selected as constituting a "representative sample" of the population being studied. Thus, if we select and interview, say, 200 adults as a sample of Champaign County's voters, and Messrs. Doe and Roe happen to be selected, not only can we state how many of our respondents say they voted for Eisenhower and how many say they voted for Stevenson, but we can also place Doe and Roe each in his proper category.

There is little doubt that the most notable development in the study of electoral behavior in the past two decades has been the growth in prestige of "sample surveys" (i.e., studies relying mainly on individual data provided by interviews of persons in selected samples), as manifested by their steadily increasing number, by their extension to the politics of many different nations, and by the eagerness of practitioners as well as students of politics to know and use their findings. Paralleling the numerous studies of particular electorates, there has also developed a considerable body of literature on survey methodology—describing, analyzing, and evaluating its presuppositions, techniques, and problems.

The prestige of the sample surveys should not, however, obscure the fact that the greater proportion of the studies of electoral behavior published since 1940 have continued to rest, as they did before, mainly or wholly on aggregate data, particularly election returns and census reports.[1] This is not surprising, for relatively few political scientists have the facilities and skills required to do sound survey research. What is surprising, however, is the paucity of commentaries on the methodology of aggregate data research. To be sure, many reports of findings contain a page or two on methodological problems encountered in the particular study, but comprehensive analyses comparable to those in which the literature on survey methodology abounds are hard to find.[2] The upshot

---

[1] This is shown by earlier surveys of the literature on electoral behavior: S. J. Eldersveld, "Theory and Method in Voting Behavior Research," *Journal of Politics,* Vol. 13 (1951), pp. 70-87; R. Heberle, *Social Movements* (New York: Appleton-Century-Crofts, Inc., 1951), pp. 206-65; and S. M. Lipset, P. F. Lazarsfeld, A. H. Barton, and J. Linz, "The Sychology of Voting: An Analysis of Political Behavior," in G. Lindzey, ed., *Handbook of Social Psychology* (Reading, Mass.: Addison-Wesley, 1954), Vol. 2, pp. 1124-75.

[2] Thus, many aggregate data studies rely on Stuart A. Rice's thirty-year-old classic, *Quantitative Methods in Politics* (New York: Alfred A. Knopf, 1928), for their methodological underpinning. V. O. Key, Jr.'s *Primer of Statistics for Political Scientists* (New York: Thomas Y. Crowell Company, 1954) discusses exhaustively and well one aspect, but is not intended to be a comprehensive discussion of the whole approach. Heberle, *op. cit.,* has a number of helpful, if scattered, comments. Perhaps the most comprehensive treatises on the subject since Rice are two French works: F. Goguel, *Initiation aux recherches de géographie électorale* (Paris: Centre d'études sociologiques, 1949); and G. Dupeux and F. Goguel, *Sociologie électorale; Esquisses d'un bilan; Guide de recherches* (Paris: Armand Colin, 1951).

is that by far the more commonly employed of the two types of research has received by far the lesser amount of critical attention.

The present paper has no pretensions of restoring the balance, but seeks only to make a modest contribution to that desirable end by attempting, in the sections that follow, four tasks: (1) a review of the principal similarities and differences among recent aggregate data studies of electoral behavior, (2) a description of some of the special advantages of such studies, (3) a discussion of some of their chief limitations, and (4) some suggestions about the use of aggregate data in the total scholarly effort to understand the world of politics.

I

Most of the recent aggregate data studies of electoral behavior [3] have been conducted by American, French, and British scholars. Despite some differences in emphasis among them (see below), they all employ what is sometimes called the "ecological" approach. This term has been borrowed from biological science, where it is usually defined as "the study of the relation of organisms or groups of organisms to their environment, or the interrelations between living organisms and their environment." [4] Thus, an ecological study of electoral behavior seeks to understand the interrelationships of political parties and voters with one another and with the social and legal environment in which they act.

Most ecological studies proceed in some such manner as the following. Election returns from subsections (counties, cities, precincts, departments, constituencies, etc.) of the electoral unit being studied are tabulated and analyzed in various ways [5] so as to identify recurring patterns of voter turnout and preference along the spatial dimension of differences among various areas or the temporal dimension of change over time within particular areas or a combination of both. These voting patterns are then juxtaposed with a wide variety of political, social, and economic data about

---

[3] Throughout this paper the term "electoral behavior" includes both the behavior of individual voters and the behavior of electorates (i.e., particular geographical aggregations of voters possessing the legal power to elect particular public officials).

[4] E. P. Odum, *Fundamentals of Ecology* (Philadelphia: W. B. Saunders Company, 1953), p. 3.

[5] A useful discussion of the principal techniques available for this purpose is provided by Key's *Primer, op. cit.*

the areas and their populations—income levels, predominant forms
of economic activity, ethnic composition, religious affiliations, party
organization and leadership, election laws, historical events, and
so on. Finally, the observed patterns of electoral behavior are
explained in terms of what the particular author regards as significant correlations (whether defined and expressed in the mathematical terms of descriptive statistics or in the "common sense"
terms of historians and journalists) with particular aspects of the
environment.

Although scholars using aggregate data now generally follow the
foregoing theme, American, French, and British scholars have each
developed national variations on it. The American studies make the
fullest use of the techniques of descriptive statistics and concentrate mainly upon ethnic, social, legal, and economic factors as explanatory devices.[6] The French studies, and the Italian, Belgian,
and other continental studies modeled on them, have been characterized by what is variously called the "electoral geography" or
"electoral sociology" approach. They differ from the American
studies mainly in their greater use of maps as descriptive and
analytical devices, and for the most part they classify electoral behavior along the single ideological scale of "left-center-right," no
doubt because they deal with multiple-party systems conventionally
viewed as spread along such a continuum.[7] British work in this field
consists mainly of the studies in "psephology" emanating from

---

[6] The leading studies are far too numerous for more than a sample to be
presented here. Eldersveld, op. cit., offers a useful summary of the studies
published up to 1950. Since then some representative examples of American
studies of state politics are: V. O. Key, Jr., American State Politics: An Introduction (New York: Alfred A. Knopf, 1956); D. Lockard, New England State
Politics (Princeton, N.J.: Princeton University Press, 1959); J. H. Fenton, Politics in the Border States (New Orleans: The Hauser Press, 1957); and L. D.
Epstein, Politics in Wisconsin (Madison: University of Wisconsin Press, 1958).
Studies of congressional politics include: M. Moos, Politics, Presidents and
Coattails (Baltimore: The Johns Hopkins Press, 1952); D. H. Ackerman, Jr.,
"Significance of Congressional Races with Identical Candidates in Successive
District Elections," Midwest Journal of Political Science, Vol. 1 (1957), pp.
173-80; T. V. Gilpatrick, "Price Support Policy and the Midwest Farm Vote,"
Midwest Journal of Political Science, Vol. 3 (1959), pp. 319-35. Some leading
studies of city politics are: E. B. Olds and D. W. Salmon, St. Louis Voting
Behavior Study (St. Louis: Metropolitan St. Louis Census Committee of the
St. Louis chapter of the American Statistical Association, 1948); and E. C.
Banfield, "The Politics of Metropolitan Area Organization," Midwest Journal
of Political Science, Vol. 1 (1957), pp. 77-91.

[7] In addition to the works of Goguel and Dupeux cited in note 2, a considerable volume of studies has been published under the sponsorship of the
Fondation Nationale des Sciences Politiques. Representative examples are:

Nuffield College, Oxford. The "Nuffield school" has produced a book describing the candidates, issues, campaigns, and results for each British general election since that of 1945.[8] For a variety of reasons, some ideological[9] and some practical (e.g., British election returns are not available for subconstituency units), the British studies have been more historical-journalistic-descriptive and less "scientific" and "behavioral" in method and tone than either their American or their French counterparts. Nevertheless, the recent British studies have made increasing use of statistical analyses of aggregate data, and the differences among the three national variations on the basic ecological theme appear to be growing steadily less distinct. In any case, the *common* advantages and limitations of all these studies are the principal concerns of this paper.

II

Aggregate data have several advantages as raw material for the study of electoral behavior. First and most obvious is the fact that, by contrast with survey data, they are available for a wide variety of electorates and relatively easy and inexpensive to obtain and analyze. Most democratic nations have for some time published election returns for their principal constituencies, and many publish returns broken down by various subconstituency units. Also, most nations periodically conduct censuses and publish reports presenting veritable avalanches of social and economic information about their populations. The result is an immense body of data, rich in its variety and coverage, and easily and cheaply accessible to individual scholars anywhere in the world. To secure reliable sample survey data, by contrast, requires not only a skilled and

---

F. Goguel, *Géographie des Élections Françaises de 1870 à 1951* (Paris: Armand Colin, 1955); and R. E. De Smet and R. Evalenko, *Les Élections Belges* (Brussels: Institut de Sociologie Solvay, 1956). See also M. Davis, "French Electoral Sociology," *Public Opinion Quarterly*, Vol. 22 (1958), pp. 35-55.

[8] The 1945 study was written by R. B. McCallum and A. Readman, that of 1950 by H. G. Nicholas, those of 1951 and 1955 by D. E. Butler, and that of 1959 by D. E. Butler and R. Rose. Growing out of these studies is a more general work by Butler, *The Electoral System in Britain, 1918-1951* (Oxford: at the Clarendon Press, 1953).

[9] Cf. the critiques of American-style behaviorism in: B. Crick, *The American Science of Politics: Its Origins and Conditions* (Berkeley: University of California Press, 1958); and D. E. Butler, *The Study of Political Behaviour* (London: Hutchinson, 1958). See also the shrewd and amusing discussion of the sources of American and British disagreements about method in A. Hacker, "Political Behaviour and Political Behavior," *Political Studies*, Vol. 7 (1959), pp. 32-40.

relatively elaborate research organization, such as that built up over the years by the Survey Research Center at the University of Michigan, but also considerable funds to support the organization and its operations. Thus survey research, unlike aggregate data research, is not something any individual scholar can do on his own in the library after he has finished his classes for the day.

Second, the accessibility and inexpensiveness of aggregate data invite replicative and comparative studies on a wide scale. To be sure, far fewer studies of either sort have actually been published than the data makes possible, but there are indications that their number and quality are growing.[10]

A third advantage of aggregate data in general and election returns in particular is that, for finding answers to many questions about electoral behavior, they are the "hardest" data we can get, in the sense that their meaning and comparability vary less from area to area, from time to time, and from study to study than do most survey data. For one thing, the aggregate data researcher does not directly interact with his basic sources of information and so has no handicap comparable to the much-discussed problem of "interviewer bias" in sample surveys. For another, recorded votes are not merely constructs established by scholars for research convenience; they play a direct and official role in the political process comparable to that played by money in the economic process. Their periodic allocations are the immediate determinants of the identity of the persons who occupy many of the most strategic positions in governments and political parties. Whatever complex socio-psychological processes may underly the voters' decisions to make particular allocations, the votes themselves constitute a basic medium of political exchange. Thus their relative "hardness" as much as their accessibility, makes election returns a significant body of data for political analysis.[11]

III

Anyone who uses aggregate data in his research soon learns that, while election returns and census reports are easier to come

---

[10] See, for example, the recent replicative studies by J. A. Robinson and W. H. Standing, "Inter-Party Competition and Primary Contesting: The Case of Indiana," *American Political Science Review*, Vol. 52 (1958), pp. 1066-77, and "Some Correlates of Voter Participation: The Case of Indiana," *Journal of Politics*, Vol. 22 (1960), pp. 96-111.

[11] Cf. Rice, *op. cit.*, pp. 93-94.

by than high-quality sample survey data, a number of minor but irritating practical problems nevertheless arise in the course of collecting and analyzing them. For one thing, some fraud and more honest error are apparently inevitable in the casting and counting of votes and reporting of results, particularly in electoral systems using paper ballots. This makes no great difference if the error has no systematic bias or if the bias is known and can be corrected, but it means that official election returns are always only an approximate, never an exact, picture of the voters' will.[12] For another, in the United States the boundaries of census tracts rarely coincide exactly with those of election precincts, and so the researcher who wishes to use these smallest of election districts as his basic units cannot rely solely on census reports for determining the various social and economic characteristics of their populations.

Of far greater methodological concern, however, is the extreme crudeness of aggregate data analysis as an instrument for describing and explaining the behavior of individual voters. A number of studies have set themselves the task of describing how particular kinds of voters vote and why they vote as they do. Most of them proceed from a premise succinctly stated in the Olds-Salmon St. Louis study:

Statistics of election results in themselves give little insight into voting behavior. In order to gain insight, it is necessary to ascertain the kind of people who vote in a certain way. It is impossible, and undesirable, to know how each individual votes, but it is possible to learn how voters in each precinct vote as a body; and since the citizens in these small election units have many characteristics in common, it is possible to generalize with accuracy regarding the relationship between a certain way of voting and a certain kind of people.[13]

Accordingly, many aggregate data studies select "homogeneous" election-reporting units—that is, small areas (preferably precincts or, at most, wards) in which most of the residents share one or more ethnic, religious, economic, or other characteristics whose influence on voting behavior is being investigated. If these election districts report a highly disproportionate allocation of preferences and/or an unusually high or low rate of turnout, the studies

---

[12] Cf. S. J. Eldersveld and A. A. Applegate, *Michigan's Recounts for Governor, 1950 and 1952: A Systematic Analysis of Election Error* (Ann Arbor: Bureau of Government, University of Michigan, 1954). This study reported error in the count of from 2 to 3 per cent, which error consistently favored the dominant party in areas with the least interparty competition.

[13] Olds and Salmon, *op. cit.,* p. A-3.

typically conclude that the particular characteristics are significantly related to (the more cautious say "highly correlated with" and the less cautious say "have a tendency to produce") the observed patterns of preference or turnout. In this manner a number of generalizations have been constructed about the behavior of such types of voters as Jews, Negroes, low-income people, farmers of various sorts, and the like.[14]

The common-sense sort of plausibility in the foregoing logic is most tempting. After all, if 90 per cent of the people in a precinct are Negroes and 85 per cent of the precinct's vote regularly goes to the Democrats, then most of the Democratic voters must be Negroes and most of the Negroes must be voting Democratic. And if one finds this pattern repeated in all or most predominantly Negro precincts, it seems entirely reasonable to conclude that there is something about being Negro that strongly impels Negroes to prefer the Democrats.

Yet no matter how plausible such an inference may appear by the canons of common sense, it has no warrant in generally accepted statistical theory and practice. In a widely-cited article of a decade ago, W. S. Robinson demonstrated that "ecological correlations" (those using aggregate data exclusively) have no necessary relation to or correspondence with "individual correlations" (those using individual data) about the same populations.[15] A number of subsequent commentaries have suggested that ecological correlations are helpful for certain other purposes, but all have confirmed Robinson's finding that correlations based on aggregate data cannot be relied upon to produce reliable descriptions or explanations of the behavior of individuals.[16] Warren E. Miller

---

[14] For Jews, see L. H. Fuchs, *The Political Behavior of American Jews* (Glencoe, Ill.: The Free Press, 1956); and W. Spinrad, "New York's Third Party Voters," *Public Opinion Quarterly*, Vol. 21 (1957-58), pp. 548-51. For Negroes and low-income people, see Olds and Salmon, *op. cit.;* L. C. Kesselman, "Negro Voting in a Border Community: Louisville, Kentucky," *Journal of Negro Education*, Vol. 26 (1957), pp. 273-80; and O. Glantz, "Recent Negro Ballots in Philadelphia," *Journal of Negro Education*, Vol. 28 (1959), pp. 430-38. For farmers, see Gilpatrick, *op. cit.;* and J. Klatzmann, "Comment Votent les Paysans Français," *Revue Française de Science Politique*, Vol. 8 (1958), pp. 13-41.

[15] W. S. Robinson, "Ecological Correlations and the Behavior of Individuals," *American Sociological Review*, Vol. 15 (1950), pp. 351-57.

[16] Cf. L. A. Goodman, "Ecological Regressions and the Behavior of Individuals," *American Sociological Review*, Vol. 18 (1953), pp. 663-64; P. F. Lazarsfeld and A. H. Barton, "Quantitative Measurement in the Social Sci-

has given political scientists a telling illustration of this point by showing how the familiar generalization from aggregate data about the pulling power of "presidential coattails" collapses when it is tested by information about the attitudes and behavior of individual voters gathered by a sample survey.[17]

IV

If aggregate data studies cannot usefully deal with questions about the behavior of individual voters, what place, if any, can they have in the more general field of electoral behavior? In the present writer's opinion, they are most likely to make valuable contributions if they bypass questions about particular individuals and types of individuals and adopt as their sole object of inquiry the behavior of *electorates.*

This opinion is based on the view that electorates,[18] no less than individual voters, are significant units for political analysis. An electorate, to be sure, is composed of individual voters, and its behavior is merely the sum of their individual behaviors. Admittedly, therefore, we cannot get an adequate understanding of the behavior of electorates without studying the perceptions, attitudes, motivations, social and economic affiliations, and other socio-psychological processes operating in the individuals who compose them. The sample survey is clearly the best tool yet developed for investigating these matters, and the studies using it have contributed a dimension badly needed by and notably missing from much of traditional political science.

Yet in investigating other aspects of electoral behavior it is useful to regard electorates not merely as arithmetic sums of individuals but rather as units playing special and significant roles in the political process and therefore worthy of analysis in their own right. After all, nations too are aggregations of individuals, but few would say that it is useless or nonsensical to speak of, for example, what "the United States" does to counter the policy

---

ences," in D. Lerner and H. D. Lasswell, eds., *The Policy Sciences* (Stanford, Calif.: Stanford University Press, 1951), pp. 189-92; and L. A. Goodman, "Some Alternatives to Ecological Correlations," *American Journal of Sociology,* Vol. 44 (May, 1959), pp. 610-25.

[17] W. E. Miller, "Presidential Coattails: A Study in Political Myth and Methodology," *Public Opinion Quarterly,* Vol. 19 (1955-56), pp. 353-68.

[18] See note 3 for the meaning of "electorate" as used here.

of "the Soviet Union," as though these two national aggregations were identifiable political actors. By the same token, a significant dimension is added to the discussion of such matters as the election of a President or the composition of a Congress if they are conceptualized not only as the result of the behavior of individual voters but also as the result of the behavior of state and district electorates. Politicians find it possible and useful to talk of what "Iowa" or "the First District" or "the Second Ward" or even "the American People" have done or are likely to do without forgetting that each electorate is composed of individual voters. Surely political scientists can do the same.

Accordingly, if aggregate data studies carefully and thoroughly identify and describe recurring patterns of preference and turnout characteristic of particular electorates and clusters of electorates over time and, by ecological correlations, relate those patterns to other traits of the electorates and their environments, they can be valuable allies to the sample surveys in the investigation of electoral behavior.

For one thing, they can provide information of great utility for the validation of the various survey studies' samples. For another, they can suggest hypotheses for further investigation by both types of studies. Perhaps the principal aid they can render, however, is to help overcome the time-bound and place-bound limitations of most sample survey studies. The great majority of the latter have, because of their great expense, been confined to particular local areas at particular points in time.[19] These limitations, in the view of some commentators, raise serious doubts about the *general* applicability of the findings to the most interesting questions about electoral behavior. Raymond Aron's criticism of the French "electoral sociology" studies, for instance, could well be applied to many sample survey reports:

On ne manque pas d'information sur les différents tempéraments politiques des Français, selon les regions au pays. Mais la recherche microscopique, dans le cadre de la circonscription, risque d'accumuler des renseignements intéressants ou curieux, sans aboutir à aucune conclusion.[20]

---

[19] An outstanding exception has, of course, been the Survey Research Center's studies of national samples in every national election since 1952, all of which consider the phenomenon of long-term change.

[20] R. Aron, "Électeurs, Partis et Elus," *Revue Française de Science Politique,* Vol. 5 (1955), p. 246.

Similarly, V. O. Key comments that "neither the particular findings (of most sample survey studies) nor the generalizations about these microscopic situations tell us much about the political order observed or political orders in general." He adds that, because of their time-bound character, most sample survey studies have not coped with the problems posed by the fact that "many of the great and really significant political actions—units of political behavior—take place over comparatively long periods of time." And he concludes: "If the specialist in electoral behavior is to be a student of politics, his major concern must be the population of elections, not the population of individual voters. One does not gain an understanding of elections by the simple cumulation of the type-findings from the microscopic analysis of the individuals in the system." [21]

V

The thesis of this paper has been that aggregate data studies can, if their advantages and limitations are properly understood and dealt with, play an invaluable role in the study of electoral behavior. If this thesis has any merit, one of the most encouraging recent developments in this field is the fact that in each of the three national "schools" mentioned previously there is a growing tendency to combine aggregate data and survey data in an effort to develop descriptions and explanations that are more precise, more widely applicable, and of greater significance for general theories of electoral behavior than either approach has produced by itself.

In the United States the most notable recent instance of this tendency is the Survey Research Center's comprehensive and impressive study of the American presidential electorate.[22] The center's forthcoming study of the 1958 congressional elections is expected to proceed even further along these lines, and most political scientists are likely to agree with Key's judgment that these studies are conspicuous examples of the possibility and desirability of combining aggregate and individual data.[23]

In France, this same trend appears in the study of the 1956 gen-

---

[21] V. O. Key, Jr., "The Politically Relevant in Surveys," *Public Opinion Quarterly*, Vol. 24 (1960), pp. 54-61.

[22] A. Campbell, P. E. Converse, W. E. Miller, and D. E. Stokes, *The American Voter* (New York: John Wiley & Sons, Inc., 1960), especially chap. 11.

[23] Key, "The Politically Relevant in Surveys."

eral election published under the sponsorship of the *Fondation Nationale des Sciences Politiques,* which adds to the usual "electoral sociology" analyses the results of a *sondage* (sample survey) in the First District of the Seine.[24] A comparable effort with perhaps even greater potential, and one deserving the close attention of scholars everywhere, is the joint attempt of the Institute for Social Research in Oslo and the Christian Michelsen Institute in Bergen to combine French "electoral sociology" techniques, content analysis of campaign speeches and documents, community surveys, and national sample surveys to achieve a broad and yet precise understanding of Norwegian electoral behavior.[25]

In Great Britain the Nuffield studies in "psephology" have increasingly added to their descriptions of campaign events and their analyses of constituency returns material from Gallup polls and other survey reports to add the dimension of the perceptions, attitudes, and reactions of individual voters.[26]

The achievements of these studies show that the student of electoral behavior who has neither the skills nor the financial resources to conduct survey research need not abjure aggregate data research. So long as he understands the limitations of his data and does not try to make them tell stories they are incapable of telling, he may contribute knowledge that even his friends doing sample surveys will find methodologically respectable and socially useful.

---

[24] M. Duverger, F. Goguel, and J. Touchard, eds., *Les Élections du 2 Janvier 1956* (Paris: Armand Colin, 1957).

[25] Cf. S. Rokkan, "Electoral Activity, Party Membership and Organizational Influence: An Analysis of Data from the Norwegian Election Studies, 1957," *Acta Sociologica,* Vol. 4, pp. 25-37; and S. Rokkan, U. Torgersen, H. Valen, and G. Dupeux, "Les Élections Norvegiennes du 7 Octobre 1957," *Revue Française de Science Politique,* Vol. 8 (1958), pp. 73-94.

[26] Survey data is used extensively in the most recent study in this series: D. E. Butler and R. Rose, *The British General Election of 1959* (London: Macmillan and Co., 1960).

Some Recent Trends in International Relations Theory and Research

Richard C. Snyder
NORTHWESTERN UNIVERSITY

This essay is intended as a bird's-eye view of selected trends in the study of international relations in the United States, with emphasis on the period 1956-61. Because of the nature of the original assignment given to the writer, no effort will be made to cover prescriptive theories, the literature embodying "policy advice," or diplomatic history, important as these are. Although what follows is perforce selective, it is hoped that anyone who addressed the same task would see fit to cover roughly the same kinds of materials. Moreover, the purpose here is not to render *ad hoc* personal judgments but simultaneously to make a report and suggest the emergent structure of the field.

GENERAL TRENDS

The bulk of our presentation will focus on specific theoretical analysis and research activities. However, certain general statements are in order.

Theory Development and Conceptual Clarification

Evidence of growing precision, explicitness, and coherence in theory-building and conceptualization has been noted by more than one commentator.[1] A trend toward visibly greater preoccupa-

[1] H. D. Lasswell, "The Scientific Study of International Relations," *Yearbook of World Affairs*, Vol. 12 (1958); C. McClelland, "The Function of Theory in International Relations," *Journal of Conflict Resolution*, Vol. 4 (1960), pp. 303-37; R. C. Snyder, "Toward Greater Order in the Study of International

tion with theoretical concerns is exemplified by Fox, ed., *Theoretical Aspects of International Relations*, by the September, 1960, issue of the *Journal of Conflict Resolution* (Vol. 4, No. 3) devoted to "The Place of Theory in the Conduct and Study of International Relations," K. Knorr and S. Verba, eds., *The International System: Theoretical Essays*, and J. Rosenau, ed., *International Politics and Foreign Policy: A Reader in Research and Theory*.[1a] Critical evaluations of theories, conceptual schemes, and frames of reference can be found in works by Hoffman, Hyvarinen, Kindleberger, Sprout, and Sondermann—to name but a few.[2] McClelland has summarized admirably the agreements and disagreements among theoreticians.[3] Criteria for the acceptability and usefulness of theories and concepts have been discussed.[4] In sum, as our purposes, operations, and assumptions are more fully revealed, it has become somewhat easier to locate, compare, relate, and extend various "approaches" and to determine the nature of disagreements.[5]

ROADS TO THEORY

Glossing over important differences is hardly conducive to progress. By the same token, exaggeration of disputes and avoidance of integrative possibilities are equally debilitating. For example, it is revealing to characterize, albeit crudely, six different roads to theory which can be found in the literature:

Politics," *World Politics*, Vol. 7 (1955), pp. 461-78; R. C. Snyder, "International Relations Theory—Continued," *World Politics*, Vol. 12 (1961), pp. 300-312.

[1a] W. T. R. Fox, ed., *Theoretical Aspects of International Relations* (Notre Dame, Ind.: University of Notre Dame Press, 1959); K. Knorr and S. Verba, eds., *The International System: Theoretical Essays* (Princeton, N.J.: Princeton University Press, 1961); J. Rosenau, ed., *International Politics and Foreign Policy: A Reader in Research and Theory* (New York: Free Press of Glencoe, 1961).

[2] S. Hoffman, "International Relations, the Long Road to Theory," *World Politics*, Vol. 11 (1959), pp. 264-74; R. Hyvarinen, *Monistic and Pluralistic Interpretations in the Study of International Politics* (Helsinki: Societas Scientiarum Fennica, 1958); C. Kindleberger, "Scientific International Politics," *World Politics*, Vol. 11 (1958), pp. 3-15; H. Sprout, "International Politics and the Scholar," *Princeton Alumni Weekly*, Vol. 59 (1959), pp. 8-10, 14-15; and F. Sondermann, "The Study of International Relations, 1956 Version," *World Politics*, Vol. 10 (1957), pp. 102-11.

[3] McClelland, *op. cit.*

[4] Fox, *op. cit.*, pp. 40-51; Snyder, *op. cit.*

[5] K. Waltz, *Man, the State, and War* (New York: Columbia University Press, 1959); and I. Claude, Jr., *Swords into Plowshares, the Problems and Progress of International Organization* (New York: Random House, 1956).

(1) avowedly deductive [6]—Kaplan's work is the closest to a full-blown attempt to construct a hypothetico-deductive theory in the classical sense;

(2) the strategy of working backward from a central question or problem and then ordering the answers systematically—Waltz [7] focuses on war and disorder as recurrent patterns of interaction;

(3) derivation of an international political theory from a more general theory of politics based on a rational actor and a dominant power motive; [8]

(4) an inductive delimitation, description, and comparison of historical international systems which have existed in the past; [9]

(5) the use of analogs usually drawn from outside political science or international relations *per se*—for example, limited theories of bargaining [10] and particular market conditions of monopoly, bilateral monopoly, or oligopoly; [11]

(6) "middle range theories" combining informing questions and hypotheses, inductive and deductive elements, and interdisciplinary borrowing and aiming at a restricted range of phenomena and/or sets of variables[12]

---

[6] M. Kaplan, *System and Process in International Relations* (New York: John Wiley & Sons, Inc., 1957); A. Wolfers, "The Actors in International Politics," in Fox, *op. cit.*, chap. 6.

[7] Waltz, *op. cit.*

[8] H. Morgenthau, "The Nature and Limits of a Theory of International Relations," in Fox, *op. cit.*, pp. 29-50.

[9] S. Hoffman, *Contemporary Theory in International Relations* (Englewood Cliffs, N.J.: Prentice-Hall, 1960).

[10] T. Schelling, *The Strategy of Conflict* (Cambridge, Mass.: Harvard University Press, 1960).

[11] C. Kindleberger, "International Political Theory from Outside," in Fox, *op. cit.*, chap. 5.

[12] K. Deutsch, *Nationalism and Social Communication* (New York: John Wiley & Sons, Inc., 1953), *Political Community at the International Level* (Garden City, N.Y.: Doubleday and Co., 1954), and "Mass Communications and Loss of Freedom in National Decision-making: A Possible Research Approach to Interstate Conflicts," *Journal of Conflict Resolution*, Vol. 1 (1957), pp. 200-211; E. Haas, *The Uniting of Europe* (Stanford, Calif.: Stanford University Press, 1958), and *Consensus Formation in the Council of Europe* (Berkeley and Los Angeles: University of California Press, 1960); H. Guetzkow, *Multiple Loyalties: Theoretical Approach to a Problem in International Organization* (Princeton, N.J.: Center for Research on World Political Institutions, 1955), and "Isolation and Collaboration: A Partial Theory of International Relations," *Journal of Conflict Resolution*, Vol. 1 (1957), pp. 48-68; H. and M. Sprout, *Man-Milieu Relationship Hypotheses in the Context of International Politics* (Princeton, N.J.: Center of International Studies, 1956), and "Environmental Factors in the Study of International Politics," *Journal*

Obviously many factors shape these different orientations to theory-building—diverse intellectual traditions and training, individual styles and perferences, philosophies of knowledge, and so on. Moreover, different conceptual foci (*field* [Wright, Hoffman]; *systems and equilibrium* [Kaplan, Liska,[13] McClelland [14]]; *communication* [Deutsch]; *power* [Morgenthau]; and *decision-making* [Snyder]) and levels of analysis (a society or nation-state, actor or action perspective [Sprout, Wolfers, Morgenthau, Guetzkow]; an *inter*nation, *inter*action perspective [Deutsch, Kaplan, Liska, Hoffman, Wright]) are associated with the alternative theoretical approaches.

Each of the foregoing strategies yields different products and has its own advantages. Thus (1) results in hypothetical propositions to be tested in various situations, and (6) results in qualified generalizations. Strategy (5) provides markedly different orientations toward familiar subject matter, while strategy (4) provides greater richness of data and hence a check against legitimate simplification and the dangers of oversimplification. As we shall note later on, the various roads to theory are not necessarily either–or choices (see Snyder, 1961), and certainly they are not all susceptible to the same criteria of evaluation. Therefore, it is highly desirable at this stage of development to consider them as mutually reinforcing phases of a multiple strategy for advancing knowledge. It is proper and indeed necessary for alternative theory constructions to evolve out of rigorous criticism of prior efforts. It is neither proper nor fruitful for this to lead to false polarities or wasteful proliferations of analytic schemes whose surface differences may obscure an underlying commonality.

CHANGE AND THE LEVEL AND UNITS OF ANALYSIS

The trend toward greater explicitness and the evidence of a struggle for increased coherence of inquiry also reflect, of course, two sources of difficulty. First, social change on a global scale has clearly produced an increase in the kinds and frequency of inter-

---

of Conflict Resolution, Vol. 1 (1957), pp. 309-28; and Q. Wright, *The Study of International Relations* (New York: Appleton-Century-Crofts, 1955).

[13] G. Liska, *International Equilibrium: A Theoretical Essay on the Politics and Organization of Security* (Cambridge, Mass.: Harvard University Press, 1957).

[14] C. McClelland, "Systems and History in International Relations: Some Perspectives for Empirical Research and Theory," *General Systems Yearbook*, Vol. 3 (1958).

national communication and an increase in the number of units of action and interaction. Hence the empirical terrain embraced by the field has grown in size and complexity. Partly in response to social change, and partly for reasons usually referred to in terms of the sociology of knowledge, students of international relations have formulated new ways of viewing their traditional domain of events and problems. Research has, fortunately, also increased in amount and significance—an additional fact which has jarred older modes of thought.

There is no paradox, then, in the juxtaposition of Lasswell's statement, ". . . it is remarkable how much agreement there is about the primary frame of reference on the subject," [15] and Fox's remark on "the lack of an agreed framework." [16] The former can be interpreted as a reference to clusters of phenomena generally categorized under such headings as conflict-cooperation, grand strategy, war and peace, foreign policies and foreign policy-making, political integration, international organization, particular systems such as alliances and markets, and values, attitudes, and opinions related to the external relations of nations. On the other hand, the latter appears to refer to conceptual ambiguities, a multiplicity of "approaches," *and* the absence as yet of a commonly accepted map of the international world which we are all supposed to be describing and explaining—a map consisting of a set of categories which logically exhausts the nature and types of units, actions, interactions, relationships, events, and trends which are of primary interest as well as explicit criteria for establishing the relevance of occurrences and antecedent conditions. Given this situation, it is sometimes difficult to know whether we are saying the same thing about apparently different phenomena, or different things about the same phenomena, or different things about different phenomena.

Obviously the nation-state is still a basic unit of analysis, but owing to the two sources of change mentioned above, complications have arisen. In the first place, the nation-state can be conceived in different ways: (1) as an ideal-typical monolithic, rational actor (Morgenthau); (2) as a social group behaving *qua* group (Guetzkow); or (3) as a pluralism of forces (Nitze). In the second place, the nation-state has been undergoing change and is no longer the only significant unit of action and interaction.

---

[15] Lasswell, *op. cit.*, p. 5.
[16] Fox, *op. cit.*, p. ix.

To repeat, we do not now have a commonly accepted map of the empirical terrain embraced by the term "international relations," if we use it as the most general designation. Of what does the contemporary international system consist? Something called the Western and Eastern blocs? Present membership of the UN? This number plus eligible countries? Do we include nonself-governing territories? What about stateless societies (e.g., the Nuer) and societies which are not nations as conventionally defined, both of which seem to play an important role in international life? Is the European Common Market a new kind of unit? How do we handle the Indian village which is closely and directly linked to a foreign government? Where does the supranational community of scientists fit into the general scheme of things? How many kinds and levels of contacts among societies do we or should we incorporate in a framework which bounds a domain from which we make our selections of targets of inquiry?

Where we seem to stand at the moment is approximately as follows. The *nation-state* is certainly a primary unit—a *governmental* unit. But Nitze, noting that influences on nation-state purposes come from loyalties both broader and narrower than the state, insists that our theory will have to embrace actions and interrelations of "those entities not usually coterminous with national boundaries." Nitze asks "who is the 'we' the U.S. or Soviet governments act for?" [17] Kindleberger admits we may need a special theory for those actions and relationships in which an "international group" (i.e., some governing group) is primary. Herz stresses the contemporary permeability of the nation-state: political and psychological boundaries have "softened." Wolfers recognizes that nonstate actors may be significant "deviations" from the otherwise paramount position of the nation-state. Wolfers does say that theory must include overlapping authorities, split loyalties, and divided sovereignty, but he explicitly downgrades the "minds of men theory" which emphasizes individuals in general as units and "decision-making analysis" which focuses on individual officials. Acceptance of the nation-state as primary unit carries with it, of course, the notion that *governmental* interactions and relationships are the key ones. On the other hand, there is more than a hint in recent writings that when the term "politics" is used something more than interrelations

---

[17] P. Nitze, "Necessary and Sufficient Elements of a General Theory of International Relations," in Fox, *op. cit.*, pp. 4ff.

between national administrative or policy-making organizations is implied. Fox notes that those now emphasizing *process* (rather than just institutional forms) tend to view world politics as "politics in the absence of government." [18] Beyond the diplomatic machinery of the state lies another layer of relevant phenomena which one might call the interrelations of political systems.

Furthermore, beyond the political system is another unit, namely, the society as a whole where a wider range of interactions and relationships is included and where what is contained within a jurisdictional boundary is treated as a total group or collectivity for the purposes at hand. The work of Deutsch (communications, trade) and Guetzkow (isolation-collaboration patterns and multiple loyalties) is illustrative, and, of course, cultural and economic relations embrace nongovernmental individual and group phenomena.

Shifting to another set of analytic and observational foci, we find other kinds of units. Everyone accepts formal international organizations as proper subjects for research. In addition, the term "system" (in its multiple usage) denotes various foci of interest. Many authors speak of *the* international system (Liska, Hoffman, Nitze), but the term is more often employed in the plural suggesting that the singular refers to the sum total, or some particular aspects, of interactions among *all* the actors or units deemed to be in the system. This latter element is usually unspecified. Liska seems to be dealing with a system made up of all nation-states, while Fox talks of a "theory of the whole," which, when coupled with his emphasis on a global perspective and transcending the patterns of an age, could be read more broadly. Some use the term international society which implies more perhaps than a throwback to the older "society of nations." [19] At any rate, the point is that we are presently groping for a "whole" as well as a "core," and the former, though vague, indicates a globalization of inquiry.

Actually, it is *systems* of interaction which have become important entities or units—a "something" not the whole, as used above, yet more than the sum of its constituent parts. As Kindleberger notes, Kaplan moves away from the "grand design" and provides a taxonomy of six types of systems (balance of power, loose bipolar,

[18] Fox, *op. cit.*, p. 36.

[19] Cf. Morgenthau, *op. cit.*; and T. Mathisen, *Methodology in the Study of International Relations* (New York: The Macmillan Company, 1959).

tight bipolar, universal, hierarchical, and unit veto). Hoffman, while opposed to Kaplan, also makes systems a focal point. The bases of his types are not yet clear; he says only that "diplomatic constellations" or "historical situations" are to be characterized by features and combinations of features which make them different and/ or similar. Binder demonstrates that *the* international system or *an* international system may have important *subsystems*—in this case one with a spatial domain, the Middle East. Polak describes an international system comprising the twenty-five nations most significantly linked by the economic collapse and depression of 1929-31.[20] Bilateral and trilateral systems have been described by Wolfers and Brebner respectively.[21] Systems as foci represent an attempt to make the "whole" manageable and to deal with inter-unit phenomena assuming the basic unit is still the nation-state or society. Those who have claimed that varieties of the nation-state focus (whether decision-making analysis or policy analysis) tend to distort the field or ignore important factors are right.[22] By far the larger amount of theorizing and research has been devoted to the behavior of single nation-states. This imbalance is now being corrected.

DELIMITATION OF "INTERNATIONAL RELATIONS"

In the preceding context, it can be suggested that the old distinction between "international relations" and "international politics" is still with us, at least implicitly. For some, this will raise a sterile definitional problem. Doubtless futile semantic exercises have surrounded the question in the past. However, recent developments prove (to this writer) that the "core" and "outer limits" of what is implied by the term international relations in its most general usage is still a relevant and unsettled issue. Moreover, it is ultimately bound up with the conviction held by some that international relations is not now, and probably never will be, anything more than a lumpy mixture of different branches of knowledge and a loose collection of topics subsumable under area study, com-

---

[20] J. Polak, *An International Economic System* (Chicago: University of Chicago Press, 1953).

[21] A. Wolfers, *Britain and France Between Two Wars* (New York: Harcourt, Brace and Company, 1940; and J. B. Brebner, *The North Atlantic Triangle* (New York: Columbia University Press, 1949).

[22] Cf. Sondermann, *op. cit.;* and Hoffman, "International Relations, the Long Road to Theory."

parative politics, foreign policy, and so on.[23] Does the *study* of international relations constitute a *discipline?* or can it be? or should it be? Admittedly these questions have not always been posed or discussed in a meaningful or fruitful way.[24] Skeptics argue that the term international relations includes "everything" and is therefore unmanageable. In this connection it is pertinent to note that Lasswell wrote an article entitled "The Scientific Study of International Relations," [25] yet he was highly critical of Wright [26] for including practically all of human knowledge.[27] At any rate, the core and boundary issue brings us back to fundamental concepts—which are far more than matters of mere definitions, for these determine, in part, what will be observed and what distinguishing properties actions and events will have in the light of our theoretical purposes.

PROBLEMS OF CONCEPTUALIZATION

In general, the trend toward greater precision and explicitness has included attention to more operational formulations and specification of the roles of various concepts in theorizing. Constructive reappraisals of *national interest* (Schilling),[28] *collective security* (Claude, 1956), and *national character* (Inkeles),[29] exemplify this concern. Other central concepts (e.g., *sovereignty, nationalism*) have not been subject to quite the same penetrating criticism.

Equilibrium is, of course, a pervasive concept in the social sciences as well as in international relations theory—particularly in connection with applications of systems notions including homeostatic mechanisms in open systems. While equilibrium is usually

---

[23] This view is rarely stated baldly in published writing but is usually voiced orally. Skepticism is more often expressed on the general ground of the undeterminacy, accident, and emotion which allegedly characterize human behavior at the international level: see D. Bell, "Ten Theories in Search of Reality," in A. Dallin, ed., *Soviet Conduct in World Affairs* (New York: Columbia University Press, 1960), pp. 1-36.

[24] However, see Kaplan, "Is International Relations a Discipline?" (paper delivered to American Political Science Association, Annual Meeting, 1960).

[25] Lasswell, *op. cit.*

[26] Q. Wright, *op. cit.*

[27] H. Lasswell, "Some Reflections on the Study of International Relations," *World Politics*, Vol. 8 (1956), pp. 560-66.

[28] W. Schilling, "The Clarification of Ends, or, Which Interest Is National?," *World Politics*, Vol. 8 (1956), pp. 566-78.

[29] A. Inkeles, "National Character and Modern Political Systems," in F. Hsu, ed., *Psychological Anthropology: Approaches to Culture and Personality* (Homewood, Ill.: Dorsey Press, 1961), pp. 172-208.

defined explicitly or implicitly by theorists (e.g., Kaplan and Liska), it has received comparatively little technical explication. Uncritical or unnecessary usage and negative criticism have tended to over-balance efforts to enhance its constructive functions. Clearly the concept is directed to phenomena of stability and change in patterns of action and interaction. For the most part, the development of *process* variables has lagged behind, and our theory is predominantly static (however, see Kaplan, *op. cit.*). As more dynamic theoretical formulations develop (i.e., a change from state of affairs one to state of affairs two will occur under such and such conditions), the identification and measurement of opposed tendencies, the rate and direction of change, and control mechanisms will be required. To this writer's knowledge, existing analyses of equilibrium do not contain instructions for its use in developing theory.

To return to the need to delimit the phenomena of international relations, two concepts have been employed as criteria for identification and relevance: *political* and *power*. Now it must be acknowledged at once that under some circumstances the discriminatory capacity of these terms is not a problem. The fact that political scientists do not seem to agree on the generic properties of predominantly political acts or relationships is not serious if one is analyzing a concrete governmental institution or organization. By the same token, a particular conception of power can be used effectively in, say, a community study without regard to its general utility in other settings. But if the two concepts are being considered as possible aids to ordering a broader field of inquiry, then leaving them undefined or employing only nominal definitions or simply saying that anything a government does or says externally is *ipso facto* political may not suffice.

It is interesting to note that Hoffman, in touching on this issue, says that politics is "different" but has no "essence." On the other hand, Rapoport argues the need for postulating an essence, and he goes back to Catlin for a possible cue, namely, "the clash of wills." [30] Whether one wishes to adopt this particular conception, the point is *not* to search for long abandoned *metaphysical essences*, but rather to adopt a working assumption that political acts and relationships do exist and then the specification of the characteristics by which such acts and relationships are to be recognized. In fact,

---

[30] A. Rapoport, *Fights, Games, and Debates* (Ann Arbor: University of Michigan Press, 1960).

this is what the Comparative Politics Committee of the Social Science Research Council has done when confronted with the similar problem that traditional categories no longer "contained" the phenomena of chief concern. The test will then be fruitfulness for research—what we can do with the "approximation," not "proof" of the existence of some corresponding "thing."

Difficulties attendant upon the employment of the power concept in international relations are doubtless familiar to most readers. The controversy surrounding this aspect of Morgenthau's theory will not be reviewed, nor will the cogent, valuable analyses of Haas, Knorr, Sullivan, and McClelland be summarized.[31] Despite dissatisfaction with the formulation of the power variables, the term is widely and meaningfully used—suggesting that many recognizable situations or relationships are thought to embody power. Nevertheless, Sullivan found seventeen different definitions of power which are usually introduced in a "framework" chapter of leading international relations textbooks and later abandoned when substantive topics are treated. Thus, contrary to appearances, power is not actually a central organizing and explanatory concept, and there is no shared *general* theory of power which orders or informs our intellectual operations. Sullivan has formulated a possibly more fruitful basis for theory embodying power as a basic concept. He has taken advantage of conceptual improvements which have been advanced by writers outside the field of international relations.[32]

Having a formula which reduces some seventeen versions of the power concept to a more general statement is not enough. No one who has seriously approached the identification and measurement of power factors takes the problem lightly. Conceptual improvements are a step forward but still leave us some distance from

---

[31] E. Haas, "The Balance of Power: Prescription, Concept or Propaganda?," *World Politics*, Vol. 5 (1953), pp. 275-88; K. Knorr, *The War Potential of Nations* (Princeton, N.J.: Princeton University Press, 1956); D. G. Sullivan, "The Concept of Power in International Relations" (paper delivered to the Midwest Conference of Political Scientists, 1960); and McClelland, "Dynamics of National Power" (lecture delivered to War College, U.S. Air Force Air University, 1960).

[32] R. Dahl, "The Concept of Power," *Behavioral Science*, Vol. 2 (1957), pp. 201-15; J. French, "The Bases of Social Power," in D. Cartwright, ed., *Studies in Social Power* (Ann Arbor: Institute for Social Research, University of Michigan, 1959), pp. 150-68; J. March, "An Introduction to the Theory and Measurement of Influence," *American Political Science Review*, Vol. 49 (1955), pp. 431-51; and H. Simon, "Notes on the Observation and Measurement of Political Power," *Journal of Politics*, Vol. 15 (1953), pp. 500-516.

a theory or from a set of rules to guide the use of a power concept in theory building. Nonetheless, recent studies do offer prime considerations for shaping future developments:

(1) The fact that there are so many definitions of power (power$_1$ . . . power$_{17}$), and that a single definition is usually abandoned by an author, indicates the concept (like many others) is not situationally and transactionally referred.[33] In turn, this suggests that propositions containing the concept should be content analyzed with a view to codifying the qualified generalizations which are asserted and to identifying the range of conditions under which "power" factors are alleged to operate.

(2) Any strategy for employing a power concept in theory ought to account for observed paradoxes such as: (a) if A has "power over" B, B nonetheless may limit A's behavior; (b) having coercive or physical power does not mean the possessor can use it under all circumstances; [34] (c) some forms of power may destroy the objective sought.

(3) Perceived power would appear to be a key aspect of power relationships about which we know very little. More is involved here than estimates of military strength and their correspondence to actuality. In an age when something loosely called "prestige" seems to loom so large in the international political process, refined conceptualization of power should include the perception by one party of the other party's control or influence over (a) the environment (e.g., science and technology), (b) other parties, and (c) self-destiny.

(4) Actions or interactions postulated to embody power ought to be conceived as transpiring in a total relationship between two parties (or more as in the case of a coalition) in which there are *a finite number of bases of reciprocal influence and control* over outcomes of vital interest to the parties and which result from the intersection of actions or moves by the parties.[35] A highly general but not vacuous hypothesis which is relevant is: the greater the number of interactions and contacts between two parties, the greater

---

[33] K. London and R. Poltoratzky, "The Problem of Contemporary Analysis in History and Psychology," *Behavioral Science*, Vol. 3 (1958), pp. 269-77.

[34] See F. Tannenbaum, "On Political Stability," *Political Science Quarterly*, Vol. 75 (1960), pp. 161-80.

[35] See M. Rosenberg, "Power and Desegregation," *Social Problems*, Vol. 3 (1956), pp. 215-23.

the number of opportunities to exercise influence or control over outcomes. This suggests the possibility of viewing internation relations in terms of an "interaction matrix" in which power is manifest in the comparative ability of A and B to affect the quality of particular outcomes desired or attained by each other.[36]

Inventories and Stocktaking

Another set of significant general trends is manifest in (1) improved reporting and communication, (2) efforts to propositionalize the literature, and (3) research planning. That incomplete circulation of research findings and lack of continuous stocktaking contribute to wasteful duplication and nonadditive activity seems self-evident. Furthermore, in the absence of evaluative summaries, consolidation, and planning, many procedural questions tend to be answered rather arbitrarily on an *a priori* basis instead of on the basis of an exploratory diagnosis of researchability. In a field as large and potentially segmented as international relations, the increase in research and writing can have disjunctive consequences. The sheer number of published items and wide range of journals in which pertinent materials may be found confront the individual scholar with a serious problem of keeping abreast of developments.

An outstanding example of a recent contribution to this problem is *Current Thought on Peace and War*, a quarterly digest of literature and research in progress on the problems of world order and conflict edited by Dr. L. Larry Leonard. The skill and comprehensiveness which characterized the first two issues (Winter and Summer-Fall, 1960) give this publication great value —a notable addition to the annotated bibliographical services rendered by other sources: *Background, Journal of Conflict Resolution, Foreign Affairs*, and *American Behavioral Scientist*. Recently, inventories of major sectors of the international relations literature have appeared—for example, a special issue of the *Journal of Conflict Resolution* on "Psychology and Aggression" edited by Elton McNeil (Vol. 3, 1959) and an issue on "The Anthropology of Conflict" edited by Robert LeVine (Vol. 5, 1961). The External Research Division of United States Department of State publishes a

---

[36] For the most applicable presentation of this perspective, see J. Thibaut and H. Kelly, *The Social Psychology of Groups* (New York: John Wiley & Sons, Inc., 1959).

descriptive list of completed research projects (annually in October) and a companion list of ongoing projects (annually in April) together with an identification of individual researchers and institutional centers.[37] The broadly conceived review essays which appear in *World Politics* also contribute to increased consolidation.

In addition to annotated bibliographies and research reports, propositional inventories are being developed as an important ordering technique. Basically, this technique involves the explicit formulation of descriptive and explanatory statements in such a way that concepts, variables, and their interrelationship can be identified clearly and analyzed in terms of their theoretical and empirical contexts. Unless skillful propositionalizing is an integral part of stocktaking, quasi-laws, qualified generalizations, and hypotheses may be buried or obscured in lengthy passages and diverse language. It is virtually impossible to estimate what causal connections and range of variables undergird international relations theory unless this structure of propositions is more fully revealed. Nor can gaps in theory and imbalances in the total research picture be assessed adequately.

The methodology of fruitful, rigorous propositionalizing is not a simple matter, and as yet no "manual of procedures" is generally available. However, the materials are at hand. Sullivan has completed the first stage of an inventory of key explanatory propositions which appear in leading international relations textbooks used in the United States.[38] A preliminary formulation of some 200 propositions which appear to underlie contemporary writing on strategic deterrence has been attempted.[39] More general inven-

---

[37] For example, U.S. Department of State, Bureau of Intelligence and Research, External Research Division, *International Affairs,* October, 1960, ER List No. 10.15.

[38] J. March, H. Simon, and H. Guetzkow, *Organizations* (New York: John Wiley & Sons, Inc., 1958); B. Collins, "The Development of an Inventory of Variables and Propositions in the Social Sciences" (Northwestern University 1960, mimeo.); and D. G. Sullivan, *An Inventory of Major Propositions Contained in Contemporary Textbooks in International Relations* (unpublished Ph.D. dissertation in political science, Northwestern University, 1962).

[39] R. Snyder, *Deterrence, Weapons Systems, and Decision-Making, Studies in Deterrence, III* (U.S. Naval Ordnance Test Station, China Lake, Calif., October, 1961). Related inventories are: S. Feldman and C. Osgood, *Literature Research on Psychological Factors in Peace and War* (Urbana: University of Illinois, Institute of Communications Research, 1962), and L. Soloman and P. Probasco, *Annotated Bibliography on Deterrence Propositions: Research Relevant to Problems of Inter-Nation Relations* (La Jolla, Calif.: Western Behavioral Sciences Institute, 1962).

tories have a direct bearing on the study of international relations—for example, on social conflict.[40]

Finally, there is a notable trend toward the identification of needed research which also embraces at least partial efforts to assess completed and ongoing studies. The Institute for International Order commissioned the preparation of five programs of research directed to the problem of war and peace: No. 1, Bernard Feld *et al.*, *The Technical Problems of Arms Control;* No. 2, Kenneth Boulding *et al.*, *Economic Factors Bearing Upon the Maintenance of Peace* (in five parts); No. 3, Arthur Larson, *The International Rule of Law;* No. 4, Richard C. Snyder and James A. Robinson, *National and International Decision-Making;* and No. 5, Ithiel Pool, *Communication and Values in Relation to War and Peace.* Some 495 projects are outlined and discussed in the light of what we know and do not know regarding the outbreak and control of violent modes of interaction between nations. Charles Osgood and Shel Feldman are preparing a sixth monograph in this series on psychological factors in peace and war. Thomas Schelling (Harvard University Center for International Affairs) has highlighted certain needs in his *Arms Control Research* (1961). The primary objective of these monographs is to achieve a more effective mobilization of relevant disciplines and qualified researchers, but in the process theory and research as well as theory and policy are related in the rudiments of a "grand research strategy" which highlights much of the empirical terrain mentioned above.

The marked growth of interest in more systematic mapping of research is not confined to the war and peace focus; it is an important by-product of the programs of centers of international relations research at M.I.T., Princeton, Chicago, Harvard, Stanford, Michigan, Northwestern, the Washington Foreign Policy Center, Johns Hopkins, Columbia, and the Brookings Institution. Two examples are furnished by W. Scott and D. Katz.[41] It would be difficult to overestimate the potential implications of such activities for greater theoretical integration despite the obvious revelation of how

---

[40] L. Coser, *The Functions of Conflict* (Glencoe, Ill.: The Free Press, 1956); and R. Mack and R. Snyder, "Toward a Framework for the Analysis of Social Conflict," *Journal of Conflict Resolution,* Vol. 1 (1957), pp. 212-48.

[41] W. Scott, "A Broad Orientation to Research on International Attitudes," *Journal of Conflict Resolution,* Vol. 4 (1960), pp. 458-68; and D. Katz, "Current and Needed Psychological Research in International Relations" (Center for Conflict Research, University of Michigan, 1960, mimeo.).

much more we need to know. If existing guidelines can be followed, future learning need not be as haphazard as it has been in the past.

Additive Research Activities

Academic organization and tradition have led to individualism and separatism in intellectual endeavor. These are cherished values, yet they have undoubtedly slowed up the accumulation of knowledge, especially in view of relatively poor communication among scholars and the lack of high uniform standards of criticism and review. One result has been discrete studies embodying little replication and often little comparability. Attempts to link closely experimental, field, and propositional inquiries are only just beginning.

Signs of greater collaboration—not to be interpreted as team research—are appearing. Deutsch's seminal ideas about international communication and integration [42] have stimulated numerous follow-up studies. Naroll (1960) is testing hypotheses formulated by J. Gillin, T. Milburn, and R. Snyder in his program of inquiry into historical deterrence situations and relationships.[43] McClelland has employed several of Kaplan's concepts and propositions in research on international crises.[44] Northwestern University and Stanford University are collaborating in an effort to reproduce in a laboratory simulation exercise some of the central features of reconstruction of events leading to the outbreak of World War I being undertaken at the latter institution.

Hopefully, we stand at the threshold of a period of further efforts to give greater depth and breadth to the confirmation of hypotheses and application of conceptual schemes.

SPECIFIC ACTIVITIES: RESEARCH AND THEORY

The works of individual scholars to be discussed were chosen because they illustrate the trends noted above and because

---

[42] K. Deutsch, *Political Community at the International Level,* and "Mass Communications and the Loss of Freedom in National Decision-Making: A Possible Research Approach to Interstate Conflicts."

[43] R. Naroll, *Deterrence in History* (San Fernando, Calif.: San Fernando Valley State College, Deterrence Project, Project No. 7, a General Report of Six Months of Research, 1961), 55 pp.

[44] McClelland, "The Acute International Crisis," in Knorr and Verba, *op. cit.*

together they constitute further evidence of an emergent multiple strategy. A range of techniques, foci, and objectives is revealed which can be viewed as a stepping stone to what Kindleberger has described as a set of theoretical models which take their shape from history and are "stripped to their essentials." [45] To characterize briefly a system of thought is always dangerous; clearly it is not possible to do full justice to these theoretical and research efforts.

Nor can the following selections be considered exhaustive, for choice is complicated by the rapid growth of related research by government agencies and private business.[46] While much of this activity centers on weapons systems, military strategy, arms control, disarmament, and deterrence, numerous projects, classified and unclassified, certainly have a direct bearing on broader aspects of international relations. In many instances government sponsored research is as basic as any done by the academic community even though policy problems are the immediate incentive. For various reasons—including the familiar one of security barriers—the total pattern of inquiry which is connected with national defense is not apparent to the outsider. The results of policy oriented thinking and investigation have only been partially fed into the mainstream of international relations literature. Hence it is difficult to predict what the effects will be.

However, it seems safe to assume that, in so far as the research supported by the armed services and by business is broadly conceived and executed skillfully, the reservoir of pertinent data and theoretical tools will be enriched. That such a consequence is likely to be true can be inferred from the example of Project Michelson,[47] a cluster of interrelated projects which includes important research not hitherto undertaken on the present scale (e.g., a comparative analysis of Soviet and United States national values hypothesized to shape the responses of the two countries to the existing situation). Many studies of the RAND Corporation and the Institute for Defense Analyses fall in the same category.

---

[45] Kindleberger, "Scientific International Politics."

[46] See E. Katzenbach, "Ideas: A New Defense Industry," *Reporter*, Vol. 24 (1961), pp. 17-22.

[47] Directed by Dr. Thomas Milburn, Naval Ordnance Test Station, China Lake, California. More than thirty projects have been assigned to academic researchers. Particular topics cover significant social, psychological, and political implications of weapons systems for international behavior. See T. Milburn, "Design for the Study of Deterrence" (Project Michelson, Naval Ordnance Test Station, 1961, mimeo.), 19 pp.

Society as the Acting Unit: Intrasocietal and Subsocietal Analyses
(Society: Nation-state, Nation, Stateless Society and Dependencies; Levels: Societal
(as a political collectivity), Institutional, Organizational, Group, and Individual)

DECISION-MAKING AND POLICY PROCESS ANALYSES

Five lines of development, which have different but mutually complementary features, are worthy of mention.

Environmental Factors. The work of Harold and Margaret Sprout is noteworthy on several counts. It is an effort to separate the wheat from the chaff in a whole group of theories which have now fallen pretty much into disrepute—monistic theories such as were purveyed by the so-called Geopolitical School and which smack strongly of environmental determinism. While their analysis does not focus on geographical factors alone, it is an attempt to integrate geography as one of the disciplines which contribute to the study of international relations. The Sprouts' method is a combination of rigorous conceptual analysis, development of hypotheses, and case studies. The term "environment" is redefined in terms of "milieu," which has a twofold aspect: the psychological or perceived and the "operational"—those properties of the milieu which set limits to what can be accomplished, irrespective of whether or how these limits are perceived by decision-makers. The Sprouts critically examine five basic hypotheses which they label: (a) environmental determinism; (b) mild environmentalism; (c) environmental possibilism; (d) probabilism; and (e) cognitive behaviorism. Their scheme, characterized as "capability analysis," falls under (c). Probabilism (a form of policy analysis) explains or predicts on the basis of a generalized model or typical decision-maker who reacts in certain ways to a given milieu—for example, Wolfers' "state as actor" concept, which bypasses depth decision-making analysis (cognitive-behaviorism), is based on a kind of ideal-typical decision-maker who is found in all (or *almost* all) states.[48]

The Sprouts are less interested in how or why a decision was made or a policy evolved than in the basic relationship between the perceived and operational environments, between the assessments and goals built into a policy and its path of action through a matrix of conditioning factors which may or may not accord with the decision-makers' perceptions and estimates. Thus the emphasis is on post-decisional outcomes or on a comparison of simultaneous, independent judgments by decision-makers and an observer. It

---

[48] Wolfers, "The Actors in International Politics."

is interesting to note Fox's insistence on a theory of international relations which aims primarily at identifying the "limits of the possible" and at distinguishing what is, and what is not, within a state's control.[49] A series of case studies may suggest the outline of such a theory. The Sprouts' first applied study is the British Defense Act of 1956.[50]

Personality Factors. Alexander and Juliette George have essayed the difficult task of applying certain concepts of dynamic psychology to historical data in their study entitled *Woodrow Wilson and Colonel House.*[51] Using the full range of existing materials, the Georges have reconstructed a portrait of Wilson's total career in terms of those aspects which reveal the impact of personality factors on his political actions—particularly the fateful and unsuccessful struggle over the League of Nations in the United States Senate. They relate Wilson's overt behavior throughout his political life to what they hypothesize were emotional needs internalized during his childhood socialization. The intent is to develop a consistently comprehensible theory to account for repeated patterns of response in different situations and for puzzling contradictions in Wilson's political style and strategy. Their theory is a logically interrelated set of observations concerning the dynamics of Wilson's personality and political behavior. One of the basic hypotheses is that power was a compensatory value for Wilson, a means of restoring self-esteem damaged in childhood. (The general form of this hypothesis was stated by Lasswell.)[52]

In a research note the authors characterize their techniques as a "developmental biography" in which personality and situational factors are studied chronologically and cross-sectionally. The Georges realize no incontrovertible proof of their Wilson theory can be offered, but we do have criteria for accepting or rejecting their explanation as compared to the many others presented in the Wilson literature. (One of the thirteen criteria advanced by Fox is consistency.)[53] However, the important thing is the tech-

---

[49] Fox, *op. cit.,* pp. 45-46.

[50] H. Sprout, "Environmental Factors in the Study of International Politics" (paper presented at the Conference on the Interrelations of Behavioral and Ecological Models, Northwestern University, 1958).

[51] A. and J. George, *Woodrow Wilson and Colonel House* (New York: John Day, 1956).

[52] H. Lasswell, *Power and Personality* (New York: W. W. Norton, 1948), p. 39.

[53] Fox, *op. cit.,* p. 41.

nique which seems to give promise of more fruitful exploitation of much biographical data now lying fallow. The Georges are now engaged in refining their analytic procedure as part of a project on the role of personality in political behavior.

The state of research and theory on personality and decision role in the field of foreign policy is primitive indeed, yet we are constantly confronted with statements and observations which indicate that a Churchill or a Roosevelt or a Dulles or a Khrushchev or a Castro make a "difference." While some sophisticated observers are skeptical about the significance of personality factors,[54] we cannot seem to escape them.[55] It is curious that there has been so little systematic follow-up on the pioneering work of Lasswell and Leites.[56] Granted the problem is extremely difficult, progress is necessary and possible. Members of the RAND staff—notably Myron Rush—have had success using personality variables as predictive tools with respect to the Soviet Union and China. Unfortunately neither the data nor the methodology is publicly available.

The Policy Process: Official and Nonofficial Actors. Aside from being a very useful and thorough description of an important American policy decision, Bernard Cohen's *The Political Process and Foreign Policy: The Making of the Japanese Peace Settlement, 1957,* is dedicated to the accumulation of more reliable knowledge about how foreign policy is made *generally* in this country.[57] He offers a framework which he hopes will make possible a "systematic comparison of the factors and the relationships comprising the overall political processes covering a wide range of policy issues arising in a variety of different circumstances." Cohen (p. 6) postulates the following five "participating elements" in the foreign policy process: (1) a general, somewhat amorphous "climate of public opinion"; (2) articulate private citizens and political interest groups; (3) the media of mass communications; (4) specific agents and agencies in the executive branch; and (5) specific committees of Congress, informal political groupings in Congress and the two houses. This is his way of organizing for "analytical purposes" the

[54] Dean Rusk, "The President," *Foreign Affairs,* Vol. 38 (1960), pp. 353-69.

[55] Dean Acheson, "The President and the Secretary of State," in D. Price, ed., *The Secretary of State* (Englewood Cliffs, N.J.: Prentice-Hall, 1960).

[56] Lasswell, *Power and Personality;* and N. Leites, "Psycho-cultural Hypotheses About Political Acts," *World Politics,* Vol. 1 (1948), pp. 102-18.

[57] B. Cohen, *The Political Process and Foreign Policy: The Making of the Japanese Peace Settlement* (Princeton, N.J.: Princeton University Press, 1957).

"chief foreign policy actors" whom he views essentially as interacting groupings. Cohen argues that the five elements listed are involved in "one form or another" in the making of "virtually *all* foreign policy." Perhaps the distinguishing characteristic of Cohen's focus is the emphasis on related factors outside (but linked to) the formal governmental machinery—the "public factors," as he calls them—and on a conception of the foreign policy-making process as a special case of "the domestic political process."

Cohen is rightly cautious, as are we all, in his generalizations from a particular case, but his book is full of more general hypotheses (often by his own admission, crudely phrased). Nor does he build a set of clear-cut general hypothetical relationships among the five elements, except for those specific to the Japanese Peace Treaty decision. This particular decision substantiates his general thesis that such factors as public opinion, mass media, and interest groups belong at the center of any theory of foreign policy-making—the low level involvement of public factors gives the government greater leeway in formulating the peace treaty, but the deep involvement of media and interest groups in the fishery treaty restricts the government's latitude. This does not state the conditions under which these two propositions will have wider application. However, Cohen does suggest strongly that what is required is typology of policy issues, public factor relationships, and characteristic patterns of the policy process.

The Policy Process: Executive and Legislative Interaction. Roger Hilsman cuts into the policy-making process via congressional-executive relations.[58] His conceptual scheme centers on a model of consensus and conflict. The emphasis here is more on informal relationships among participants—"the pattern of pressure and counterpressure, debate, persuasion and coercion that marks their interaction." This is not unlike the broad concept of influence which Cohen employs. Hilsman views the decision-making process in the United States government as much looser and inconclusive than a rational model would imply. Using an "incremental" concept of policy-making developed by Lindblom,[59] Hilsman argues that even within the government it is a *political* process. This process has

---

[58] R. Hilsman, "The Foreign Policy Consensus: An Interim Research Report," *Journal of Conflict Resolution*, Vol. 3 (1959), pp. 361-82.

[59] C. Lindblom, "The Science of 'Muddling Through,'" *Public Administration Review*, Vol. 19 (1959), p. 79.

three characteristics: (1) reconciliation of diversity of values and goals, means and ends; (2) competing groups who are identified with these alternatives; and (3) relative power of the participating groups which has a direct bearing on the outcome. Out of the mixture of these ingredients comes the combined conflict and consensus-building essence of the process. Rejecting the case method, Hilsman is concentrating on "areas of policy"—"broad streams of thought, debate, activity, compromise, decision, and action." He has chosen three: foreign policy, military policy, and East-West relations. He proposes essentially to see what, if any, recurrent patterns of involvement develop in these three areas of policy. His underlying hypothesis turns on the differentiating functions of two major variables: (1) roles or interests of active participants and (2) type of issue. His focus is somewhat narrower than Cohen's, but he goes further in conceptual refinement of one phase of the former's framework. His data gathering technique is the unstructured interview in contrast to Pruitt (see p. 127).

James Robinson is also concerned with the interrelationship of the executive and legislative branches in foreign policy-making. In his examination of the communications network linking Congress and the State Department, Robinson discusses the reciprocal effects of the way decisions are made and policy content.[60] Two key variables which are employed in this study are satisfaction of members of Congress with the process and the flow of information. Initial results indicate that satisfaction with the policy process depends on satisfaction with policy content and that consensus between the two branches of the federal government will increase as the amount of information exchanged increases. In a case study of congressional initiative in foreign policy-making, Robinson concludes that the organization and internal processes of the legislature and the degree of technicality of information involved, rather than the content of an issue, will determine when Congress will initiate foreign policy successfully.[61] Thus Robinson, unlike Hilsman and Cohen, tends to stress interorganizational structure and process variables, not issue variables or nonorganizational influence patterns. On the other hand, his research could be viewed as throwing

---

[60] J. Robinson, *Congress and Foreign Policy Making* (Homewood, Ill.: Dorsey Press, 1962), chap. 6.

[61] J. Robinson, *The Monroney Resolution: Congressional Initiative in Foreign Policy-Making* (New York: Henry Holt and Co., 1959).

light on the conditions under which *some* of the same actors (or roles) Hilsman and Cohen analyze do influence each other. Furthermore, the latter theorists are less concerned with "inner" aspects of process (e.g., the perceptions of the actors) than in what actors become involved and why. In this respect, Robinson's scheme is closer to the decision-making approach discussed below.

The Decision-making Process: Official Actors in an Organizational Context. The ingredients of this system of analysis are to be found in Richard C. Snyder, H. W. Bruck, and Burton M. Sapin, *Decision-making as an Approach to the Study of International Politics* (1954); R. Snyder, *An Analysis of Case Materials on the U.S. Decision to Resist Aggression in Korea* (1957); and R. Snyder and Glenn Paige, "The United States Decision to Resist Aggression in Korea: The Application of an Analytic Scheme." [62] This approach conceives of state action as resulting from the way identifiable official decision-makers define the situation of action. It seeks to determine why a decision is made at all and why a particular decision is made rather than some other. It postulates that decision-making behavior takes place in a complex organizational setting and can be accounted for by interrelations of three clusters of variables: *organizational roles and relations, communication and information,* and *motivation.* The basic assumption is that if a sufficient number of factual propositions concerning the behaviors and activities implied by these variables can be established, the interrelations of the three sets of propositions become the empirical foundation for an explanation of a decision.

In contrast to both Cohen and Hilsman, this scheme regards as actors only those decision-makers who are members of the decisional unit responsible for a decisional outcome. The decisional unit may be concrete (e.g., an office in the Department of State or an interdepartmental committee) or analytic (i.e., individuals who play key roles but who are abstracted from their permanent group or organizational homes for purposes of a particular mission). Cohen's public factors are introduced via either motivational variables (norms and values of the decision-makers) or communi-

[62] R. Snyder and G. Paige, "The United States' Decision to Resist Aggression in Korea," *Administrative Science Quarterly,* Vol. 3 (1958), pp. 341-78. The Snyder-Bruck-Sapin monograph was reprinted by the Free Press of Glencoe, Inc., under the title *Foreign Policy Decision-Making;* it contains supplementary materials.

cation-information variables (the state of public opinion, group goals, etc.). Hilsman's conflict-consensus factors would be treated as aspects of the sequence of decision-making activities leading to choice and as factors entering into sequential definitions of the situation (see below). However, this not to say that this framework embraces everything Cohen and Hilsman stress or that the decision factors are conceived the same way. The latter formulations have additional advantages. On the other hand, there are obviously noticeable convergences.

The depth reconstruction of the decision-making events of June 24 to June 30, 1950, when the United States decided to intervene militarily in Korea, has been used to sharpen and extend the crude frame of reference presented in the first publication listed above. Three advances seem to have resulted from the Korean decision case study (to be published as a full-length book by the Ronald Press): first, some forty *general* hypotheses have been formulated which can be applied to, or tested by, other case materials; second, certain explicit, two-way connections among the three sets of variables have been identified; and third, the motivation concept has been narrowed by means of an operational formulation of "definition of the situation" consisting of five component elements into which available data can be coded. These elements are: (1) categorization of an event in terms of past experience and existing "givens"; (2) specification and clarification of generalized values and the bearing of the objective situation on them; (3) perceived relevancies—factual aspects "added to" the objective situation; (4) the establishment of a set of goals—a desired state of affairs to be attained; and (5) assessment and selection of one combination of available means and desired goals.

Some of the methodological problems arising out of this approach have been discussed (Snyder and Paige, *op. cit.*), but some procedural developments have not yet been published. For example, the pertinent data have been coded into Marschak's mathematical model of a consistent decision-maker.[63] Though this application has not yet been subjected to the test of independent judgment, there does seem to be a "fit"—United States policy-makers did conform to the rules derived from the model.

---

[63] M. Shubik, *Readings in Game Theory and Political Behavior* (Garden City, N.Y.: Doubleday and Co., 1954), pp. 22-33.

Robert Elder and Dean Pruitt both focus on the Department of State. Elder's study is the richest data pool on the executive branch which we have, but his more than four hundred interviews were apparently conducted with little or no theoretical orientation. Nonetheless, much light is thrown on the decisional role structure of this agency and the data are a fruitful source of hypotheses. Pruitt's research is a deeper probing on a pilot basis of a subunit of the Department of State—the Office of British Commonwealth and Northern European Affairs. All personnel in this office have now been interviewed twice at different time periods (1958-59; 1960). Like Robinson, Pruitt's theoretical purpose is to identify and assess the interrelations of structure and process on the one hand and policy outcomes on the other.[64]

After an analysis of the nature and implications of formal organizational context derived from manuals of procedure, job descriptions, and interviews, Pruitt goes on to trace the course of a typical problem through its various phases. He lays particular stress on the initiation and assignment of problems, the development of proposals for solving problems, procedures for resolving disagreements among policy-makers, and, finally, validation and action as final phases of problem-solving. Authority, communication, and the substantive features of specific problems are among the important variables affecting the problem-solving process. Pruitt's interview schedule included some fifty propositions which embodied variables drawn from the research discussed immediately above and from such sources as March, Simon, and Guetzkow.

The empirical work of Elder and Pruitt add flesh to the conceptual framework developed by this writer and others which emphasizes the general significance of the organization of decision-making for the way personality, societal, external, and environmental factors structure national responses.

Criticism and an Alternative. It would be as unwise to overestimate as to underestimate the results of the foregoing policy process and decision-making analyses and research. Limitations have been recognized: the possible culture-bound nature of con-

---

[64] R. Elder, *The Policy Machine* (Syracuse, N.Y.: Syracuse University Press, 1960); D. Pruitt, *Problem Solving in the Department of State* (Program of Graduate Training and Research in International Relations, Northwestern University, 1960, mimeo.), 125 pp.

cepts and findings; the problem of the single case; data lacks; the as yet small number of cases which makes it hard to tell what population of events we are sampling; uncertain comparability; and *ex post facto* explanations. Critics have been quick to point these things out and rightly so.[65]

Nevertheless, we have moved beyond documentary data, formal description, and simple enumeration of causal conditions. Taken together, the systems of analysis reviewed provide a clearer identification of relevant variables, levels, and units; more adequate descriptions of policy-making behavior; more precise and fruitful conceptual definitions; and improved guidelines for cumulative research. Numerous explicit hypotheses which appear to transcend particular instances can now be further tested. One reason for stressing complementarity is that as these incipient theories develop, we will one day know when and how to predict outcomes (within limits) from the content of issues or problems or from personality or from constants in the organizational context or from stable national responses to the operating environment. The criticism that many of the studies are historical and unique (in some sense) is valid, but the answer is that one of the ways we achieve theoretical control over future events (prediction) is to examine past events with rigorous procedures. We must study in depth before we can learn what we can safely discard given certain theoretical purposes. Case studies in foreign policy decision-making have temporarily outstripped the development of theory.[66] However, despite wide variance in depth, policy substance, and method, the materials are susceptible of coding and interpretation in the light of the foregoing conceptual schemes.

One way to cast decision-making perspectives into bold relief is to cite a competing strategy. As stated earlier, Wolfers favors a unit-centered, "states as actors" approach which requires postulation of general goals and responses typical of "almost" all actors

---

[65] Cf. Hoffman, "International Relations, the Long Road to Theory"; H. McClosky, "Concerning Strategies for a Science of International Politics," *World Politics,* Vol. 7 (1956), pp. 281-96; W. Gibbons, *Political Action Analysis as an Approach to the Study of Congress and Foreign Policy* (unpublished Ph.D. dissertation, Princeton University, 1961), pp. 1-46; and J. Frankel, "Towards a Decision-Making Model in Foreign Policy," *Political Studies,* Vol. 7 (1959), pp. 1-11.

[66] See R. Snyder and J. Robinson, *National and International Decision-Making* (Program of Research No. 4, Institute for International Order, 1961), pp. 76-82.

and which seems to imply common reactions to certain kinds of objective conditions (e.g., deprivation of some value such as territory). Thus Wolfers offers this generalization: states tend to use their most powerful weapons. Hence "Hiroshima . . . requires little of any decision-making analysis to explain the American action." [67] Wolfers is trying to find a more economical mode of explanation than "going down" to the level of individual decision-makers in particular nations. He admits this proposition does not account for the restraint on the use of nuclear weapons in the Korean war. Accordingly, he suggests a deeper analysis or another theory to account for "deviant" outcomes. Assuming for the moment this is not a trivial proposition, do we accept an explanation which does not, apparently, account for crucial variance? How do we know whether we have adequately explained Hiroshima if Korea constitutes an important exception? If deviant cases are significant, why bother with two theories *if* one will do? Clearly the predictive and explanatory power of the Wolfers' hypothesis is a matter for empirical testing. In any event, it is difficult to see how we can be prepared to handle what he calls deviant cases without concepts and theories which are *situationally referred* which is one of the aims of a program of selected case studies and general characterizations of the impact of types of decisional systems and processes in typical situations. Unless we have sufficient grasp of both response factors and situations, we shall be unable to determine why different actions are compatible with the same general motives, why one of these possible actions is chosen on occasion, and whether deviant cases are really deviant at all except by surface inspection.

VALUES, ATTITUDES, AND OPINIONS

Pool (1961) provides a very able outline of this sector of research and theory and its problems. Despite a voluminous literature, the topics implied remain largely unconnected theoretically and despite substantial collections of survey data, there are significant gaps in our knowledge. In short, as Pool concludes, we do not have satisfactory answers to the question: *What is the role of attitudinal factors in international relations?* [68] Dissatisfaction boils down to two main elements: first, conceptually, we have not pro-

---

[67] Wolfers, "The Actors in International Politics," pp. 93, 97.

[68] I. Pool, *Communication and Values in Relation to War and Peace* (Program of Research No. 5, Institute for International Order, 1961).

gressed much beyond Almond's earlier imaginative analysis; [69] second, the imposing technology of attitude research perfected over the past dozen years has not been applied systematically to the study of international phenomena. Furthermore, whether one is interested in policy or in theory, we need much better knowledge about the processes of attitude and opinion formation and how these processes are influenced.

A Conceptualization of the Opinion-Policy Relationship. The most thorough critique of existing concepts and most sophisticated attempt (known to this writer) to conceptualize this problem is James Rosenau's recent book, *Public Opinion and Foreign Policy* (New York: Random House, 1961). Rosenau conceives the public opinion–foreign policy relationship in terms of three distinct, yet related, social processes (governmental decision-making process, the opinion-submitting process, and the opinion-making process). He then employs an accessibility scale to differentiate opinion-makers and opinion-holders and a motivation-information scale to differentiate two basic types of opinion-holders in terms of manner and extent of their participation in the policy process. The public is stratified along the lines of the earlier Almond model—mass, attentive, and opinion-making publics. Sixteen types of opinion-makers are identified. Finally, three primary and seven secondary channels of communication are described.

Like all initial conceptual efforts in complex areas, this is probably overly elaborate. However, the scheme was heavily influenced by a case study of the Conference on Foreign Aspects of U.S. National Security (with particular reference to the foreign aid program) held in Washington, D.C., February 25, 1958. Some 1400 participants—corporation executives, educational leaders, labor leaders, scientists, heads of voluntary organizations, and officials from the executive branch and Congress attended. Three months later, 1067 conferees were sent an eight-page questionnaire soliciting information about social backgrounds, experiences at the conference, and subsequent behavior regarding foreign aid. Hence, Rosenau's conceptualization is, to a marked degree, empirically inspired. His conceptual map is not in itself, of course, a theory, but it does locate the crucial points at which causal factors linking the policy process and public opinion are to be found. His case study is

---

[69] G. Almond, *The American People and Foreign Policy* (New York: Harcourt, Brace and Company, 1950).

valuable in its own right and stands in contrast to Mills' *The Power Elite* and Hunter's *Top Leadership U.S.A.*[70]

Elite Studies. Certainly it is true that we know more about how various elites perceive and evaluate international events, foreign policy issues, and other countries than we did ten years ago. Rather large-scale interviewing and questionnaire projects have brought the scholar closer to individuals and groups deemed to be politically important. Outstanding examples are: Free—legislative personnel; Bell—comparative judgments of the United States and the Soviet Union by Jamaican elites; Speier, and Speier and Davison—West German military and political leaders; Pye and Berger—military groups in developing nations; Shils—intellectuals in India.[71] While more recent elite studies do not employ essentially different techniques (except in the case of improved scaling procedures) from the earlier ones, one trend is toward asking how and why elites are self-activated to influence larger publics and governments in the ways they do.[72]

There still remains the problem of incorporating this data into our theories of national behavior. Clearly in many societies there is not one single, cohesive elite with an unchanging involvement in foreign affairs. Rather there are elite groupings who play potentially different roles in determining external responses in varying situations. In other instances the degree of societal complexity may tend to limit the number and size of elites. One set of ques-

---

[70] C. W. Mills, *The Power Elite* (New York: Oxford University Press, 1957); and F. Hunter, *Top Leadership, U.S.A.* (Chapel Hill: University of North Carolina Press, 1959).

[71] L. Free, *Six Allies and a Neutral* (Glencoe, Ill.: The Free Press, 1959); W. Bell, "Attitudes of Jamaican Elites Toward the West Indies Federation," *Annals of the New York Academy of Science*, Vol. 83 (1960); H. Speier, *German Rearmament and Atomic War: The Views of German Military and Political Leaders* (Evanston, Ill.: Row, Peterson and Co., 1957); H. Speier and W. Davison, eds., *West German Leadership and Foreign Policy* (Evanston, Ill.: Row, Peterson and Co., 1957); L. Pye, "The Military and Political Power in Developing Countries" (paper delivered to the American Political Science Association, Annual Meeting, 1959); M. Berger, *The Military Elite and Change* (Princeton, N.J.: Center of International Studies, Princeton University, 1960); and E. Shils, *The Intellectual Between Tradition and Modernity: The Indian Situation* (New York: Supplement No. 1, Comparative Studies in Society and History, 1961).

[72] For example, R. Bauer, I. Pool, and L. Dexter, *Business and Public Policy: The Reciprocal Trade Act of 1953-55* (to be published); K. Deutsch and L. Edinger, *Germany Rejoins the Powers* (Stanford, Calif.: Stanford University Press, 1959).

tions for theory is, then, what are the effects of different *elite struc-tures* in various societies? How do elite structures correlate with the number and kinds of interactions a society engages in? How are local elites related to elites in other countries? Are there emerging cross-national elites, and, if so, what are the consequences for policy and action?

The data cited need to be assessed for the following purposes: possible sources of innovation and limits on policy alternatives; possible relation to patterns of change and stability in policies; and possible relation to self-help and collaboration as responses to external situations.

Attitudes and Opinions of Unorganized Publics. Survey data gathered in many countries on many issues and problems has been accumulating at a rapid rate through the continuing activities of the Wilson Poll, Gallup affiliates, the Center of International Studies at M.I.T., and the United States Information Agency. The latter organization has a mass of data collected from fifty countries where identical questions and repeated samplings have been employed. It seems safe to say that only a small proportion of the total data pool is available to scholars. With one or two exceptions, the significant surveys conducted by the USIA have remained classified. Thus systematic theoretical exploration has not been possible up to this time.

Current unclassified studies do, however, reveal several important trends. First, a resourceful effort to explore the actual impact of public opinion on foreign policy-making is under way. The Survey Research Center of the University of Michigan has begun an extensive, long range study of the relationships between foreign policy attitudes and congressional behavior. Three of the center's staff, Stokes, Miller, and Converse, have applied a Likert scale of internationalism to samples of four populations: (1) congressmen's attitudes; (2) constituents' attitudes; (3) congressmen's perception of constituents' attitudes; and (4) congressmen's votes on salient issues. This project has not been completed, but its design and magnitude suggest that it will supply descriptive data which has been lacking hitherto. The results should help narrow the search for explanations concerning the role of public opinion because the project explicitly relates an official group and unofficial groupings to whom the former respond in some manner and because attitudes are at least correlated with behavior—in this case votes in Congress.

Second, empirical investigations are pushing beyond momentary opinions on issues which change from time to time to the mapping of more enduring attitudes and images.[73] Third, these investigations are increasingly cross-cultural, which makes possible a preliminary analysis of crucial similarities and differences in national perceptions and judgments. Fourth, relatively new research techniques have been devised. These trends are more or less simultaneously illustrated in ongoing projects. Under the direction of Charles Osgood, the cross-cultural generality of meaning systems is being investigated. Through the use of Osgood's "semantic differential" in such countries as India, Egypt, Turkey, Japan, Brazil, Chile, Finland, Iraq, United States, Germany, Greece, and Italy, the objective is to discover commonness of meanings which are obscured by obvious differences in language structure. This appears to be the first time, so far as I know, that a yardstick for making the measurement of values and attitudes directly comparable between different cultures has been applied on this scale. The familiar notion that people who speak differently think differently (the Whorfian hypothesis) will have to be modified if the early results of research continue to hold. It might be that similarities and dissimilarities of meanings and evaluations are not basically determined by formal language or boundaries. To the extent this is true, it has significance for ideological explanations of international conflict and for communication strategies.

Campbell and LeVine have developed a detailed "ethnocentrism interview" which is now being tested in several cultures. It is designed to elicit from a given people their attitudes toward neighboring people—stereotyped images, historical relations, traditional treatment of strangers, and so on. Once the instrument has been perfected, it will be administered to a large number of independent cultures by field researchers. The ultimate result should be a set of maps of reciprocal stereotypes.[74] Hadley Cantril has developed a "striving scale" which is being administered to United States, Norwegian, German, Indian, Philippine, and Bantu samples

---

[73] The concept of "images" has been formulated by: K. Boulding, "National Images and International Systems," *Journal of Conflict Resolution*, Vol. 3 (1959), pp. 120-31; and W. Scott, "Psychological Structure and Social Correlates of International Images," in H. Kelman, ed., *International Behavior* (to be published). See also the research reported by Harold Isaacs in *Scratches on Our Minds* (New York: John Day, 1958).

[74] D. Campbell, "A Proposal for Cooperative Cross-Cultural Research on Ethnocentrism," *Journal of Conflict Resolution*, Vol. 5 (1961), pp. 82-108.

to determine "felt needs" at different stages of political and economic life.[75]

Value Analysis.[76] Disillusionment with certain ideas and factors loosely grouped under the term "national character" is well-known. The basic deficiency has been lack of data, there being only a half-dozen studies which meet minimal standards of reliability and validity and even these did not use common procedures. However, in a recent paper, Inkeles argues convincingly that, given operational political concepts (e.g., a syndrome of personality characteristics required for the maintenance of a democratic society)[77] and existing devices for probing personality dynamics, it is now possible to tackle the problem of identifying and locating modal adult personality types. Once conceptual difficulties are overcome, then particular techniques such as Osgood's Evaluative Assertion Analysis,[78] projective tests, and survey procedures can be used in uniform or complementary research strategies.

Scott has undertaken a project to determine whether and to what extent attitudes toward international events and toward particular countries are anchored to personal values. His underlying hypothesis is that the same value orientations which direct or guide the manner in which people relate to daily life will also affect their judgments of external phenomena—in other words, a person's value system is generalized to international relations. Initial results tend to confirm the underlying hypothesis. An instrument is being developed which can be applied to a much larger population of respondents.[79] Building on the work of Rosenberg *et al.*, and others,[80]

---

[75] H. Cantril, *The Politics of Despair* (New York: Basic Books, 1958).

[76] The reader is referred to the following items which indicate the recent direction of stocktaking, conceptualization, and empirical research: E. Albert and C. Kluckhohn, *A Selected Bibliography on Values, Ethics, and Esthetics in the Behavioral Sciences and Philosophy, 1920-1958* (Evanston, Ill.: Row, Peterson and Co., 1959); H. Lasswell, "Clarifying Value Judgment: Principles of Content and Procedure," *Inquiry*, Vol. 1 (1958), pp. 87-98; and M. McDougal *et al.*, *Studies in World Public Order* (New Haven, Conn.: Yale University Press, 1960).

[77] A. Inkeles, *loc. cit.*

[78] In I. Pool, ed., *Trends in Content Analysis* (Urbana: University of Illinois Press, 1959), pp. 44ff.

[79] W. Scott, "Correlates of International Attitudes," *Public Opinion Quarterly*, Vol. 22 (1958-59), pp. 412-26, and "Rationality and Non-rationality in International Attitudes," *Journal of Conflict Resolution*, Vol. 2 (1958), pp. 8-16.

[80] M. Rosenberg *et al.*, *Attitude Organization and Change: An Analysis of Consistency Among Attitude Components* (New Haven, Conn.: Yale University Press, 1960).

Scott is also exploring the conditions under which international attitudes will or will not change. A basic concept here is "cognitive consistency," the general notion being that individuals and groups tend toward consistency in their perceptions and judgments even when the facts indicate a change is in order. Hence, as Charles Osgood points out, "it is cognitively inconsistent for us to think of people we dislike and distrust as making honest, conciliatory moves. . . ." [81]

Angell and Singer have begun a program of research to compare Soviet and American value systems with special reference to conflict and competitive coexistence. One objective is to arrive at an adequate description of "the dominant, politically relevant collective values" held by decision-makers, elites, and publics in the United States and the Soviet *and*, more important, to attempt to discover the conditions under which these values lead to foreign policy goals and strategies. Their method consists primarily of content analysis and statistical analysis of data already in existence by means of a theoretical framework which will relate values to policy-making.[82] Closely related to the foregoing is a major project under the direction of Philip Jacob at the University of Pennsylvania: Studies of Social Values and Public Policy. The first stage has consisted of formulating an explicit conceptual scheme within which comparative case studies have been initiated.

Problems of Bridging Disciplines and Levels of Analyses. A discussion of primarily psychological variables provides a fitting occasion to highlight briefly a set of problems which is peculiarly raised by the research just reviewed. We can best do this by additional samples.

Guetzkow has applied psychological theory to a large body of survey and other data to construct a basis for a theory of the nature, sources, and focus of national allegiances. In his analysis of "multiple loyalties" as a problem of international organization, he sets forth a precise and operational definition of loyalty and then examines seven types of loyalty and seven different sources of

---

[81] C. Osgood, "Cognitive Dynamics in the Conduct of Human Affairs," *Public Opinion Quarterly*, Vol. 24 (1960), pp. 341-65.

[82] R. Angell and J. D. Singer, *Value Systems, Foreign Policy and Soviet American Co-Existence* (preliminary report to Project Michelson, Naval Ordnance Test Station, 1961, mimeo.). Compare D. Gray, "The Foreign Policy Process in the Emerging African Nation: Nigeria and Ghana" (research prospectus, University of Pennsylvania, Studies of Social Values and Public Policy, memorandum no. 2, 1962).

loyalty. A sound use of propositions concerning underlying psychological mechanisms enables him to state the conditions under which loyalty to both nation and supranational entities, and transfers of loyalty from the former to the latter, are possible and likely.

The procedure followed by Guetzkow has key relevance for the problem of interdisciplinary bridge-building. He first locates national loyalty in a traditional framework of nationalism, supranational community building, and international organization. Then he defines loyalty as a special case of the more general category "attitude" which enables him to tap a larger body of knowledge. Evidence on the types, sources, and expression of loyalty comes from both political and nonpolitical studies. By conceptualizing the phenomena as he does—including the functions loyalties fulfill for the individual and the kinds of punishments and/or rewards attached to behaviors based on them—he is able to interrelate loyalties as well as to analyze their adaptiveness. With all this as a basis, he addresses himself to questions which have been posed by international relationists or which might be posed by a policymaker. Although the data is not sufficient to permit a high degree of certainty in answers, Guetzkow pretty well destroys the hidden assumption that there is a limited "fund" of loyalty which must be distributed among competing objects.[83]

Many of the hypotheses relating values, attitudes, and opinions to international relations embody more fundamental mechanisms, e.g., the frustration-aggression hypothesis. This body of thought is ably summarized by McNeil.[84] It has often been pointed out that hypotheses concerning the outbreak of war tend to fall into two categories: those which attribute war to the machinations of rulers, to the rational calculations of official policy-makers, or to accident and those which locate the trouble in "the minds of men," to widespread hostility and fear on the part of the man in the street. The relevant questions are easy to pose: (1) What is hostility or tension and how does one measure it? (2) If one *has* measured something, what difference does it make to policy-makers? (3) Is tension or hostility a necessary or sufficient condition of critical conflict or war?

---

[83] H. Guetzkow, *Multiple Loyalties: Theoretical Approach to a Problem in International Organization,* esp. pp. 53-62.

[84] E. McNeil, "Psychology and Aggression," *Journal of Conflict Resolution,* Vol. 3 (1959), pp. 195-233.

Unless something like Stuart Dodd's proposed "tension barometer"[85] can be perfected into an adequate measuring device and unless the conceptual problems associated with the opinion-policy nexus and with the personality-decision role nexus, answers to the first two questions will remain unsatisfactory. In his book, *Man, the State and War: A Theoretical Analysis,* Waltz himself does a good job of laying bare the assumptions which lead to (or underlie) the choices of one of the three levels included in his title (war refers to the state-system) and the implications which follow. He concludes that the state-system is the most appropriate *level of explanation* for war as a mode of conflict interaction. Thus he attacks strongly the "behavioral scientists" (whom he labels optimists with respect to man's nature) because one group he cites (mainly a particular group of psychologists) explains war in terms of mechanisms at work in the individual.[86] It is to be noted that "man," in this context, represents *both* a high level of abstraction and a level of explanation. The same is true of most of the analyses of "national character" where we seem to leap from the individual to the nation with a long, free fall occurring in the course of the leap.

The point is that our attempts to clarify theoretical operations make it possible to illuminate blind alleys and to formulate alternatives. We can reject the over-simple assumption entailed by many propositions containing individual psychological variables, namely, that those who make war decisions are a good sample of "men" and will be influenced by these factors, without necessarily giving up the assumption that individual decision-makers *may* be fruitful units of analysis or the assumption that, *under certain conditions,* psychological variables *may* account (partly at least) for what a government does in a given situation. Specifying these conditions is not always easy, but the absence of a careful, explicit chain of reasoning which links levels of explanation is usually the source of complaints. The question of how these are to be related or combined is not to be answered on an *a priori* basis. Premature and unwarranted reduction is to be resisted, but Guetzkow's work shows

---

[85] S. Dodd, "A Proposed Barometer of International Tensions," *Journal of Conflict Resolution,* Vol. 3 (1959), pp. 430-34. A very fruitful effort in this same direction is M. Zamnovich, "Patterns of Dimensional Behavior Within the International System: The Sino-Soviet Example" (Stanford University, Studies in International Conflict and Integration, 1961, mimeo.).

[86] K. Waltz, *op. cit.;* D. Singer, "The Level of Analysis Problem in International Relations," in Knorr and Verba, *op. cit.*

that the charge of "reducing politics to psychology" is often unfounded.

QUANTIFIABLE INDICATORS OF SOCIETY-AS-UNIT CHARACTERISTICS

More than any other student of international relations, Karl Deutsch has engaged in the imaginative use of statistical techniques to describe and interpret interaction flows among nations and societies, particularly trade and communications. His research has been done in both historical and contemporary settings. Recently Deutsch has interrelated quantitative indices of selected societal characteristics and external transactions (1960). This research is directed to such questions as: What are the basic changes in interaction patterns among nations? Is the world becoming more "international"? What is the impact of contemporary changes in intersocietal relationships on internal conditions? It has two related and fundamental purports: first, his findings begin to illumine, and suggest new insights into, the reciprocal connections between the unit and interunit levels; second, at the interunit level, the statistical mapping is a basis for describing the total external involvement of individual nations, the "closeness" of pairs (or other groupings) of nations, and the correlation of independence or dependence measures with more subjective factors such as hostility or friendliness.[87] In a similar vein, Kling (1959) uses taxes on foreign trade as an index of political behavior in certain Latin American countries and finds that when taxes derived from foreign trade fall clearly below 30 per cent, the pattern of internal politics has shifted or is shifting from "*caudillismo* to the contours of interest group politics."[88] This technique suggests the possibility that other significant internal indicators of external patterns might be discovered.

Another facet of this trend is represented by the revival and extension of the pioneering work of Raymond Cattell[89] by John Sawyer, a psychologist at the University of Chicago. Using Cattell's formulation of "dimensions of nations," Sawyer is comparing eighty

---

[87] K. Deutsch, "Toward an Inventory of Basic Trends and Patterns in Comparative and International Politics," *American Political Science Review,* Vol. 54 (1960), pp. 34-57.

[88] M. Kling, "Taxes on the 'External' Sector: An Index of Political Behavior in Latin America?," *Midwest Journal of Political Science,* Vol. 3 (1959), pp. 127-50.

[89] R. Cattell, "An Attempt at More Refined Definition of Centrality in Modern Nations," *American Sociological Review,* Vol. 17 (1951), pp. 408-13.

nations along three hundred variables. A refinement of factor analysis techniques will permit the utilization of both hard and soft data in the same matrix. That is, subjective data such as opinion surveys and objective data such as population characteristics can be combined in the construction of a single descriptive index which can then be compared. The end result of the Sawyer project will be a series of ways of comparatively describing many nations as one means of laying bare hidden likenesses and unlikenesses. Cattell's analysis was based on League of Nations' compilations, while Sawyer is basing his on United Nations' sources. The latter, of course, contain many more categories of data and are probably more reliable because of improvement in statistical techniques and information gathering skills.

The examples cited are complementary to the rating scales applied by Russell Fitzgibbon to Latin American countries.[90] In general, the theoretical significance of this type of analysis would seem to lie in a marked extension of the possibilities of fruitful correlations. Gross data indices can be related to other known facts (e.g., policy responses or coalition patterns) so that new hypotheses are suggested.

Interunit and Interaction Foci
(System and Subsystem at the Intersocietal Level; Patterns of Interaction and Relationships; The Global Environment)

It is no accident that interunit analyses are, on the whole, more general in scope, more formal, and more quantitative than is true of societal-action analyses. The inspiration for this comes primarily from economic theory, game theory, statistical techniques, general systems theory, and communications models. The universe of observation is (in one sense) more removed and is more populated with entities. Things (e.g., transactions) can be counted. Powerful collectivities must be dealt with. Perhaps it is also not an accident that the tillers in this part of the vineyard (e.g., Hoffman, Liska) are especially critical of the work discussed in the previous section. Granted that the criticism has been a useful corrective, a basic theoretical problem is that neither level of analysis can escape the other. No "system" approach can escape the properties of participants of "the" or "a" system. Conversely, the notion of system

---

[90] R. Fitzgibbon, "A Statistical Evaluation of Latin American Democracy," *Western Political Quarterly*, Vol. 9 (1956), pp. 607-19.

implies much more than the summation of these properties. This is an ancient merry-go-round, memorialized in the juxtaposition of the individual and the group. Fruitful research and theory at each level is reaching toward the other. Often the reachings do not meet. Very few significant propositions linking the two levels have been formulated.[91] For many purposes such linkage is unnecessary. However, the choice of level alone cannot determine this. It was remarked earlier that Kaplan presents a logico-deductive theory in the classical tradition. It is an exercise in free-floating theorizing. This is one reason the theory is attacked—because of its "unempirical" appearance, because of "purely abstract hypotheses," or because it is "too *remote* to be tested." [92] Further, says the same critic, "systems scientism" does not "capture the stuff of politics" and besides, "international relations" is not an "integrated system." The general drift of this kind of comment does raise an important issue, namely, the nature and status of theoretical entities.[93] General statements about unobservable entities—the invention of that which empirical generalizations are supposed to be about—are *not* subject to the twofold test of truth and adequacy, only to the latter. That is, do they supply premises from which empirical propositions can be deduced which are in "close accord" with the facts? Nonempirical concepts which are not inferred from subjects (such as gravity) may be useful provided we know what we are doing, which includes *not* acting as though they "stand for" something "real." These concepts do not point to new or old facts but ascribe properties to entities which permit, in turn, deductions. Hoffman is a self-avowed nominalist, yet in his capacity as critic he becomes a meticulous empiricist. The expectation or requirement that *all* concepts "correspond" (note this in itself is not self-evident and unambiguous) to a real, objective world seems to be the result partly of the use of nonabstract nouns (electron), which are actually theoretical concepts, to point to "things," and partly because of a habit of insisting that theoretical explanations be both true and adequate. Hoffman himself uses the term "force" or "forces" and speaks of an "index of intensity" which seems to stand for something but actually is an ascribed property. Aristotle, whom Hoffman

---

[91] See Sondermann, *op. cit.*

[92] Hoffman, "International Relations, the Long Road to Theory," p. 358.

[93] One of the best and clearest treatments of this problem is B. Mayo, "More About Theoretical Entities," *Science News*, Vol. 39 (1956), pp. 42-55.

quotes, made a qualitative distinction between natural and violent motion from which no deductions were possible. This may be one reason why the concept of power appears to wander back and forth between an empirical and a nonempirical status.[94]

Now the point is not that those who prefer the low road to theory (e.g., induction, inferred properties of concepts) are wrong or that for most purposes concepts should not be operational or that the Kaplan route and the Hoffman route are mutually exclusive alternatives. Rather, our purposes and tests should be clear and appropriate. As Rapoport has so cogently put it: the remoteness of theory is no indication *per se* of relevance or irrelevance, and not every conclusion of an exact theory has to be translatable into observation.[95]

Most of the research and theory-building activities to be discussed here will be divided into two familiar categories: (1) conflict, crisis, strategy, and war—the *counterpulls*; and (2) cooperation, collaboration, consensus, and integration—the *adhesives*. However, one general type of analyses which for the most part transcend these categories must be noted before we move on.

SYSTEMS AND EQUILIBRIUM ANALYSES

McClelland has, more than any other theorist, explored the potential contributions of general systems theory to the study of international relations. His specific effort to suggest empirical applications to history has not received the attention it deserves—partly because it was published in a source not widely read by those in the field. A systems orientation to the problems of organized complexity is now a common form of attack on widely different subject matters (ranging from the brain to traffic control), and more is involved than is conveyed by the common sense words "system" or "systematic." [96]

---

[94] Hoffman, "International Relations, the Long Road to Theory," pp. 347, 371.

[95] A. Rapoport, "Various Meanings of Theory," *American Political Science Review*, Vol. 52 (1958), pp. 972-88.

[96] C. McClelland, "Applications of General System Theory in International Relations," *Main Currents in Modern Thought*, Vol. 12 (1955), pp. 27-34; "The Function of Theory in International Relations," and "Systems and History in International Relations: Some Perspectives for Empirical Research and Theory," pp. 222-34. See also K. Boulding, "Political Implications of General Systems Research" (Presidential address before the Society of General Systems Research, 1957, mimeo.).

One of the criteria of fruitful theory is the questions it leads us to ask. Basically, McClelland asks: can we get any extra mileage by viewing our phenomena (or any segment thereof) as an "open system" related to, and interacting with, its "environment"? Three questions follow: [97] (1) What are the operating parts of the system (call these parts "components")—what do they do, how are they arranged, how are they coordinated, how do they fluctuate, grow, or change, and how are they replaced? (2) What are the boundaries between the system and environment—what functions do the boundaries serve, how are they structured, maintained, and changed? (3) What is the character of the influence of the environment on the system and of the system on the environment—how do these hypothecated complexes interact?

Note that a system could be the relationships of states A and B (interaction focus) or state A and its environment (action focus). The three questions can be asked at different levels of complexity or generality.[98] We shall not list these, but simply mention in passing that they can be connected empirically to such intuitive distinctions as that between, say, NATO and those countries in the southern hemisphere who trade with each other. Depending on the level of complexity, the three fundamental questions will be of a different order. McClelland goes on to argue that the systems perspective may be a most fruitful way to organize the simplistic tools we have for understanding a very complex range of phenomena which can and should be divided analytically in many useful ways. It also may provide a basis for re-examining old concepts; power may be "defined in systems terms as the efficiency with which a system is able to give and get from its environment, whatever the need, purpose or goal may be." Then, again in systems terms, we can ask: what is the effect of increasing organizational complexity on a nation's power? Furthermore, if we ignore territorial boundaries for a moment,[99] we can ask: What are the boundaries of the United States foreign relations system? What are the forces operating to expand and contract these boundaries through time?

---

[97] C. McClelland, "The Acute International Crisis."

[98] See K. Boulding, "General Systems Theory—The Skeleton of Science," *General Systems Yearbook*, Vol. 1 (1956), pp. 3-17.

[99] J. Herz, *International Politics in the Atomic Age* (New York: Columbia University Press, 1959).

Kaplan's *System and Process in International Politics,* also grounded in systems analysis, has been more controversial because it is a formidable attempt at rigorous, highly abstract thinking. There are four aspects of his theory: *systems of action; processes* (integrative and disintegrative); *values;* and *strategy.* Rather than an impractical summarization of Kaplan's analysis, attention will be drawn to some of the key issues which have been raised concerning it.[100] To recall briefly, Kaplan postulates the rules which actors follow in, and the equilibrium conditions for, six different models or kinds of international systems and identifies (or rather hypothesizes) the transformations which will occur when disequilibrium occurs. Integrative processes tend to maintain equilibrium; disintegrative processes tend to create disequilibrium. Individuals, nation-states, or blocs may be the actors—the subsystem components—of the six systems. The conditions of equilibrium may be regarded as the resultant of the operation of certain limits, rules and norms, and goal pursuits. As Kindleberger notes, Kaplan develops "partial equilibrium" models for treating certain significant types of interaction systems in contrast to Liska's single equilibrium system which combines balance of power and collective security.[101]

While apparently rejecting systems theory in the McClelland-Kaplan sense, Hoffman proposes to define and compare historical systems of international relations in terms of four correlated sets of data: (1) structure of the system (number and nature of basic units, etc.); (2) *all* of the forces which cut across or operate within many of the units; (3) impact of domestic factors (e.g., distribution of power) on foreign policy; and (4) outcomes of international relationships. Whether Hoffman is simply using system in a crude denotative way or not, he comes remarkably close to a systems perspective: there are two levels interrelated in *any* system—"unit" actions resulting from the pursuit of postulated, very general goals (the Wolfers threefold classification of self-preservation, self-extension, and self-abnegation) and the "system as a whole," the "world" tasks being performed by postulated basic process-conflict, accommodation, and diffusion. In a footnote (p. 370) Hoffman says his approach differs from Kaplan in that only two of the latter's systems have empirical referents (the balance of power and the

---

[100] The part on strategy is informed by game theory, but there are real difficulties encountered, and it is not the essential feature of his contribution.
[101] Liska, *op. cit.*

loose bipolar).[102] Richard Rosecrance is the only writer so far to actually do the kind of systematic historical analysis implied by Hoffman's position. In his highly useful unpublished manuscript *International Systems*, he examines the modes, objectives, and techniques of diplomacy in nine "systems-periods": (1) 1740-89, (2) 1789-1814, (3) 1814-22, (4) 1822-48, (5) 1848-71, (6) 1871-90, (7) 1890-1918, (8) 1918-45, and (9) 1945-60. This work can be considered a companion piece to Adda Bozeman's *Politics and Culture in International History* (1960), which contains less explicit theory and concentrates on the pre-1500 period. Together, the two are harbingers of a new historical approach.

If we are going to use a systems orientation, or describe a system, there is a crucial problem of what "it" is that we are calling a system. This is, of course, the persistent boundary question. Karl Deutsch has proposed an empirical test of the reality of social units,[103] and, in an earlier era of social science, Stuart Rice set forth a "statistical view of a perceptual world." More recently Donald Campbell demonstrates how it is possible to test the hypothesis that an aggregate of persons (or other units) behaves as a system; he defines precisely a method for distinguishing whether "it" is a system or just an arbitrary fragment. His line of reasoning is that among aggregates, some meet the test of being entities, some do not, and this is capable of empirical representation. Among aggregates which are entities, only some meet the criteria of being organic systems, and this too is capable of operational definition. Thus the question of whether there is *an international system or particular international systems* is subject to empirical determination. Campbell also reminds all of us that our knowledge processes make it appear that "stones" are more real than "groups" or that NATO is more real than a loose bipolar system.[104]

It seems necessary to work with both empirical systems and analytic systems,[105] and not all analytic systems need have empirical referents. The latter constructions simply involve our say-

---

[102] Hoffman, "International Relations, the Long Road to Theory," esp. p. 370.
[103] Deutsch, *Political Community at the International Level.*
[104] D. Campbell, "Common Fate, Similarity, and Other Indices of the Status of Aggregates of Persons as Social Entities," *Behavioral Science*, Vol. 3 (1958), pp. 14-25.
[105] See M. Levy, *The Structure of Society* (Princeton, N.J.: Princeton University Press, 1952), chap. 2, for an analysis of the distinction between analytic and concrete.

ing: let us as observers act (for the moment at least) *as though* there were gravitational pulls among bodies called nations (note our use already of the term satellite); then let us imagine how these pulls would act under certain conditions; then let us see if we cannot represent these conditions by some set of indicators and look at how the bodies (nations) interact with each other under these conditions. Admittedly, these operations involve tough problems of finding counterparts for the artificial elements in the nation of gravitational pull. Initially, however, the problem is not to quantify the unquantifiable, but to create indicators which might lead to observations which could be at least roughly scaled. To the extent that our conventional perceptions rule out such possibilities (a persistent barrier in the advance of knowledge), we shall not even try. Hoffman recommends a Copernican revolution—let's treat domestic problems *as though* they were a function of international politics. This is an act of the mind—it does not change the real world nor was the idea given by the real world.[106]

To return to Kaplan, the test of adequacy is the appropriate one for his axioms and nonempirical concepts. It is to his *theorems* or derived propositions that testability and truth apply. Kaplan generates over one hundred such statements, concerning which several reviewers have said they doubt their testability, usually without giving specific examples. Here is an example of a proposition which is testable: "In a loose bipolar system, the more hierarchical the bloc actors and the greater the antagonism and incompatibility between the blocs, the more rigid the alignments become and the greater the tendency of the loose bipolar system to be transformed either into a tight bipolar system or into a hierarchical system." [107] Certainly there are logical imperfections in Kaplan's theory; for example, his treatment of integrative functions is often unconvincing, and there are places where logical closure has not been attained. But Kaplan is actually aware of the need to test his propositions which leads him to identify, not always with saliency, a variety of data pools and methods. Therefore, Kindleberger, who approves highly of his effort, chides him for his suggestion that balanced power propositions can be tested by small group experiments.[108] How-

---

[106] Hoffman, "International Relations, the Long Road to Theory," p. 347.
[107] Kaplan, *Systems and Process in International Relations*, p. 41.
[108] Kindleberger, "Scientific International Politics." Experiments using a small number of subjects do not have to be directed to small group theory. Guetzkow

ever, it is unfortunately true that Kaplan's book is sprinkled only lightly with concrete references, thus contributing to the over-all impression that it has little empirical import. But the job of verification is not Kaplan's alone. To quote Rapoport again, a highly general deductive theory is a "system of credit," and somewhere there are "assets." Given reformulation of some propositions and a distinction between indirect and direct testability, we have been headed in the direction of several "banks" (to carry on Rapoport's metaphor)—including large amounts of so-called traditional descriptive data. Harold Guetzkow has noted that if Kaplan and Liska (who also spawns over one hundred propositions) had known about Deutsch *et al.*, *Political Community and the North Atlantic Area: International Organization in the Light of Historical Experience*, they might have discovered the relevant data for two propositions: (1) *Effective safeguards for the weaker parties may easily be the decisive factor in federation* (Liska, p. 166; Deutsch *et al.*, p. 58), and (2) *If a decision-making unit must adjust to its immediate social environment in the system for which it makes decision, it will be unable to expend its capacity on external problems and will manifest rigidity with respect to its specific role function in that society* (Kaplan, p. 108; Deutsch *et al.*, p. 58; p. 66).

Would McClelland and Kaplan have posed the same questions or advanced the same hypotheses in the absence of the systems point of departure? Would either have been able to borrow from so many sources or relate things previously only implicitly related if at all? Yes, possibly, but it is doubtful. Kindleberger in reviewing Liska and Kaplan asks: Is the behavior of a country related to its national system and subsystems and to what extent? Is it necessary for the stability of an international system for countries (or those acting for them) to *understand* it? This line of questioning probes a critical underlying nexus: Are there autonomous system properties (particularly rules and goals independent of the properties of participating units or particular actors)? If so, what is their status —are they *resultants* of the normative behavior of participating units, or are they *internalized* in the latter, and thus each level is the opposite side of the same coin?

has simulated complex organization in the laboratory: "Isolation and Collaboration: A Partial Theory of International Relations." For a clarification of some of the issues raised here see S. Verba, *Small Groups and Political Behavior* (Princeton, N.J.: Princeton University Press, 1961).

Liska's central concept (drawn from economics) is institutional equilibrium (equilibrium is also central in Kaplan, but Liska's is a more general equilibrium system transcending Kaplan's five situations). The basic proposition is that equilibrium exists when the distribution of power "outside" any international organization "corresponds to" the location of power "within" that body. What is implied is a "relative temporal stability uniquely or otherwise upset by change." States seek to maintain the best equilibrium instead of the best power position; hence the system acts as a kind of social control mechanism which provides an acceptable distribution of welfare, prestige, and other values.

Both Kaplan and Liska carry the burden of well-known disabilities of the equilibrium concept.[109] As suggested earlier, it has been a very pervasive concept. (Even Morgenthau, with whom Kaplan and Liska are in disagreement, quotes Cannon.) Like rationality or normality in psychology, equilibrium tends to be a mixed analytical-normative concept (at least implicitly)—a stable equilibrium is a "good" thing, disequilibrium is a "bad" thing. In the present instance, this is more true of Liska than Kaplan. Furthermore, the concept leads more easily to static generalizations than to process or change generalizations. To escape the static quality, modifications such as "dynamic equilibrium" must be introduced. Finally, explanations from classical mechanics are often introduced inappropriately. If equilibrium is also an ideal-typical model for Liska, the test is still not truth but deductive potential. It is very helpful to have two theorists, each using partly similar and partly dissimilar deductive platforms to generate propositions about overlapping phenomena (Kaplan's balance of power system and Liska's balance of power; Kaplan's universal system and Liska's collective security) because their disagreements give us competing hypotheses and their agreements give us greater conviction.

To reiterate, equilibrium theorizing still retains its heavily static flavor; we have few propositions which tell us how and why we move from one system state to another or from one system to another. Despite often experienced difficulties, we have not yet fully exploited a concept which, though often ambiguous, points to "something" we all come back to sooner or later. We ought to postulate a greater variety of equilibria situations and compare the

---

[109] E.g., D. Easton, *The Political System* (New York: Alfred A. Knopf, 1953), pp. 266-307; Wright, *op. cit.*, pp. 514-17.

accompanying assumptions and stability conditions. Such a suggestion is reinforced by Kindleberger and March and Simon.[110] Neither of these sources is prone to fuzzy thinking.

INTERNATION SYSTEMS: EXPERIMENTAL TECHNIQUES [111]

Gaming in many forms—business, political, diplomatic, and war—has now become a familiar training and planning technique. Games focused on diplomacy and war were pioneered at RAND and have spread to academic centers—M.I.T., Harvard, Columbia, Northwestern, Oklahoma, San Francisco State College, Stanford, and the Army War College. Variations in this technique have been described.[112] With the exception of the RAND versions, which have been problem or policy oriented, much of the interest has centered on simulation as a teaching or training aid. But it is the potential value of gaming and experimentation in theory-building and research that will be stressed here. The activities alluded to mean that the experimental approach, the laboratory, has first entered political science on a significant scale via international relations. The recent National Science Foundation grant to Schelling (Harvard Center for International Affairs) to continue his experiments in bargaining related to international relations and the long range simulation program being developed by Guetzkow at Northwestern are signs of an important recent trend.

Laboratory experimentation is, of course, not the only relevant type. A recent experiment in an actual social setting which bears

---

[110] Kindleberger, "International Political Theory from Outside," pp. 69-82; and March and Simon, *Organizations*, chap. 4.

[111] For a general survey, see H. Guetzkow, C. F. Alger, R. Brody, and R. Noel, *The Use of Simulation for Teaching and Research in International Relations* (to be published).

[112] J. Goldsen, *The Political Exercise, an Assessment of the Fourth Round* (Washington, D.C., the RAND Corporation, D-3640-RC, 1956, mimeo.); H. Goldhamer and H. Speier, "Some Observations on Political Gaming," *World Politics*, Vol. 12 (1959), pp. 71-83; M. Kaplan *et al.*, "Theoretical Analysis of the Balance of Power," *Behavioral Science*, Vol. 5 (1960), pp. 240-52; H. Guetzkow, "A Use of Simulation in the Study of Inter-Nation Relations," *Behavioral Science*, Vol. 4 (1959), pp. 183-91; C. McClelland, "A World Politics Game" (San Francisco State College, International Studies Project, 1959, mimeo.); O. Benson, "A Simple Diplomatic Game" (University of Oklahoma, 1958, mimeo.); L. Bloomfield, "Report and Analysis of Political Exercise held in September, 1958" (Center for International Studies, M.I.T., mimeo.), and "Political Gaming," *United States Naval Institute Proceedings*, Vol. 86 (1960), pp. 57-64.

closely on the mixture of conflict, competition, and cooperation found also in the international realm is Muzafer Sherif *et al., Intergroup Conflict and Cooperation: The Robbers Cave Experiment.*[113]

Simulation or gaming exercises take many forms. Multiple explorations and "loose experiments" are especially appropriate for initial applications to international relations because the technique is difficult in itself and because of the mixture of hard and soft variables which are present. Fortunately, the group of scholars who are carrying on this work have kept in close touch with each other (a special panel at the 1959 convention of the American Political Science Association presented reports of four exercises), and results should be cumulative in some sense. While it is a risky simplification, different simulation techniques may be divided into the *more programmed* and *less programmed* and then subdivided into two each. More programmed games, e.g., RAND Santa Monica games 1955-1958, lead to determinant outcomes (solutions) and are generally concerned with war and strategy. Some games of this sort are played with teams representing real countries (RAND), but some employ a single experimenter or a staff of experts using a complex computing machine through which various alternatives (e.g., strategies) can be "played out" (Benson). Less programmed games usually allow the players more latitude and do not necessarily end in a determinant outcome (i.e., somebody "wins"). Soft variables, not easy to reduce to computations, are given freer run. Some less programmed games are more realistic, i.e., the country teams will consist of experienced personnel (e.g., Soviet experts) to represent real nations (actual role playing) in an exercise directed to a real problem such as the Berlin crisis of 1949. The less realistic games do not normally use experienced players, countries are fictitious (though they embody certain basic properties such as differences in economic and military strength), and particular runs are not problem oriented. Within these crude categories there are many other variations (e.g., number of countries, size of teams, rules for communication, etc.) and these are often related to the experimenter's purpose—professional training, operations research, or teaching.

What can be learned from all this? How can the complex world of international relations be imitated or reflected in a game or lab-

---

[113] M. Sherif *et al., Intergroup Conflict and Cooperation: The Robbers Cave Experiment* (University of Oklahoma, Institute of Group Relations, 1961).

oratory exercise? To put the worst possible face on it, how can inexperienced students playing five fictitious nations without real life equipment help in the building of theory? We are not sure of the answers to these questions yet, but everyone concerned seems to be sufficiently convinced of worthwhile payoffs to invest substantial resources. We shall sketch briefly a rationale, although acceptance will depend primarily on one's understanding of experimental techniques and their role in the accumulation of knowledge.

In the first place, to undertake a miniature simulation of some phase or aspect of international reality requires that the experimenter be explicit about his theory, about what happens, how, and why. Since he cannot *duplicate* reality, with all its scale and detail, he has to choose the essentials—those parameters, rules, and structural features which will produce the desired effects or establish the necessary and sufficient combinations under which certain kinds of expected actions and interactions are likely. *What is simulated is not the real world* per se, *but the relationship among variables under approximate conditions.* Through repeated trials these relationships can be subjected to controlled variation. (The Northwestern Program spent two years preparing for the control stage, so it is not reached quickly.) The second point grows out of a statement by Hoffman to the effect that experimental methods available in the social sciences cannot "demonstrate" causal laws.[114] At the present time, no one expects direct, rigorous testing of hypotheses, but certain hypothetical relationships *can* be shown to hold or not to hold under specified laboratory conditions. The *generation* of new hypotheses is also a valuable result to be anticipated. In both cases, internation simulation must be closely coordinated with field research in a continuous two-way process. Thus a major advantage of experimentation is its heuristic fruitfulness, its help in building theory. From this writer's experience, the insights which emerge from laboratory exercises are not the same as those which emerge from armchair musings. For example, the following hypothesis has emerged from an internation simulation: the less trustworthy one nation-team is in the eyes of the others in a given system, the more likely negotiation is bilateral rather than multilateral. Is this self-evident?

Third, though gaming is expensive, if the number of controlled

---

[114] Hoffman, "International Relations, the Long Road to Theory," p. 357.

runs is to permit statistical inference, it is a fairly quick way of tracing or identifying effects which might require a long, costly field research operation. Precisely because the elements of the simulated system are visible to, and controllable by, the experimenter, the loss entailed through the lack of realism is counterbalanced by the capacity to observe the gross systemic consequences of such factors as the invention or acquisition of new weapons, a change in decision-makers, an economic setback in one country and so on. Such observations may suggest critical locations of influences and changes which are, or tend to be, obscured by the complexity and "noise" confronting us in the real world.

Gaming exercises geared to theory building are more likely to be open-ended—there is no "optimal solution," no winner or loser. The objective is either to discover how the imposed rules, conditions, and player characteristics affect the choice process or how these antecedents give rise to patterns of interaction—the evolution of cooperation, coalitions, and war. In a series of controlled runs at Northwestern in the summer of 1960, an effort was made to examine what happens when universal distribution of nuclear capability is introduced into a loose bipolar system.[115]

A fourth potential utility of internation simulation lies in the exploration of events or problems which are still in the future and for which there is no relevant past experience. An example is the so-called n-country problem which looms as a consequence of the spread of nuclear capabilities. It is stated, almost without contradiction, that the acquisition of the new weapons by ten to twenty countries will automatically destabilize the international system. That possibilities of "accidents" will increase seems logically entailed by the multiplication of installations, but beyond this, what is the evidence for the dogmatic assertion? Why not an alternative prediction? It is of more than passing interest to note that in the series of controlled runs in the summer of 1960 an effort was made to discover what happens when universal nuclear capability was introduced into a loose bipolar system. The results suggest another hypothesis: whether destabilization follows the spread of nuclear weapons depends on the state of system at the time the change occurs.

---

[115] H. Guetzkow et al., "An Experiment on the N-country Problem Through Inter-Nation Simulation: Two Case Study Examples" (paper delivered at the Social Science Institute, Washington University, 1960, mimeo.).

To reiterate, gaming exercises geared to theory building are more likely to be open-ended—there may be no "optimal solution," no winner or loser in the usual sense. The objective is to discover how the imposed rules, conditions, and player characteristics affect the choices of action responses and how these antecedents give rise to patterns of interaction—communications, cooperative bargaining, coalitions, war, and so on. Therefore, loose, but not unstructured experimentation, is desirable, particularly in the light of the variability observed in everyday reality. The reciprocal impact of the intraunit and interunit levels on each other is complex and inevitable. Intimations of what the range of effects when the dependent and independent variable status of the dual set of factors are reversed can be better detected if outcomes are allowed to proliferate. In addition, the illumination of the influence of subtle personality characteristics can be approached in at least two ways: they can be "washed out" by controlling other variables *or* pretests of participants in the exercise becomes a way deliberately introducing different ideologies and cognitive orientations. The latter procedure will be employed in the Stanford-Northwestern collaboration in the replication of some features of the World War I analyses. After a careful attempt to isolate the personal attributes of decision-makers which appear to have played a key role in 1914, simulation participants will be chosen by means of tests designed to identify individuals possessing similar attribute clusters. It hardly needs to be said that the search for a latter-day Kaiser Wilhelm is not a proper description of this procedure.

INTERSOCIETAL CONFLICT

A major attempt to redefine and update the problem of war and peace as a research focus (i.e., The Institute for International Order's Five *Programs of Research*) and the relatively recent body of thought connected with deterrence, weapons systems, and strategy [116] have already been mentioned. Obviously, the critical

---

[116] For a discussion of deterrence theorizing, see R. Snyder, *Deterrence, Weapons Systems, and Decision-making.* Useful introductions to bibliographical sources are: R. Brody, "An Annotated Bibliography on Deterrence," *Journal of Conflict Resolution,* Vol. 4 (1960), pp. 443-58; C. Wright, "Selected Critical Bibliography," *Daedalus,* Vol. 89 (1960), pp. 1055-70; and M. Halperin, "Nuclear Weapons and Limited War" (to be published in the *Journal of Conflict Resolution*). Among political scientists who have contributed to this literature and who are also identified with the broader field of international

postwar period has left its mark. New questions about old problems,[117] re-examination of familiar concepts in the light of changed conditions,[118] formulation of less familiar concepts (e.g., credibility of deterrent capability, automaticity of response to nuclear attack, accidental war, counterforce strategy, etc.), and preoccupation with the safe and effective management of radically different destructive power as well as with the escalation of limited wars— these are all evident.

The research and theory challenge can be summarized as follows: the identification and relating of process, situational, and unit-action variables to the end that the prediction and explanation of violent or nonviolent patterns of interaction among societies are made possible. This requires the description and explication of conflict processes, situations, and pertinent societal characteristics in order that theories, concepts, and hypotheses can be applied and tested in the appropriate context.

The fruitful application of theories and analytical tools depends in large part, first, on their existence and accessibility; second, on the specification of the kinds of relevant events and outcomes which are to be accounted for, and third, on the accumulation of studies of actual conflicts. So far as the first condition is concerned, the storehouse is far richer than it was ten years ago.[119] Kenneth Bould-

---

relations are: M. Kaplan, "The Calculus of Nuclear Deterrence," *World Politics*, Vol. 11 (1958), pp. 20-43; R. Osgood, "Stabilizing the Military Environment," *American Political Science Review*, Vol. 55 (1961), pp. 24-39; G. Snyder, "Deterrence and Power," *Journal of Conflict Resolution*, Vol. 4 (1960), pp. 163-78; and J. Singer, *Deterrence, Arms Control, and Disarmament* (to be published). Bernard Brodie's *Strategy in the Missile Age* (Princeton, N.J.: Princeton University Press, 1959) remains the standard work. Among contributions primarily from nonpolitical scientists are: H. Kahn, *On Thermonuclear War* (Princeton, N.J.: Princeton University Press, 1960); A. Hadley, *The Nation's Safety and Arms Control* (New York: Viking Press, 1961); T. Schelling and M. Halperin, *Strategy and Arms Control* (New York: Twentieth Century Fund, 1961); D. Frisch, ed., *Arms Reduction: Program and Issues* (New York: Twentieth Century Fund, 1961); D. Brennan, ed., *Arms Control, Disarmament, and National Security* (New York: George Braziller, 1961); Symposium, "Psychology and Policy in a Nuclear Age," *Journal of Social Issues*, Vol. 27 (1961).

[117] E.g., is there a "point of no return" on the road to war? Deutsch, "Mass Communications and the Loss of Freedom in National Decision-making."

[118] E.g., stability, R. Osgood, *op. cit.;* rationality, T. Milburn, "What Constitutes Effective Deterrence?," *Journal of Conflict Resolution*, Vol. 3 (1959), pp. 138-45.

[119] E.g., UNESCO, *The Nature of Conflict* (1957); Coser, *op. cit.;* Mack and Snyder, *op. cit.;* Rapoport, *Fights, Games, and Debates.*

ing has recently given us an admirable survey of conflict theories.[120] With respect to the second condition, we are beginning to develop typologies of conflict situations.[121] Rapoport's somewhat primitive but applicable threefold delineation of fights (violence), games (interdependence of strategic moves), and debates (persuasion) as ideal types is helpful in deciding when certain theories are appropriate. Modelski and Huntington provide discriminations among kinds of internal violence. The former enlarges the sample of instances upon which to base possible predictions concerning the escalation problem by his conception of "internal wars" as a special case of a more general class, namely, limited wars. These two writers also propose analytic and empirical links between intrastate and interstate violence. Modelski outlines a conceptual scheme for the analysis of the "international structures" of internal wars and Huntington cites historical examples for a set of propositions which make intersocietal violence dependent on societal circumstances such as alternative outlets for skills and energy. Thus Modelski makes war more than an interstate system phenomenon (cf. Waltz, *op. cit.*) by extending it to the domestic realm, and Huntington's hypotheses seems to run counter to theories of Lewis Richardson and Herman Kahn.[122]

Related to the third condition, we note an increase in empirical studies: North's research into World War I, McClelland's analysis of the Berlin and other crises, and R. Naroll's project [123] focused on historical deterrent relationships. The first of fifteen case studies commissioned by the Carnegie Endowment for International Peace

---

[120] K. Boulding, *Conflict and Defense* (New York: Harper and Brothers, 1962).

[121] E.g., Rapoport, *Fights, Games, and Debates;* C. Modelski, *The International Relations of Internal War* (Princeton University, Center of International Studies, 1961), the first report on the Internal Wars project being carried out by the Princeton Center; S. Huntington, "Arms Races: Prerequisites and Results," *Public Policy,* Vol. 8 (1958), pp. 41-86; and S. Huntington, "Politics, Violence, and the Military: Some Preliminary Hypotheses" (paper delivered to the American Political Science Association, Annual Meeting, 1960).

[122] L. Richardson, *Statistics of Deadly Quarrels* (New York: Quadrangle Books, Inc., 1960), *Arms and Insecurity* (New York: Quadrangle Books, Inc., 1960).

[123] Naroll, *op. cit.* This appears to be the only substantial effort to find analogs to the present situation in past confrontations of two other powers, one of which attempts to deter the other. Through careful selection of numerous cases, it is hoped that factors significant in the success or failure of deterrence can be identified. Imaginative approaches to methodological problems such as data quality control in historical research also promise fruitful results.

has been published—Jacques Freymond's *The Saar Conflict, 1945-55*.[124] This program of research is unfinished, and Robert MacIver's general conclusions are not yet available.

For our purposes, the work of North and McClelland (to be discussed below) is of more immediate interest because of their concentration on the formation of theory and experimentation with novel techniques of analysis. North's reconstruction of the events leading up to the outbreak of World War I probes the interrelations of policy declarations, perceptions of threat, communications within and between the protagonist nations, and personality factors. McClelland's crisis studies are intended to discover whether certain unstable situations generate a structure of rules and responses as events unfold which is or is not susceptible to the outer limits desired by the participants. Both of these lines of inquiry share two significant features: first, each offers promise of propositions which link the unit-action and interunit, interaction levels; second, each explicitly develops an analytic scheme in the context of specific situations, thus permitting the isolation of generalizable variables which can be applied to other cases. Together they point to an ultimate ability to identify more clearly the combination of factors which puts a crisis beyond control.

An economist, Thomas Schelling, has pushed his concern for the present politico-military environment to a consideration of more fundamental processes and mechanisms in international relations —negotiation and bargaining.[125] Hitherto, our knowledge of why negotiations over conflicts succeed or fail, of the consequences of various bargaining strategies and tactics, of how bargaining relationships are established and maintained, and of the range of acceptable points of agreement under particular circumstances has been scant indeed. It still is. But the significant theoretical implication lies in viewing certain intersocietal interactions from this perspective. Assuming that conflict is inherent in all of social life, and assuming further that it is not a polar opposite of cooperation (a misleading dichotomy), the development or existence of effective bargaining techniques would seem to be one of the necessary elements in the institutionalization of nonviolent modes of handling clashes of interest among nations.

---

[124] J. Freymond, *The Saar Conflict, 1945-55* (New York: Praeger, 1960).
[125] T. Schelling, *The Strategy of Conflict*, and "Experimental Games and Bargaining Theory," in Knorr and Verba, *op. cit.*

Conflict Processes: Games of Strategy and Arms Races. A comment on game theory is in order although a thorough examination of all the problems which arise in the application of game theoretic analysis to social conflict is not possible. It was perhaps inevitable that attempted applications to international conflict should appear to verge on fadism.[126] Under the sophisticated guidance of Luce and Raiffa, *Games and Decisions* (1957), as well as other writers, we have recoiled from earlier optimism.[127] The need to use empirical grounds for some of our choices of techniques has already been emphasized, but there is more to it than this. Thus far, for those political scientists who have been interested at all, the elements of game theory have been sources of metaphors and analogies —both useful in the early stages of systematization if care is used. But metaphorical usage has resulted in critics not being able to see the relationship between where the user jumps off from and where he lands—as in the case of game theory leading to a non-game theoretical examination of diplomatic strategy.[128] Moreover, analogies have been only partially pursued—one set of words, "game" or "player" is substituted for another set, "international politics" or "nation."

To the question "What good is it?" there is no categorical answer. One reason has to do with "it," and the other has to do with the questioner. A fundamental issue is whether we are willing or able to regard the assumptions and concepts of game theory as idealizations of what politics is, namely, interaction between individuals and groups whose interests are partly conflicting and partly convergent and who in some sense calculate when choosing their course of action. It is instructive to read Braithwaite's *Theory of Games as a Tool for the Moral Philosopher* (1955) in the light of traditional formulations of the nature of political phenomena.[129] A second reason concerns the need to advance beyond the zero-sum game for which the theory was initially most highly developed.

---

[126] See Kindleberger's criticism of Kaplan, "Scientific International Politics"; R. Quandt, "On the Use of Game Models in Theories of International Relations," in Knorr and Verba, *op. cit.*

[127] D. Luce and H. Raiffa, *Games and Decisions* (New York: John Wiley & Sons, Inc., 1957).

[128] S. Perry, "International Relations and Game Theory," *Bulletin of the Research Exchange on the Prevention of War*, Vol. 4 (1956), pp. 1-8.

[129] R. Braithewaite, *Theory of Games as a Tool for the Moral Philosopher* (New York: Cambridge University Press, 1955).

This form of games of strategy clearly has much more limited application in the social realm. As Raiffa, Luce, and others have refined and extended non-zero-sum game theory, more fruitful applications are possible as is evident in Schelling's work.

Nonetheless, we shall still have to be careful to ask in what "game" (in a sociological sense) our actors are involved or whether their interactions can be characterized properly as a game of strategy at all.[130] Then we must ask whether the data to determine the values of the intersection of "moves" are available, for, as Luce points out, this is the difficult part. Furthermore, we must distinguish between descriptive-explanatory functions and normative functions. The former assumes a structure of action and interaction in which decision-makers or nations are following certain rules, or *trying* to, while the latter offers a prescription which might require the actors to follow these rules *if* they wish to optimize, maximize, or strike an acceptable bargain.

Game theories are, of course, models of, or for, rational behavior. Most of the theories and conceptual schemes discussed here could be classified according to the presence or absence of built-in elements of rationality even though the particular definition of rational conduct might differ. When used as descriptive models, game theories provide a standard, deviations from which, or conformity to, are to be accounted for, but the basic question of what rational rules (if any) actors are actually following may not necessarily be revealed. That is why some research and theory-building must also be free of postulated rationality and allow the rules of action to be a matter for empirical discovery. Game theories cannot tell us why actors are not rational or why they may be guided by different conceptions of rationality. Herein lies the importance of decision-making and crises research which may explain why rational rules are not followed or are followed unsuccessfully. The constant pull between rational and irrational interpretations *a priori* and *post hoc* suggest the strong likelihood that only some areas of action and interaction permit rationality and it is a combination of rational, irrational, and nonrational elements which is operating.

The most full-blown mathematical theory is that of Lewis Richardson, whose collected statistical analyses and ideas have finally been published in the United States.[131] Fortunately, this body of

---

[130] See Rapoport, "Various Meanings of Theory."
[131] Richardson, *Statistics of Deadly Quarrels,* and *Arms and Insecurity.*

writing has been lucidly interpreted [132] and critically reviewed.[133] A theory of this kind raises many complex issues. Whether Richardson has been altogether successful in facing the arms race problem head-on is less important perhaps than whether his efforts will or can be seminal in the further development of theory. The statistical materials add to our historical data pool—a fact easy to overlook when one is dazzled or repelled by the mathematical formulations. Apart from this, an effort to check Richardson's equations will most certainly raise the old question of what variables and parameters will comprise our theory about arms race processes. In this respect, the quantitative and formal exercises perform the same function as gaming—we are forced to be explicit and, so far as possible, parsimonious.

Although his theory is predominantly labeled mathematical, and statistically analyzes interactions, Richardson does not ignore the psychological or microlevel, which confronts him with a problem which has recurred in this essay. At one level—the interaction of armaments—nations appear from his data to be caught in a vicious cycle of defense coefficients; at another level—the actions of decision-makers—particular choices determine whether war will occur or not. What is the relationship between the two levels in this instance? Do the statistics simply reflect consistent patterns of decision-making response under the condition of distrust and spiraling armaments? Does the pattern suggest that strategic policy thinking is based on an implicit minimax rule (i.e., do that which is protective in the face of the worst your opponent can do)? Or are the statistics indicators of systemic factors which, in effect, operate as "givens" for policy-makers? If the answer to both questions is affirmative, then the theoretical task is to probe the inter-level connectives. From this point of view, Richardson's theory is not just an interesting attempt to do something relatively unimportant.

Conflict Processes: Bargaining and Negotiation. Schelling's theoretical analyses, hitherto scattered, have been brought together in a book *The Strategy of Conflict* (1960). While he roams over a

---

[132] Rapoport, "Various Meanings of Theory," and "Lewis F. Richardson's Mathematical Theory of War," *Journal of Conflict Resolution,* Vol. 1 (1957), pp. 249-300.

[133] O. Sutton, reviews of Richardson's works in *Scientific American,* Vol. 204 (1961), pp. 193-200.

wide range of conflict situations, his central interest is in international conflict. However, the latter is conceived as a special case of a generic type. Schelling queries why formal game theory has contributed so little to theorizing about certain problems—limited war, deterrence, surprise attack, atomic blackmail, and massive retaliation. The key to his basic conceptual thinking is in chapter two, "An Essay on Bargaining" and chapter four "Toward a Theory of Interdependent Decision." In contrast to the essentially restrictive, unilateral zero-sum game in which one player *always* loses or wins less and the aim is to play the best strategy regardless of what an opponent does, Schelling focuses on the most general form of the non-zero sum game which he calls the "mixed motive" game. In this game, the mixture lies in the presence of conflict *and* mutual dependence which demands some kind of collaboration or accommodation between the parties, i.e., tacit or explicit *bargaining*. What makes this a game of strategy is the interdependence of expectations, i.e., each player's proper choice of action depends on what he expects the other to do. Bargaining is necessary because the range of alternative outcomes is such that any one point within the range is better for both players than no agreement at all. From this framework of assumptions about the nature of the mixed motive game, Schelling pursues two significant lines of development: if bargaining is to result in the "convergence of mutually consistent expectations," there must be perceptual and suggestive cues exchanged by the parties; and collaboration and accommodation are carried on by basic moves (commitment, promise, or threat) and structural elements which these moves depend on (enforcement, communication). Much of his theory consists of descriptive elaboration of moves, tactics, and structural elements, of analysis of their interrelations, and of hypothesizing the consequences of particular bargaining and negotiation tactics under particular conditions. Emphasis is put on special conditions and problems—the possible existence of certain focal points (or *one* focal point) within the range of outcomes (the *prominence* of a given solution); the effects of limited or poor communication which leads to *tacit* bargaining misperception; how threats and promises are affected by their manner of communication, by the distribution of information between the players (e.g., the knowledge they have of each other's values), and by institutional factors.

Even with this brief picture, it is clear that Schelling has moved somewhat beyond the usual formulations of game theory. Restrictive assumptions have been relaxed (e.g., there is no longer shared information between the players about what the outcome matrix looks like), a sequential flow of moves has been added so the model is dynamic, the secrecy of the zero-sum game has been abandoned, indeterminant solutions or outcomes become a condition of the conflict situation not a difficulty in the application of the theory, and the range of strategies and tactics is greater. The mixed motive game has much more psychological and sociological richness. In short, the theory embraces a wider variety of situations which have real world counterparts. Not only can one see more fruitful empirical fit to the problems and events of interest to the international relationist, but theories of perception, organizational theories, and decision theories (of the nongame sort) can be brought within the game of strategy framework. Furthermore, the depth explication of such concepts as "threat" and "bargaining strength" show there is much more than meets the eye. Schelling stresses the essential paradox in strategic bargaining: one party manipulates the incentive and responses of the other by *relinquishing* its initiative and freedom of choice, not by preserving these while the opponent is persuaded or forced to give them up. The age-old question of sovereignty looks somewhat different if we reject the assumption that it is a "thing" that is completely present or completely absent, and the argument for giving up freedom of choice in order to preserve it can have a strong pragmatic base. In non-zero-sum games, self-interest is not a self-evident concept. Power and balance of power may look substantially different, too. Power may be the resultant of skill in communicating appropriate, credible cues. "Balance" may consist in the coincidence of reciprocal expectations concerning what will not damage the parties to conflict rather than equal capability for inflicting damage in the absence of a test.

Although the application of Schelling's analysis thus far has been directed to limited war, deterrences, and arms control problems, wherever the interdependence of expectations and action is empirically given, the theory is relevant. As hinted earlier, Schelling is an unusual economist in that he is subjecting some of his hypotheses (e.g., if it is obvious that two players can achieve a 50-50 division of a value, this will invariably condition their joint choice) to experimental validation (chapter six is entitled "Game Theory and Experimental Research"). Moreover, his ideas are being incorporated in the experiments of psychologists and economists who are not directly concerned with international relations.[134] One of the most interesting patterns to emerge from this research is the tendency to convert a non-zero game into a zero-sum game and for players to be more interested in "looking good" or "scoring points" rather than in reaching collaborative bargains of benefit to all concerned.[135] Some examples in the international arena might be viewed profitably in these terms.

Conflict Processes: Intersocietal Communications. It is pertinent to mention here the current theoretical work of Ithiel Pool. Basically, Pool is attempting to move from the somewhat atomistic perspective of the classical communications model—who says what to whom with what effect—to a more systemic or "society as a whole" perspective which may be more fruitful for political scientists or international relationists. One phase of his general theoretical framework involves communication between open and closed societies. An open society is one whose capabilities *and* intentions can be assessed with some degree of confidence by another; that is, it is possible to assign subjective probabilities to a range of possible actions and to decide how much confidence one has in the assigned probabilities. A closed society is one whose capabilities can be so assessed but not its intentions. He applies his model to a bargaining situation between two major powers (i.e., nations capable of inflicting severe damage on each other) who are hostile and one of which is closed and the other open. (This is actually one of seven conditions which can be derived from his model.) Clearly this situation is not without its real world counterpart. From this scheme, propositions concerning the outcome of certain communication strategies can be derived. For example, Pool argues that while it is disadvantageous on some grounds for the United States not to be able to control and pinpoint completely its information program, the inability to send only one au-

---

[134] S. Siegel and L. Fouraker, *Bargaining and Group Decision-Making Experiments in Bilateral Monopoly* (New York: McGraw-Hill Book Company, Inc., 1960); and R. Willis and M. Joseph, "Bargaining Behavior I: Prominence as a Predictor of Games of Agreement," *Journal of Conflict Resolution*, Vol. 3 (1959), pp. 102-13. B. Lieberman, "Experimental Studies of Conflict in Some Two- and Three-Person Games" (Harvard University, Center for International Affairs, 1961, mimeo.), 41 pp.

[135] Scodel *et al.*, "Some Descriptive Aspects of Two Person Non-zero Sum Games," *Journal of Conflict Resolution*, Vol. 3 (1959), pp. 114-19.

thoritative message (or group of messages) is an advantage because it reduces the possibility that an opponent could become *highly certain* about his subjective probability estimate for *one* of our possible actions or reactions. This brief presentation does not do justice to Pool's theory, but it represents a significant reorientation of comunications analysis. His other applications include competitive communications, the Berlin Blockade, economic growth, and problems of underdeveloped countries.

Conflict Processes: International Crises. That recurrent crises are a significant feature of international life needs no demonstration, but actually we know little about the anatomy and internal process features of a crisis. Their generic properties are thus obscure and no real comparison is possible. Charles McClelland has devised a method for describing an "acute" international crisis as an interaction flow.[136] His aim is, first, to provide an objective description of the sequence of actions and reactions by the parties to a crisis. His first reconstruction is the 1948 Berlin crisis and he projects similar studies of the Korean crisis (1950), the Matsu Quemoy crisis (1954) and the Suez crisis (1956).

McClelland defines three kinds of single acts: a *bid* (a move which establishes a new position, bargaining point, or change in the status quo); a *claim* (which defends the situation against a change in the status quo); and a *withdrawal* (an act which signifies an intention not to participate further). A sequence or pattern is a number and combination of unit acts and patterns are distinguished as *trade off* (a competing bid claim or withdrawal); a *backoff* (a withdrawal in the face of a bid or claim); *duplication* (in effect a special form of trade off in which the counter move is by indirection—a parallel structure of interaction); *reinforcement* (repetition and reiteration of bids and claims); and *level shifts* (shift in locale or negotiators). Recorded events from public sources are coded into these categories. The chronology of the Berlin crisis runs from December, 1947 (Council of Ministers Meeting, London), to February 2, 1950 (announcement by the United States that the Soviet Union is violating the Paris agreement of June, 1949). Some 656 events are included in the chronology. Flow charts for particular time segments and topics (e.g.,

---

[136] McClelland, "The Acute International Crisis," *loc. cit.;* also, McClelland, "Tacit Communication by the Physical Act at Berlin and Quemoy: An Approach to Interaction Analysis" (unpublished paper, October, 1961).

transportation restrictions) are prepared on the basis of the chronologically numbered events and coded single acts and patterns. This
particular crisis is viewed as a recurrent aspect of the cold war
within the bounds set by the prevailing international system (closely
akin to Kaplan's loose bipolar system).

McClelland analyzes the patterns of the crisis (as reconstructed
via the categories mentioned) as consequences which result from
the logic of the situation given certain properties of the system.
Ten interesting propositions—generalized descriptions and explanations of the interactions—are formulated. I shall list only two:
(1) An acute crisis is marked by a crescendo of interactions and
in this particular system every point in the sequence may take the
form of "maximum conflict" up to the limit imposed by the rules
of the system (one of the nine rules is that both blocs must be prepared to fight World War III to avoid destruction of a bloc);
(2) With the growth of experience, the processes of the cold war,
including the spectacular manifestations of crises may become increasingly "traditionalized" and "automatized," but the blocs may
also seek new methods and forms in pursuit of objectives.

The second proposition is cited because despite McClelland's
attempt to confine his analysis to phenomena at the interaction
level, the logic of the "system situation" level, he found his data
forcing him to the action or unit level for explanations or interpretations which would make sense. This proposition is, implicitly,
based on a learning proposition, and it draws a distinction between
routinization and innovation which is not deductible from system
rules, but rather from the way choices are made by the actors
within the discretionary limits permitted by system rules. At any
rate, McClelland has provided the first reasonably systematic attempt to lay bare the structure of interaction in a prolonged acute
crisis and to interpret patterns in terms of an explicit framework.
His study should be compared with Davison's excellent *The Berlin
Blockade: A Study in Cold War Politics* [137] where the data is essentially the same but the underlying pattern (in McClelland's sense)
is hidden.

Robert North and his associates at Stanford University are developing a novel and significant set of techniques for comparative

---

[137] W. Davison, *The Berlin Blockade: A Study in Cold War Politics* (Princeton, N.J.: Princeton University Press, 1958).

analyses of international conflicts.[138] Although a systematic recon-struction of the interactions during the six-week period prior to the outbreak of World War I in August, 1914, is the main empirical focus of this research in its initial phase, the design and the theo-retical framework are applicable to any conflict situation for which required data is available. (The North group is preparing the same kind of reconstruction for the Bosnian crisis.)

By incorporating (a) the perceptions of decision-makers, (b) action and policy decisions, and (c) objective reality in a viable analytic scheme and by the application of recent developments in coding and statistical techniques to historical documents, consid-erable light can be thrown on such critical problems as: How do wars start? How do limited armed encounters escalate? How does a deepening crisis affect the responses of decision-makers? How does the prehostilities balance of national armaments enter into calculations? Briefly, the research strategy rests on a precise con-ceptualization of the nature of conflict interaction, specification of the units (e.g., policy condition: statements of goals, preferences, or intent), interims of which the interaction is to be analyzed, and content analysis of official messages within and between the parties to conflict. Coding of historical documents with explicit theoretical purpose has involved progressive change and refinement of cate-gories as well as close attention to the level of inter-coder re-liability. The five basic perceptions which lie at the heart of this method are: (1) perceived power–strengths and weaknesses; (2) frustration–satisfaction; (3) hostility–friendship; (4) capability; and (5) resolution of conflict.

Preliminary results appear most intriguing. Among the emergent hypotheses are: *the stronger the perception of injury to the state, the less weight is given by decision-makers to insufficient military capability; as a conflict crisis intensifies, the less emphasis there is on rational calculation of means–ends relationships and the more emotions tend to influence crucial choices;* and, *as the emotional component increases, the greater the tendency of the parties to conflict to form their own image of the conflict and to select only that information about the objective situation which is compatible with the image.* Needless to say, these propositions must be sup-ported by further rigorous inquiry, but their relevance to the whole

---

[138] R. North *et al., The 1914 Conflict Study Seminar, a Statement of Progress* (Stanford University, October 1, 1959, mimeo.).

questions of the respective role of rational, irrational and nonrational factors in the use of large-scale violence as a mode of international conflict resolution is undeniable.

Conceptual clarification and empirical studies focused on crises
have progressed to the point where a program of additive research
is now possible. The papers on crisis decision-making given at a
Stanford conference in January, 1962, will be published in a forthcoming issue of the *Journal of Conflict Resolution.*

INTERSOCIETAL INTEGRATION AND POLITICAL COMMUNITY

Wolfers argues there are two trends in the world: one en-
hances the position of the nation-state, the other diminishes the
paramount position of the nation-state. There are so many complex
factors, says Wolfers, "we cannot tell which will gain the upper
hand." [139] Why must one gain the upper hand? Cannot both trends
be juxtaposed? Are international centralization and decentralization
opposed tendencies, or are they both the result of increasing organizational complexity inside societal units and in intersocietal interactions? Do law and government *always follow* the formation of
a minimal community, or can this process also work in reverse?
I shall discuss briefly two research and theory foci which bear on
these questions.

Security Communities: Historical Case Studies. Karl Deutsch
and six historians have produced a notable example of group research involving the combination of social science conceptual tools
and the skills of the historians.[140] Aside from the task of establishing an effective working relationship among the team, the problem
here was quite obviously to devise a conceptual scheme which
would facilitate the reordering of existing historical data or the
acquisition of new data in such a way as to make some generalization from individual historical instances which from one point of
view were unique. The conceptual foundations, drawn largely but
not exclusively from communications models, were laid in Deutsch's
earlier work *Nationalism and Social Communication* and *Political
Community at the International Level.* Ten case studies (admit-

---

[139] Wolfers, "The Actors in International Politics," pp. 101-04.

[140] K. Deutsch *et al., Political Community and the North Atlantic Area*
(Princeton, N.J.: Princeton University Press, 1957). This was one of a series
of studies initiated by Richard Van Wagenen when he was director of the
Center for Research on World Political Institutions at Princeton University.

tedly confined to the North Atlantic Area) are analyzed in terms of operational definitions of *community, integration, peaceful change,* and differentiation of *security community* as a special type having two subtypes: *amalgamated and pluralistic.* Emphasis is on the specification of the minimal requirements for a peaceful political community, which, of course, is the elimination of violent conflict problem. Certain popular beliefs are reexamined and found more or less wrong, e.g., that modern life is more conducive to the formation of supranational institutions because the technological revolution throws nations closer together.

The general findings of this study provide a much clearer picture of the conditions under which security communities and integration evolve or decline. Nine essential requirements for an amalgamated security are stated with sufficient clarity and generality to be applied to other cases where required data exists. Though the nine requirements are not identified as being necessary or sufficient or both, relatively heavier stress is laid on compatible values, minimal capabilities, mobility of persons, multiplicity and balance of transactions, and mutual predictability of behavior. While a pluralistic security community (roughly the present situation in the North Atlantic area) is less integrated than the other type, the authors feel it is a more promising approach to the elimination of war than was originally thought and indeed may be a safer device for dealing with man's new weapons.

Integration is a continuous process, crossing and recrossing a "threshold" which divides the probabilities of war or no war, and the evidence shows that the political, economic, and social capabilities of participating units is a crucial factor for the future of the process. Capabilities are divided into power—capacity to act (including administrative efficiency)—and responsiveness—capacity for self-control and redirection of attention. Increased integration puts a load on capabilities. An interesting proposition drawn from the historical analysis is: political amalgamation tended to increase the load because decisions for larger areas and populations had to be made by fewer central institutions, and claims and burdens had to be accelerated faster than decisional capabilities.

International Organization. Generally speaking, this sector of the field is slowly adding more explicit theorizing, quantitative analysis, interviewing, and direct observation to its traditional stock in trade, namely, the description of formal institutions based on documentary sources. This trend can be seen in the work of Bloomfield, Hovet, Padelford, Alger, and Haas.[141]

Ernst Haas is in many ways the leader in this sector because of the breadth of his interests, his empirical inquiries, and preoccupation with generalization. Like Deutsch, Haas's basic interest lies in the development of political community at the international level. However, the latter concentrates more on group attitudes and motives, the changes these may undergo in particular situations, the processes whereby governmental and private groups reach consensus on supranational integration, and the interrelations of institutions and attitudes with respect to community building. The chief organizational foci of his research has been in western Europe —postwar agencies involved in economic, military, and political functions and their role in integration.

In a recent study, *Consensus Formation in the Council of Europe* (1960), Haas first wrestles with the problem of an operational definition of consensus and the possible ways of measuring whether it has or has not occurred. Transnational or international political parties and parliamentary norms and behaviors are seen as significant influences on consensus formation in the absence of operating power vested in the organization. Haas states nine "developmental" hypotheses (p. 14) relating such variables as growth of shared values among the membership and the unity of national delegations; the emergence of a "catalyst" party and with federal or uncommitted groups; and shared values in the parliamentary context and national party commitments. He then tests these hypotheses against a statistical analysis of *all* roll call votes in the consultative assembly from 1949 to 1958. The main source of data is 114 nonunanimous votes tabulated in terms of a fivefold classification of issues. An "index of cohesiveness" is constructed.

The concepts and propositions employed in the foregoing study

---

[141] L. Bloomfield, "Law, Politics, and International Disputes," *International Conciliation*, No. 516, January, 1958, and *Western Europe and the United Nations: Trends and Prospects* (Cambridge, Mass.: Center for International Studies, M.I.T., 1959); T. Hovet, Jr., *Bloc Politics in the United Nations* (Cambridge, Mass.: Harvard University Press, 1960); N. Padelford, *Elections in the U.N. General Assembly* (Cambridge, Mass.: Center for International Studies, M.I.T., 1959); C. Alger, "Non-resolution Consequences of the United Nations and Their Effect on International Conflict," *Journal of Conflict Resolution*, Vol. 5 (1961), pp. 128-45; and E. Haas, *The Uniting of Europe, Consensus Formation in the Council of Europe*, and "The Comparative Study of the United Nations," *World Politics*, Vol. 12 (1960), pp. 298-322.

are drawn from Haas's earlier case study of economic integration in western Europe: *The Uniting of Europe—Economic, Social, and Political Forces, 1950-1957* (1958). A partial analysis of the Western European Union has also appeared [142] in which the hypothesis that the behavioral consequences of institutional ambiguity may work toward supranational integration is tested and disproved. Thus Haas is developing a kind of middle range theory based on case studies of regional functional organizations where the cultural background is held constant. Whether the propositions will hold for other regions remains to be seen. At any rate in attempting to isolate the conditions under which there is an actual shift in decision-making from the national to the supranational level, Haas has created a framework which is sufficiently general to appear applicable elsewhere. The central ingredients of this framework are certain key concepts—procedural and substantive consensus, the "catalyst" party, shared parliamentary (i.e., nonnational) role expections and perceptions, and the interplay of governmental and nongovernmental groups functioning in the home capital and in the international organization.

Haas [143] joins with Hoffman [144] in negative criticism of Kaplan and Liska for failing to offer "a limited-purpose theory" which can "immediately be made to dovetail with our hopes for a theory of international relations." But he adds, "Yet I persist in creeping up on such a theory from behind. . . ."Arguing for studies "which seek to generalize by remaining true to the empirical material" and approving Hoffman's comparative description of historical systems, Haas then states, "The comparisons presumably would yield the inductively obtained laws of a theory, *perhaps not dissimilar from Kaplan's deduced hypotheses.*" Following this, he outlines what an empirical theory of international organization might look like if it assumed a world-wide, post-1945 system consisting of three blocs (in tension) *and* a global institutional structure (the need for interaction) and if it attempted to describe the evolution of the system in terms of global tasks. At this point, Haas says emphasis on systemic properties should give way to a focus on institutions.

---

[142] *International Organization*, Vol. 14 (1960), pp. 37-59.

[143] E. Haas, "The Comparative Study of the United Nations," p. 302. See also E. Haas, "Systems and Process in the International Labor Organization—A Statistical Afterthought," *World Politics*, Vol. 14 (1962), pp. 332-52.

[144] Hoffman, "International Relations, the Long Road to Theory."

Nonetheless, Haas' statement about a possible convergence of the inductive and deductive approaches brings us full circle in this section.

CONCLUSIONS

Major Themes

An initial stage of a trend toward greater explicitness and coherence has been outlined and some problems of theory development and conceptualization have been noted. Current research efforts and techniques have been discussed. It has been suggested that an emerging multiple strategy for ordering observations and explanations is discernible.

These themes seem worth stressing:

(1) Greater clarity of differences in levels of observation and explanation with particular reference to the unit-intraunit and inter-unit levels and improved identification of key variables operating to determine action and interaction and the initial establishment of linkages among levels and units have been shown.

(2) More skillful borrowing among disciplines and bodies of theory together with increasing recognition of the need for putting "international relations" content into propositions derived from the analysis of more general phenomena has occurred.

(3) "Islands of theory" which highlight particular portions of the total empirical terrain have been developed, and bridge-building between them begun.

(4) A closer relationship has been shown between theory construction and research with the result, among other things, that deductive and inductive approaches are joining hands, that new analytic and research techniques are being developed in the course of confronting a problem of investigation, and that there is more additive testing across projects.

(5) The range of methodological and theoretical choices has expanded and the special advantages of each of several "roads to theory" are seen as complementary at this stage.

Toward Greater Theoretical Integration

The combination of changing reality and diverse "handles" for grasping and interpreting this reality implies a need for a

meta-framework within which the accumulation of reliable knowledge can be guided and monitored. There are not sufficient resources to do everything, and the choices of future intellectual
activities in the field of international relations ought ideally to be
determined in part by an overview of where we stand in the light
of stated purposes. The task of constructing a meta-framework has
just begun, but the ingredients may be at hand. We have useful
examples in the work of McClelland, Kelman, Frankel, Gibbons,
and Brody.[145] McClelland provides a taxonomic framework for
theories based on a general systems scheme. Gibbons compares and
relates various approaches to the determination of foreign policy.
Brody demonstrates a common linkage (i.e., feedback) among systems theory, field theory, and decision-making theories.

Two possible lines of integration might be kept in mind. First,
we need a device for *reviewing* theories, not just accepting or rejecting them. The exact model of what is needed here is found in
Estes *et al.*,[146] namely, a set of categories and questions for a comparative analysis of different theories. It seems likely, however,
that not all international relations theories are so well developed
and formally presented as to justify the application of this scheme.
At any rate, a modification of the foregoing scheme for a comparative review ought to include the following: (1) purposes—description, explanation, prediction (specificity), heuristic aid; (2) delineation of empirical area-data language, variables, and criteria;
(3) theoretical concepts—primitive terms, principal constructs,
relations among constructs; (4) procedural characteristics—assumptions, derivations; (5) empirical content and adequacy—range of
data, sensitivity to evidence.

Second, and to return to an earlier point, we need a more systematic, although empirically open, specification of levels and units
of analysis, including the possibility of the development of a loosely
integrated world society, a greater differentiation of subsocietal
units, and a mapping of interactions and interaction systems. This

---

[145] McClelland, "The Function of Theory in International Relations," and
"A Classification of International Relations Theory," *PROD*, Vol. 2 (1959), pp.
32-34; H. Kelman, "Societal, Attitudinal, and Structural Factors in International
Relations," *Journal of Social Issues*, Vol. 11, 1955), pp. 42-56; Frankel, *op.
cit.*; Gibbons, *op. cit.*; and R. Brody, "Three Conceptual Schemes for International Relations," *Journal of Student Research*, Vol. 2 (1960), pp. 8-25.

[146] W. Estes *et al.*, *Modern Learning Theory* (New York: Appleton-Century-
Crofts, 1954), pp. xiii-xiv.

will necessitate a set of typologies (including societies-as-units) and an attempt to solve the boundary problems which arise from both social change and the use of different analytic perspectives. It will be helpful also to specify "populations of events" which are of theoretical concern and which can be correlated with unit and interunit variables. Perhaps at long last, Lasswell's repeated plea for trend analyses could be undertaken with intersocietal transactions and relationships as a point of departure.

Such a program is relatively easy to cast out, but it will require the talents of many. If this excursion through the field of international relations has revealed anything to him, perhaps the reader will think the next steps feasible and urgent.

Behavioral Analyses of Representative Bodies

John C. Wahlke
VANDERBILT UNIVERSITY

This paper undertakes to consider where behavioral study of representative bodies appears to be going and what problems are involved in getting there. But, "Where to start the chronicle and what to include? Few legislative studies bear a behavioral label and many are significant only as suggestive prototypes."[1] The relevant literature displays the same diversity in topics studied and in techniques of research which characterizes political and social study in general. For here, as in the more inclusive fields, the adjective "behavioral" designates an approach and not a body of theory or knowledge. The field of inquiry can perhaps be delimited with sufficient precision for present purposes, however, if the term "behavioral studies" is taken to refer to analyses whose data directly concern those human beings known as representatives, the persons who constitute the various representative bodies historically known to man.

VARIETIES OF BEHAVIORAL ANALYSIS

The works marked out by such a definition appear to fall into three generally distinct types which differ both in the questions they seek to answer and in the methods of data collection and

---

[1] N. Meller, "Legislative Behavior Research," *Western Political Quarterly*, Vol. 13 (1960), p. 134. Professor Meller's article provides an excellent review of the most relevant literature. See also J. C. Wahlke and H. Eulau, eds., *Legislative Behavior: A Reader in Theory and Research* (Glencoe, Ill.: The Free Press, 1959).

analysis they use. They are also distinct in that works in one category tend to make references primarily to other works in the same category and to relate less often to works in the others.

The Character and Recruitment of Representatives

One variety of study often erroneously thought to be distinctively "behavioral" is that which ascertains certain demographic characteristics of the membership of particular representative bodies. The character of representatives' constituencies, for example, was the object of attention as early as 1895.[2] Since that time descriptions of various representative bodies in terms of representatives' age, sex, tenure, occupation, religion, ethnic origin, social class, and similar characteristics have become so numerous and familiar, especially in America, that some legislatures regularly publish such information about their own membership.[3] A closely related but more ambitious line of effort is that represented by the *History of Parliament* project, which, following the earlier work of Sir Lewis Namier,[4] attempts to "record the names, and . . . the careers of the persons elected to serve in Parliament from the reign of Edward I to a date as far into the nineteenth century as circumstances may permit."[5] A more recent subtype of the variety of study in question is that which explores career-configurations or general political-attitude configurations of persons who become or aspire to be representatives.[6] Although such studies often range very widely in their attempts to relate career- or attitude-patterns to various antecedent or causal factors and although they frequently share some of the characteristics of the next variety of study to be

---

[2] G. H. Haynes, "Representation in New England Legislatures," *Annals of the American Academy of Political and Social Science*, Vol. 6 (1895), pp. 58-71.

[3] A convenient listing and discussion of the most important of these studies can be found in Meller, *op. cit.*, pp. 141-43. Meller notes that the characteristics studied include, in one case, the cranial capacity of the representatives' heads.

[4] L. B. Namier, *The Structure of Politics at the Accession of George III*, 2 vols. (London: Macmillan and Co., 1929).

[5] F. M. Stenton, "The History of Parliament," *London Times Literary Supplement*, January 6, 1956. See also G. P. Judd, *Members of Parliament: 1734-1832* (New Haven, Conn.: Yale University Press, 1955).

[6] H. Eulau *et al.*, "The Political Socialization of American State Legislators," *Midwest Journal of Political Science*, Vol. 3 (1959), pp. 188-206, and "Career Perspectives of American State Legislators," in D. Marvick, ed., *Political Decision-Makers* (Glencoe, Ill.: The Free Press, 1960).

considered, they may be said to conclude usually by tabulating various patterns as "characteristics" of the membership of specific representative bodies.

The chief point to be noted about all the sorts of study here discussed is that they tend to be purely descriptive. The reader of the statistics is ordinarily left to infer for himself what the facts presented have to do with the structure, functioning or performance of the representative body, or the behavior of the members described. The case for amassing quantities of such descriptive information about the careers and the demographic characteristics of representatives is best argued by W. O. Aydelotte, who foresees the possibility of discerning in these numerous data (chiefly by statistical methods) "revealing correlations." [7]

For such data to be most useful, however, more is needed than simple tabulations for particular representative bodies or simple intercorrelations among one or more of the characteristics surveyed. Logically, two sorts of hypotheses are needed: first, hypotheses concerning the circumstances which lead to the presence or absence of representatives with certain characteristics; second, and more important, hypotheses concerning the consequences of variations in these characteristics for the behavior of individual legislators and, thereby, for the working of the representative body.

What appear to be hypotheses of this second sort are often encountered. For example, it has been said that lawyers more than representatives from other occupations act as brokers, or "professional representers," or, alternatively, that they act as "precedent-mongers" and conservers of the legal *status quo*.[8] A more complex example is provided by the assertion that political integration of local government units with central government is better promoted where many representatives in the central government have had prior experience in local government offices.[9] So commonplace that they are hardly recognized as hypotheses of this sort are the beliefs implicit in innumerable studies that representatives from rural areas act as agents of farmers, that representatives from working-class

---

[7] W. O. Aydelotte, "A Statistical Analysis of the Parliament of 1841: Some Problems of Method," *Bulletin of the Institute of Historical Research*, Vol. 27 (1954), p. 141.

[8] C. S. Hyneman, "Who Makes Our Laws?," *Political Science Quarterly*, Vol. 55 (1940), pp. 556-81.

[9] W. J. M. Mackenzie, "Local Government in Parliament," *Public Administration*, Vol. 32 (1954), pp. 409-23.

occupations act as agents of the working class, or that representatives from managerial and entrepreneurial occupations act as spokesmen for business interests. In fact, propositions such as these are generally guesses put forward to justify presentation of the descriptive factual information; they rarely function as hypotheses to be tested by the research which is being reported.[10]

Motivations and Behavior of Individual Representatives

A second variety of research is less concerned with what representatives are than with what they do and why they do it. Works of this variety seek explanations of the actions of representatives in the form of general propositions about their behavior as individuals. With some exceptions, they do not ordinarily refer to the characteristics discussed in the preceding category in making their explanations.

A few analysts have attempted to examine representatives' actions in the light of theories and principles of general psychology. John B. McConaughy's assessment of representatives' personality characteristics,[11] for example, suggests that one important psychological hypothesis about political behavior (Harold Lasswell's, that a prevailing psychological mechanism in the behavior of politicians is displacement of feelings of personal inadequacy) probably does not hold for representatives generally. But this study has never been replicated for members of other representative bodies nor extended beyond McConaughy's small sample. Similarly, Garland C. Routt's application of hypotheses taken from theories of group dynamics to study of the interactions among representatives on the floor in one legislature [12] has not been followed up by others.

Instead of working within some explicit psychological framework, most analysts in this category attempt, without psychological trappings, to measure the proportionate influence of various po-

---

[10] See, however, D. R. Matthews, *The Social Background of Political Decision-Makers* (Garden City, N.Y.: Doubleday and Co., 1954), chaps. 1, 2, and 5, for an excellent discussion of relevant theories and hypotheses which might be applied. See also his "U.S. Senators and the Class Structure," *Public Opinion Quarterly,* Vol. 18 (1954), pp. 5-22.

[11] J. B. McConaughy, "Certain Personality Factors of State Legislators in South Carolina," *American Political Science Review,* Vol. 44 (1950), pp. 897-903.

[12] G. C. Routt, "Interpersonal Relationships and the Legislative Process," *Annals of the American Academy of Political and Social Science,* Vol. 195 (1938), pp. 129-36.

litical forces or factors suspected to influence representatives' individual decisions. A number of studies, for example, describe the ways representatives receive and react to information from various sources, such as mass media, letters from constituents, or public opinion polls.[13] Others describe the relationships of representatives to their political parties,[14] to their constituencies,[15] to pressure groups,[16] to other actors, and to such abstract influence as their cultural environment.[17] Some analysts concentrate upon a particular problem, such as the dilemmas of the representative who is also a leader of an interest group.[18] A very important group of more recent studies consists of those which examine the group life of the representative body in terms of its members' perceptions of the norms of the group.[19] And closely related to these are studies of the formation of personal friendship and other cliques within the larger body [20] or of informal structures of authority such as develop, for example, around subject-matter experts within the representative body.[21]

The findings of all these and similar studies, viewed individually, are highly informative; collectively they span a wide range of representatives' behavior. But they use such a diversity of terms

---

[13] Meller, *op. cit.*, discusses most of these.

[14] D. MacRae, Jr., "Roll-Call Votes and Leadership," *Public Opinion Quarterly*, Vol. 20 (1956), pp. 543-58.

[15] L. A. Dexter, "The Representative and His District," *Human Organization*, Vol. 16 (1957), pp. 2-13; H. Eulau *et al.*, "The Role of the Representative: Some Empirical Observations on the Theory of Edmund Burke," *American Political Science Review*, Vol. 53 (1959), pp. 742-56; W. W. Crane, Jr., "Do Representatives Represent?," *Journal of Politics*, Vol. 22 (1960), pp. 295-99.

[16] W. W. Crane, Jr., "A Test of the Effectiveness of Interest Group Pressures on Legislators," *Southwestern Social Science Quarterly*, Vol. 41 (1960), pp. 335-40; J. C. Wahlke *et al.*, "American State Legislators' Role Orientations Toward Pressure Groups," *Journal of Politics*, Vol. 22 (1960), pp. 203-27.

[17] E. A. Shils, "The Legislator and His Environment," *University of Chicago Law Review*, Vol. 18 (1951), pp. 571-84.

[18] J. H. Millett, "The Role of an Interest Group Leader in the House of Commons," *Western Political Quarterly*, Vol. 9 (1956), pp. 915-26.

[19] R. K. Huitt, "The Morse Committee Assignment Controversy: A Study in Senate Norms," *American Political Science Review*, Vol. 51 (1957), pp. 313-29; D. R. Matthews, *U.S. Senators and Their World* (Chapel Hill: The University of North Carolina Press, 1960), chap. 5.

[20] S. C. Patterson, "Patterns of Personal Relations in a Legislative Group," *Public Opinion Quarterly*, Vol. 23 (1959), pp. 101-18.

[21] W. Buchanan *et al.*, "The Legislator as Specialist," *Western Political Quarterly*, Vol. 13 (1960), pp. 636-51.

and concepts and focus on such a variety of questions that it is very difficult to cumulate them into any concise and coherent statement of the present status of knowledge. One major reason for this difficulty is the common failure to be guided by some carefully formulated and clearly recognized model of the representative actor, which failure, in turn, promotes the implicit use of a great variety of models. The most familiar of these are the classical "rational-man" model (the representative individually measuring proposed courses of actions against an objective standard of the public interest), the social-class-interest model (the representative acting according to the dictates of norms and values acquired by virtue of his class status), and the simple pressure-politics model (the representative passively moving according to the mechanical combination of forces which happen to impinge on him). Future research could profit from specification of a psychological theory or model sufficiently general to accommodate the great diversity of research interests displayed in this field and sufficiently reliable to be generally accepted as a framework for future research.

One promising line of development is suggested by the fact that the basic terms and concepts used to date seem to refer not just to gross physical actions of representatives ("behavior" in the technical sense of that word in Watsonian psychological theory) but to their attitudes, judgments, and perceptions concerning the persons and forces in their political world. Several provocative works have pursued inquiry in this direction more directly and more generally than most of those previously discussed.[22] Further pursuing this line of reasoning and investigations, some analysts (the writer included) have reached the conclusion that role-theory, as set forth in social-psychological and sociological literature, promises to be both a means of systematizing the great quantities of information already set forth and a powerful theoretical weapon for future research.[23]

---

[22] R. K. Huitt, "The Congressional Committee: A Case Study," *American Political Science Review*, Vol. 48 (1954), pp. 340-65; O. Garceau and C. Silverman, "A Pressure Group and the Pressured: A Case Report," *American Political Science Review*, Vol. 48 (1954), pp. 672-91; C. Silverman, "The Legislator's View of the Legislative Process," *Public Opinion Quarterly*, Vol. 18 (1954), pp. 180-90.

[23] J. C. Wahlke *et al.*, *The Legislative System: Explorations in Legislative Behavior* (New York: John Wiley & Sons, Inc., 1962), chap. 1; Eulau *et al.*, "The Role of the Representative"; Wahlke *et al.*, "American State Legislators' Role Orientations."

Decisions by Representative Bodies

A third (and most numerous) variety of analyses focuses upon the actions which members of a given body engage in simultaneously and collectively. Instead of microcosmic examinations of patterns of behavior of the individual representative, these studies undertake a macrocosmic examination of patterns found in aggregates of actions by component individuals at particular points in time. They rarely seek or specify the individual psychological mechanism bringing about a given pattern of actions for the collectivity of representatives. On the whole, they display more careful formulation of hypotheses and greater methodological sophistication than do most analyses.

In one way or another, almost all these studies involve the attempt to discover and measure the influence of the various factors productive of cleavage in representative bodies, i.e., the determinants of collective decisions. Earliest in time and easily most numerous of all works in this category are those which assess the significance of political parties.[24] More recent studies, of which Julius Turner's [25] is probably the best-known example, attempt not merely to measure the influence of party but to compare it with the influence of other factors. Thus investigation has been pushed beyond the examination of party and constituency pressure to the examination of sectional bases of cleavage, including urban-rural influences,[26] cleavages stemming from the activity of pressure groups,[27] from members' relationships to their party leadership or their state delegations,[28] and from ideological and policy-interest differences among members,[29] to name only a few of the topics covered by the most significant works of recent years.

---

[24] A. L. Lowell, "The Influence of Party Upon Legislation in England and America," *Annual Report of the American Historical Association* (1901), Vol. 1, pp. 321-43. For a convenient listing of the many works appearing subsequently, see Meller, *op. cit.*, pp. 146-47.

[25] J. Turner, *Party and Constituency: Pressures on Congress* (Baltimore: The Johns Hopkins Press, 1951). See also D. MacRae, Jr., "The Relation Between Roll-Call Votes and Constituencies in the Massachusetts House of Representatives," *American Political Science Review*, Vol. 46 (1952), pp. 1046-55, and "The Role of the State Legislator in Massachusetts," *American Sociological Review*, Vol. 19 (1954), pp. 185-94.

[26] See the listing in Meller, *op. cit.*, p. 146.

[27] *Ibid.*, pp. 147-48.

[28] D. B. Truman, *The Congressional Party: A Case Study* (New York: John Wiley & Sons, Inc., 1959).

[29] D. MacRae, Jr., *The Dimensions of Congressional Voting* (Berkeley and Los Angeles: University of California Press, 1958).

Increasingly, such studies seek not merely to assess the amount of influence exerted by one or another factor but to investigate the circumstances under which their influence varies. Among the circumstances investigated and found significant are the degree of interparty competition in representatives' districts,[30] the character of the issue facing the representatives,[31] the majority or minority status of the parties,[32] the institutional structure of the legislative party,[33] the socio-economic characteristics of representatives' constituencies,[34] and various combinations of these.

These studies frequently sharpen and amplify the meaning of commonly used concepts. MacRae's analysis of congressional voting, for example, demonstrates the importance of distinguishing between economics and civil-rights liberalism and suggests that congressional liberalism-conservatism is explained better in terms of politics than personality.[35] Both MacRae and Truman [36] push analysis of party-cohesion well beyond simple numerical comparison of the opposing parties' cohesion and explore the nature and stability of intraparty divisions as well as the types and extent of interparty cleavage.

There is an obvious relationship of interest between studies of the influence of such factors as party, constituency, and pressure group on the decisions of representative bodies and studies of individuals' patterns of response to the same entities. Search for the causes of different patterns of group action tends to overlap or link up with the search for the bases of individuals' behavior even more clearly. For example, to understand why constituents' interests and ideology should outweigh party demands for organizational loyalty as a factor influencing the representative body's actions, it is necessary to speculate about the psychological mechanism through which these forces affect the behavior of the individual representative.[37] The same can be said of the desire to learn whether the influence of constituency comes about through "pressure" applied

---

[30] *Ibid.*, pp. 284-89; MacRae, "Roll-Call Votes and Constituencies."

[31] W. W. Crane, Jr., *The Legislative Struggle in Wisconsin* (unpublished Ph.D. dissertation, University of Wisconsin, 1959); MacRae, *The Dimensions of Congressional Voting.*

[32] Truman, *op. cit.*, especially pp. 285ff.

[33] *Ibid.*, pp. 94-144, 193-246.

[34] MacRae, "Roll-Call Votes and Constituencies."

[35] MacRae, *The Dimensions of Congressional Voting*, p. 231.

[36] *Ibid.*; Truman, *op. cit.*

[37] MacRae, "Roll-Call Votes and Leadership."

to representatives or through political selection of representatives typical of their districts.[38] Works which approach questions in this way are not easily classifiable exclusively as studies of either individual behavior or group action; they contribute to knowledge on both accounts. They also suggest further why development of psychological models of the individual representative is essential to future research.

Questions concerning the political model of the representative body are more pertinent, however, to the variety of studies being discussed. The most common model is a loose conception of a "decision-making process," wherein decisions at each step along the way are the product of forces or pressures, injected into the system. The findings of many an analysis, therefore, offer little more than a snapshot of the particular constellation of forces or pressures which happen to be exerted at whatever time the analysis is made. But there is a strong tendency toward converting concern with "process" in a loose sense into concern with structure in a more precise sense. More recent studies appear less concerned with comprehending why each particular decision comes out as it does or with predicting successfully the outcome of each future decision than with determining the general framework within which all decisions are made. The finding that southern congressmen's positions on racial issues are arrived at on a state-wide basis instead of on the basis of their individual constituencies' stands,[39] for example, is a bit of structural information in this sense. It does not tell us whether or not Congress will have to decide on some racial issue or what it will decide, but it does tell us something about *how* it will decide *if* it faces such an issue. Likewise, Truman's exploration of the ways in which party leadership groups mediate the various influences affecting the work of Congress [40] tells us about something that is relatively permanent in the system that is Congress.

In short, studies of the decision-making process in representative bodies are usually more than mere inventories of the quanta of force expended in dividing the body for purposes of decision. They are more likely to resemble blueprints, however sketchy, of structures of authority and channels through which power and influence

---

[38] MacRae, *The Dimensions of Congressional Voting*, p. 256.

[39] *Ibid.*, p. 270.

[40] Truman, *op. cit.*, pp. 193-246. See also Wahlke and Eulau, eds., *op. cit.*, pp. 355-413.

flow. Before pursuing the implications of this proposition, it will be helpful to consider some questions about methodology raised by the foregoing thumbnail sketch of recent research.

METHODOLOGICAL PROBLEMS

Perhaps because the literature is extremely heterogeneous with respect to methods and techniques of research, questions of methodology often receive explicit and exhaustive attention from analysts, both in separate sections on methodology in various research reports and in articles or monographs dealing only with questions of methodology.[41] But for the long run methodological problems are neither the most difficult nor the most critical to be faced.

Types and Sources of Data

The requirement (by definition) that the data of behavioral studies consist ultimately of some record of the specific actions or characteristics of specific human beings is neither rigorous nor restrictive. It does not single out any particular class of actions as the only legitimate object of research attention nor does it specify that data about representatives' actions be drawn from any one particular source.

Records of roll-call votes have so far been the most widely used source of data, and roll-call voting has therefore been the class of actions most thoroughly inspected. Analyses of the third type discussed above rely principally upon such data, but analysis of representatives' individual behavior often make inferences from the same. On the other hand, data from official journals and reports concerning related actions, such as speeches and motions in debate, sponsorship of bills, resolutions and amendments, or conduct in committee and in hearings, which constitute one of the most frequently used sources of data for studies of representatives' individual behavior and the most common source for studies of their demographic characteristics, are ordinarily used in analysis of the action of representative bodies only for background information or illustra-

---

[41] MacRae, *The Dimensions of Congressional Voting*, pp. 298-382; Truman, *op. cit.*, pp. 10-14, 320-30; D. MacRae, Jr., "Some Underlying Variables in Legislative Roll-Call Votes," *Public Opinion Quarterly*, Vol. 18 (1954), pp. 191-96.

tive purposes. The record of actions provided by newspapers and other secondary sources, however, has been very little used by any analysts, one good and probably sufficient reason being the wholly unsystematic and (for purposes of analysis) inadequate attention paid by these sources to the manifold activities of representatives and representative bodies.

Few would deny that the formal actions of voting and related forms of participation in the representative body's more visible official activities are a critically important class of actions. On the other hand, a major reason for past concentration upon these has no doubt been their easy accessibility to data collectors. Unquestionably research must take into account a greater variety of actions by the representative actors.

Direct and systematic *observation* of activities to this end has been used in at least one case as the chief source of data,[42] and in some cases as one of several major sources,[43] and in others as a source of background information.[44] The limitations of this data source are obvious. The legislature is a finite body of men engaging in a series of actions which, though not infinite, are certainly innumerable. They cannot all be observed simultaneously, let alone recorded for future analysis. And representatives' behavior includes a large class of actions—the often-mentioned "backroom deals," secret interchanges, communications by tone and gesture, etc.— which are forever inaccessible to any observing analyst.

An increasingly important source of data about representatives' behavior is *systematic interviews* with the representatives themselves. From representatives' responses (verbal actions) analysts can make two sorts of inference about other characteristics or behavior: informational (did or did not some particular representatives do such and such?) and attitudinal (do or do not particular representatives think, feel, or perceive a certain way?). Particularly the second usage is becoming more frequent, not only in the study of American representative bodies [45] but in both Western and non-

---

[42] Routt, *op. cit.*

[43] Crane, *The Legislative Struggle in Wisconsin.*

[44] Truman, *op. cit.;* Buchanan *et al., op. cit.;* Eulau *et al., op. cit.;* Wahlke *et al., op. cit.*

[45] S. C. Patterson, *Toward a Theory of Legislative Behavior: The Wisconsin State Assemblymen as Actors in a Legislative System* (unpublished Ph.D. dissertation, University of Wisconsin, 1958); Crane, *The Legislative Struggle in Wisconsin;* Buchanan *et al., op. cit.;* Wahlke *et al., op. cit.;* Eulau *et al., op. cit.*

Western bodies elsewhere.[46] One advantage of this data source is that it can yield bases for inferences about many classes of actions for which either no data whatever or only still more indirect data are provided by the other sources described. That interviews provide data from which inferences are made rather than direct data about the behavior to be analyzed is not really a unique feature of this data source. In a strict sense, *all* data provide only bases for inferences. Moreover, the experience of all who have used this method of data collection testifies that many frequent objections— representatives will not talk, sophistication of respondents is unjustifiably presumed, words have no relation to behavior, etc.— while they call attention to pitfalls to which researchers must be alert, are insufficiently grounded to justify refusing to consider the use of interviews at all.

It seems almost platitudinous to say that all the above-mentioned sources of data have their legitimate place in future research, that researchers, whatever source they use, should recognize the limitations of their data as well as their potentialities, or that there is need for the exercise of still greater ingenuity in discovering and utilizing new sources of data. But it is imperative to recognize that any thought of some day finding ways to amass data about every action of every representative is quixotic. It is also unnecessary. Productive analysis does not proceed from collecting "*all* the facts"; it begins when the analyst, guided by some theoretical conception and purpose, knows *what* kinds of facts he needs and then finds appropriate methods for collecting and analyzing the data he has found necessary to his purposes.

Techniques of Analysis

Just as the term "behavioral study of representative bodies" is occasionally taken to refer to some particular type or source of data, so also it is sometimes erroneously identified with particular (especially mathematical) techniques of analyzing its data. It is true that such techniques as *scale analysis* and *factor analysis* find increasing use in behavioral studies.[47] It is also true that be-

---

[46] Professor Norman Meller has used this method in the Marshall Islands. Mr. William H. Hunt in 1960 completed intensive interviews with selected members of the French National Assembly. Professor Wilder W. Crane, Jr., is presently completing a study of an Austrian regional body using this method.

[47] MacRae's *Dimensions of Congressional Voting,* representing the most ex-

havioral analyses tend to rely on increasingly rigorous *statistical techniques,* although the prevailing standards and techniques are not really as new or as sophisticated as is sometimes thought.[48] In most cases, these techniques have made possible findings which probably could not have been reached by less quantitative methods. In most cases, their mathematical character provides us with standards for judging how reliable and conclusive the findings are. But, while adequacy of research techniques to research objects and high standards of evidence and proof are characteristic of many analyses, these characteristics do not, themselves, constitute "behavioral study."

In the same way, the term should not be confused with a particular type of analysis, such as the *case study* or the *comparative study,* the *developmental* or the *cross-sectional study.* Each of these is represented in the arsenal of behavioral studies.[49] In each case, the type of analysis is dictated by considerations of research strategy (questions to be attacked) and not just by research economics (availability of time, personnel, and money). In each case, the limits of generalization from a particular study are set by the type of analysis chosen.

---

tensive use of scale analysis to date, contains a discussion of that method in relation to alternative approaches, pp. 298-312. George M. Belknap, "A Method for Analyzing Legislative Behavior," *Midwest Journal of Political Science,* Vol. 2 (1958), pp. 377-402, explains the use of this method in considerable detail. Factor analyses have been much less frequent. For an example of this technique, see H. B. Carlson and W. Harrell, "Voting Groups Among Leading Congressmen Obtained by Means of the Inverted Factor Technique," *Journal of Social Psychology,* Vol. 16 (1942), pp. 51-61.

[48] The concept of a "party vote" devised by Lowell, *op. cit.,* is still used regularly with only minor modifications. Truman's analysis, *op. cit.,* follows a method devised by Stuart Rice and Herman Beyle over thirty years ago: H. C. Beyle, *Identification and Analysis of Attribute Cluster Blocs* (Chicago: University of Chicago Press, 1931). The index of party cohesion was developed by Rice even earlier: S. A. Rice, "The Behavior of Legislative Groups," *Political Science Quarterly,* Vol. 40 (1925), pp. 60-72.

[49] The works of Buchanan, Eulau, and Wahlke cited above are all part of a comparative study of legislators in California, New Jersey, Ohio, and Tennessee conducted by them and Professor LeRoy C. Ferguson with the aid of a grant from the Social Science Research Council having as one of its major purposes the promotion of comparative study. Other examples of comparative study are found chiefly but by no means exclusively in analyses of party voting in representative bodies. Examples of developmental study are found mainly among analyses of various characteristics of legislators: Namier, *op. cit.;* A. W. Martin, "The Legislative Assembly of New South Wales, 1856-1900," *Australian Journal of Politics and History,* Vol. 2 (1956), pp. 46-67.

In general, it would appear that comparative analysis is becoming more frequent, though case studies are not becoming less so, but that relatively little attention is yet being given to developmental, as distinguished from cross-sectional, questions. Although the causes for this pattern of emphasis no doubt lie partly in mundane considerations of mechanical feasibility, they probably stem even more from theoretical problems. Once theoretical clarification brings out the questions which research must answer, problems of methodology become essentially technical questions about the adequacy of means to ends. Solving those problems will undoubtedly require the invention of new tools and devices as well as mastery of existing ones. But it also goes without saying that the tools will not operate themselves, nor will they produce if used by mechanics untrained in the objectives to be served by their use.

THEORETICAL PROBLEMS

In other words, it is the theoretical problems facing behavioral study of representative bodies which are ultimately the most important and most difficult to solve. They all involve making clear the long-run objectives shared by all research in the field. To avoid possible misinterpretations of the discussion which follows, it should be said immediately that "solving" the theoretical problems does not require choosing among mutually exclusive alternatives. It does, however, require clarity about the nature of the alternatives, about their relation to one another, and about the relation of any given piece of research to them.

Politics and Behavior: Psychology or Political Science?

By studying the behavior of representatives, one can learn something about the political behavior of human beings. Does a desire for power operate differently when men act in this particular institutional context than when they act in others? In what ways? Why do some men satisfy that desire by seeking representative office while others satisfy it in other ways? By the same token, studying the behavior of representatives can contribute to the understanding of human behavior even more generally. What gratifications does the holding of representative office provide men? What ego needs are served by different types of behavior in that office? The answers to such questions take the form of propositions which hold true for all human individuals. The ultimate aim is to learn how and why people act.

Our sketchy review of the literature shows that, contrary to the beliefs of some, few analysts of representative bodies have been concerned to discover universalistic propositions about political behavior. Still fewer have sought general psychological laws. The concern of almost all has been with the consequences of behavior which follows certain laws or principles, not with its causes. How does that behavior affect the distribution of power and authority in society? How does it affect (and how is it affected by) the political institutions which embody power and authority and through whose working other values are distributed?

It would therefore seem that the analyst of representative bodies can work best when he is able to start from a model embodying acceptable and general psychological propositions. He ordinarily will use that model to arrive ultimately at propositions which are of a quite different order. In the imperfect world of research, however, where labor must be divided, "psychological" research aimed at the production of models or the establishment of general propositions about political behavior can be a welcome ally of the analyst of representative bodies. The fundamental requirement is only that each researcher know what he seeks, how it relates to what others seek, and how reliable his findings are.

Politics, History and Political Theory: Uniqueness and Generality

David Truman's statement about his congressional case study is applicable to legislative study in general: its objective "is not history, not description of the unique elements in a stream of events, but identification of the features . . . that are basic and permanent." [50] But a critical question not squarely faced by analysis to date is, "basic and permanent features" of what? Of each particular system individually and uniquely? Of groups of similar systems? But what does "similar" mean in this case? Of all representative bodies in all times. If so, what differentiates "representative" bodies from other bodies of men?

---

[50] Truman, *op. cit.*, p. 15. Note the similarity of MacRae's comment: ". . . even the most transient issues can be used to illuminate more lasting problems, for we may abstract from each issue to consider the procedural, tactical, and strategic features of the political system within which it is posed," *The Dimensions of Congressional Voting*, p. 212.

The tradition of political science since Plato and Aristotle has been to aim at the highest level of generalization. It may therefore be suggested that the long-run objective of analysis of representative bodies is understanding of "*the* representative body." In other words, one cardinal standard for evaluating any study is its contribution to the development of a general theory of representative bodies.

Analytical energy and talent have so far been concentrated on comprehensive understanding of single systems as unique entities. Even comparative studies have usually been limited in their aims, seeking out the unique characteristics of the bodies compared more often than analyzing features shared by all of them as representative bodies. Even so, it is possible to detect a trend toward recognizing the more general theoretical objectives of analysis.

The particular direction of the trend has already been obliquely suggested; it is toward increasing concern with institutional aspects of the representative body. This is manifested, for example, by the effort to describe norms and informal structures of the representative group [51] or to discover patterns and channels of influence which are stable over long periods of time.[52] It is manifested by the effort to link "psychological" understanding of representatives' behavior to understanding of the structures of decision-making processes through such theories and concepts as that of "role." [53] Terms like "power," "process," and "institution" are beginning to take on more precise meanings; their theoretical relationships to one another are becoming more clear.

Conceptual clarification at this level seems the most pressing need if the requisite theoretical progress is to be made. To make that progress requires also that more and more representative bodies, in all cultures and at all levels of government, be subjected to comparative analysis. This does not mean that intensive analysis of particular individual systems is *passé*. The areas of our ignorance about many representative bodies is vast. Nor does it mean that more ambitious comparative analysis should be postponed until we are provided with some acceptable general theory. Theory and research necessarily progress in lock step, not independently of each other. It does mean that progress will be most rapid where analysis,

---

[51] See p. 179.
[52] See pp. 183-84.
[53] See note 23.

comparative or individual-system, aims at contributing to the development of general political theory.

Politics and Sociology: System and Function

The preceding remarks can be summarized as follows: behavioral analyses have made and promise to make still further substantial contributions to our understanding of the internal workings of representative bodies as a type of political institution. They lead beyond realistic description of the structure and processes of particular institutionalized groups to investigation of the differential consequences to all representative institutions of various forms of power and influence brought to bear on them, of the conditions of stability, and of the causes of changes in institutional structure and to other important questions of a general theoretical nature.

One other point requires conceptual and theoretical clarification which probably cannot be provided by behavioral analysis of representative bodies alone. This concerns the function and purpose of representative bodies in the larger political and social systems of which they are a part. Such concepts as "legislation" and "representation" are of crucial significance here. They must be given precise meaning in terms of a general political or social theory if they are to direct attention to the relevant aspects of representatives' behavior. Indeed, unless they are precisely defined from a theoretical standpoint, it is impossible to know what bodies qualify as objects of analysis by students of "representative" bodies. Only on the basis of clear theory on this point can analysts know what it is about representative bodies they should compare, even if they have no doubts about which bodies are representative ones and which of them they wish to subject to comparative study. Beyond such obvious political concepts and questions lie still more abstract concepts of general sociological theory, such as the origins and the management of conflict and tension in society,[54] to which also analyses of representative bodies must ultimately be relevant.

This kind of theoretical problem, of course, faces all students of government and not just "behavioral" ones. But it is incumbent on behavioral analysts to recognize that they are responsible, like all other students, for utilizing and ultimately helping to develop theory at this level, too.

---

[54] Professor Heinz Eulau is presently engaged in research in this area.

CONCLUSION

The main points we have covered can be summarized very briefly. (1) "Behavioral study of representative bodies" should not be identified with any particular methodology or methodological school. (2) Analyses of this kind have contributed greatly to our knowledge of how particular representative bodies work, but their ultimate objective is knowledge of a more general nature. (3) The knowledge sought is knowledge about government and politics, not general psychology. (4) The problems most immediately facing such analyses involve articulating "psychologist" and decision-process studies into a coherent attack on questions about the institutional character of representative bodies, a contribution to development of a general theory of representative bodies. (5) Progress toward such a theory requires articulation of behavioral analyses with political theory in a still more general sense, particularly with respect to the political functions of representation and legislation. (6) Problems of methodology can be dealt with as individual technical problems in proportion as theoretical problems are solved.

In reality, none of these problems will ever be "solved" in the sense that knowledge about representative bodies will be complete and final. Behavioral research aspires to knowledge which, though it may increase in generality and probable truth, will always be fragmentary and hypothetical. To some, this prospect may appear to condemn researchers to a labor of Sisyphus. If so, there is some comfort in the thought that we do not know certainly that our stone must periodically roll back on us forever. But we must still resign ourselves to knowing that the basic tools of future researchers will remain that of their forebears: minds which are finite and human.

Some Recent Substantive and Methodological Developments in the Theory of Organizational Decision-Making*

James G. March

CARNEGIE INSTITUTE OF TECHNOLOGY

Organizations are ubiquitous institutions. They appear to consort freely with many aspects of the political, social, and economic systems. This generality of organizational phenomena has led to anomalies within the various academic disciplines. One of the most important studies of a political organization is by a sociologist.[1] Two political scientists have written a recent book dealing extensively with business organizations.[2] A psychologist is working on a biological model of some economic organizations.[3]

One of the consequences of such promiscuity is a tendency to underestimate the significance of differences between governmental

---

* This paper draws heavily on the work of a number of my colleagues. In particular, the ideas expressed depend on my collaboration with Richard M. Cyert in the development of a behavioral theory of the firm and with Herbert A. Simon in work on organization theory. Either or both of these estimable gentlemen should properly have been coerced into co-authorship of the paper were it not for the fact that either or both of them would probably object to some of the things that are said and almost certainly to how I say them. For treatments of the same general subject, see J. G. March and H. A. Simon, *Organizations* (New York: John Wiley & Sons, Inc., 1958), and R. M. Cyert and J. G. March, *A Behavioral Theory of the Firm* (to be published in 1962).

[1] P. Selznick, *TVA and the Grass Roots* (Berkeley: University of California Press, 1949).

[2] March and Simon, *op. cit.*

[3] M. Haire, "Biological Models and Empirical Histories of the Growth of Organizations," in M. Haire, ed., *Modern Organization Theory* (New York: John Wiley & Sons, Inc., 1959).

organizations and nongovernmental organizations, to assume that the same theory will do for all types of organizations. Though I recognize at least some of the difficulties involved, I am sympathetic with such tendencies. As a result, neither the theoretical nor the methodological ideas expressed below distinguish between the study of political organizations and the study of other kinds of decision-making systems. Perhaps they should; I am inclined to think they should not.

THE THEORY OF ORGANIZATIONAL DECISION-MAKING

Organization theory is a collection of incongruous elements. In fact, a recent symposium on "modern organization theory" is an impressive monument to heterogeneity.[4] Such a state of affairs does not distinguish organization theory from many other theories, but it leads to problems for general discussions of the study of organization. Either we attempt the substantial task of theoretical integration or we condemn ourselves to parochialism.

With apologies to my co-workers in the field, this is a parochial essay. It is concerned with that part of organizational theory dealing with the analysis, prediction, and explanation of human behavior in large, complex, more or less purposive organizations. Thus, it excludes from consideration the important tradition of prescriptive organization theory. Even within the field of positive organization theory, the paper is parochial. It is concerned with the study of organizations as information-handling and decision-making systems. Thus, on this score it excludes significant recent work on the internal dynamics of organizational systems, particularly as those dynamics are reflected in growth and decay.

The classic theory of organizational decision-making suffers from two critical deficiencies. First, it consists of largely unverified propositions about how organizations behave. Some of these propositions are empirically meaningless, some are simply wrong, some are probably correct. Second, the theory lacks a language of sufficient power to permit anything more than the simplest derivations of its empirical implications. Neither the language of poetry (analogies, paradoxes, puns, etc.) nor the language of classical mathematics has been adequate for examining the implications of the theory.

---

[4] Haire, ed., *op. cit.*

Thus, the theory of organizational decision-making has traditionally lacked models that combine substantive sensibility with formal power. In large part, we lacked models having either attribute until roughly twenty-five years ago. Since that time, field studies of various kinds have provided information that allows us to formulate at least some rudimentary notions of a sensible literary model. In turn, these substantive developments have permitted the use of new methods for dealing with the verification and the model-construction needs of the theory. On the basis of recent work, I will argue that major advances seem to be promised by substantive revision of the theory, by the introduction of computer program models, and by the utilization of laboratory experimentation and structured field studies in the verification of theoretical propositions. To elaborate the argument, this paper is devoted to a discussion of (1) some of the major recent substantive developments in the theory of organizational decision-making, (2) the use of computer program models to develop the theory, and (3) the use of experimental studies to test and clarify the basic assumptions and implications of the theory.

DEVELOPMENTS IN SUBSTANTIVE THEORY

Revisions and Elaborations of the Concept of Organizational Goals [5]

Few organization theories escape the need for postulating a concept either labeled as, or analogous to, organizational goals. In normative organization theory, the efficiency criterion obviously relates to costs and returns measured in terms of goal achievement. The difficulties in developing a useful criterion of efficiency are notorious, not only in the case of public organizations but also in the case of such presumably uncomplicated institutions as business firms. On the one hand, the traditional organizational engineer is likely to measure efficiency in terms of such factors as the clip-to-paper ratio without concerning himself much with the implications such a measure has for the content of organizational goals. On the other hand, the sophisticated observer is likely to equate what the organization is currently achieving with organization

---

[5] See R. M. Cyert and J. G. March, "A Behavioral Theory of Organizational Objectives," in Haire, ed., *op. cit.*

goals, thereby reducing the question of efficiency to a giant tautology.

Positive theorists face a related problem. The problem can be paraphrased in terms of the following: (1) People (i.e., individuals) have goals; collectivities of people do not. (2) To develop a positive theory of organizational decision-making, we seem to need something analogous—at the organizational level—to individual goals at the individual level. For the moment, let us assume that we accept these propositions. Not everyone does. The theorist's problem then becomes one of introducing some concept of organization goals that is consistent with the apparent denial of their existence. There are two classic solutions to the problem. The entrepreneurial solution is to describe an organization as consisting of an entrepreneur (either the top of the managerial hierarchy or some external control group, such as stockholders, or congress) and a staff. The goals of the organization are then defined to be the goals of the entrepreneur. Conformity to these goals is purchased by payments (wages, interest, love, etc.) made by the entrepreneur to the staff and by a system of internal control that informs the staff of the entrepreneurial demands. This solution to the problem is characteristic of the economic theory of the firm, some politcal theories of public bureaucracies, and most theories of management.

The second classic solution to the problem is to identify a common or consensual goal. This is a goal that is shared by the various participants in the organization. It may be *a priori* sharing, as in many theories of political institutions in which the goal of "public interest" or "social welfare" is introduced. Or it may be *a posteriori* sharing, as in some theories of small group goal-formation through discussion. In either case, conflict is eliminated through consensus.

Neither solution is entirely happy. As a number of observers have pointed out, the existence of unresolved conflict is a conspicuous feature of organization. Organizations seem to have one goal at one time and another at another time. Different parts of the organization seem to have different goals at the same time. It is exceedingly difficult to construct a useful, positive theory of organizational decision-making if we insist on goal-consistency, either from subunit to subunit or from time to time.

As a result, recent theories of organizational objectives describe goals as the consequence of a continuous bargaining-learning process. In this process we can distinguish three subprocesses. The first is bargaining among the potential members of the organization. The organization is a coalition, and it gradually changes its composition through arriving at bargains with new members and rescinding bargains with old ones. In the course of such coalition formation, side payments are exchanged, much as is anticipated in the entrepreneurial theory of goals. What distinguishes most organizations, however, is that many of these side payments are not monetary payments but policy commitments and that internal consistency is not maintained.

Where bargaining is in terms of policy rather than money, some of the familiar framework of game theory seems less useful than it might be with respect to coalition formation where side payments satisfy the requirements of unrestricted transferability and conservation of utility. Rather, we require some way of describing the complementaries among various subsets of policy demands and some procedure for predicting which subsets of demands will be met. For the decisions on meeting demands are, in fact, the decisions on organizational goals.

The second subprocess is the internal organizational procedures through which objectives are stabilized and elaborated. We have ample reasons from field studies of organizations to specify that a theory of organizational objectives must take account of the powerful institutional forces directed toward stabilizing policy commitments and elaborating them through secondary bargaining. The allocation of functions, the use of budgets, the maintenance of precedents, the institution of standard operating procedures all serve to reinforce existing policy commitments.

The third subprocess is the process by which objectives change as a function of experience. On the one hand, organizational objectives are subject to the usual aspiration level phenomena. Thus, the quantitative level of a particular objective is a function of past achievement by the organization and past achievement by other organizations with which it is compared. On the other hand, since the organization has a rather large number of demands, experience effects which among the total set of potential demands are considered at a particular point in time and by whom. Different subunits will attend to different demands at different times.

If we adopt such a theory of organizational goals, we can tentatively explain some of the conspicuous features of organizational goals as we observe them in actual organizations. In particular, we can predict the rather crude internal rationalization of goals, the widespread use of nonoperational goals, the shifts of objectives over time, and the sequential attention to goals within organizations.

Revisions and Elaborations of the Theory of Organizational Expectations [6]

Organizations have some quality of purposiveness. As has been suggested above, it is a purposiveness having certain exotic characteristics. But it is possible to talk meaningfully about organizational goals. Consequently, a theory of organizational decision-making ordinarily postulates some connection between the choices made by the system and the objectives pursued by the system.

The classic theory of decision-making is built on three basic postulates of rationality: (1) all alternatives are known; (2) all consequences of all alternatives are known; and (3) a unique preference order exists over the set of consequences and all subsets of consequences. The organization chooses that alternative that has as its consequence the most preferred subset of consequences.

Empirical studies of organizations, however, indicate a wide disparity between the information requirements indicated by such a theory and the actual information used by an organization in making a decision. In particular, there have been four major objections to the classic concepts of expectations in organizational decision-making. First, the classical theory implies a continuous competition at the margin among all alternatives for organizational resources with extensive use of expectational data and planning. Observations of organizational decision-making suggest, however, that (within some relatively loose constraints) decisions will reflect local adaptation to local problems rather than adjustment through overall marginal planning. Feedback is often substituted for planning. Second, the theory makes information-seeking simply one of the

---

[6] See R. M. Cyert, W. R. Dill, and J. G. March, "The Role of Expectations in Business Decision Making," *Administrative Science Quarterly*, Vol. 3 (1958), pp. 307-40; R. M. Cyert and J. G. March, "Organizational Structure and Pricing Behavior in an Oligopolistic Market," *American Economic Review*, Vol. 45 (1955), pp. 129-39; R. M. Cyert and J. G. March, "Organizational Factors in the Theory of Oligopoly," *Quarterly Journal of Economics*, Vol. 70 (1956), pp. 44-64; and H. A. Simon, "A Behavioral Model of Rational Choice," *Quarterly Journal of Economics*, Vol. 69 (1955), pp. 99-118.

alternative courses of action to be evaluated by the organization and selected or rejected in terms of its expected cost and expected return. Empirical observations seem to indicate that search activity is stimulated by failure, that some alternatives are more conspicuous to an organization than others, that alternatives are considered sequentially rather than simultaneously, and that only crude comparisons are made between search costs and potential returns. Third, the theory implies substantial computational ability on the part of the organization and the use of rather refined tools of comparison. Actual observation indicates that most organizations use very limited computational techniques, that they treat various considerations as independent constraints rather than reduce them to a single dimension, and that the informational demands they make are quite modest. Fourth, the theory seems to imply that the process by which information is obtained and processed is entirely neutral. This appears unlikely. Organizational information is likely to be replete with a full complement of conscious and unconscious selective perceptions and bias.

The major implication of these comments on the classic theory of expectations and choice is that an adequate theory of organizational decision-making must include a well-defined theory of search. Information is not given; it is obtained. Before it can be obtained, there must be motivation for the organization to obtain the information—motivation either on the part of the organization, some subunit of the organization, or some external information source. A theory of search must answer three major questions: (1) When will an organization institute search activities? (2) When will it stop? (3) Where will it search?

Recent theories of organization search suggest at least partial answers to each of these questions. In simplest terms, the theories specify that an organization will search for new alternatives when its current goals exceed its current achievement; that it will examine alternatives sequentially and in a more or less predictable order until a satisfactory one is obtained; and that it will then stop searching.

Unfortunately, the theory of search is not well developed with respect to the order of search. Perhaps the most interesting proposition (with respect to organizational search—there is a related but different theory with respect to individual problem-solving) builds upon the general characteristics of the division of labor in an organization. If we postulate that the division of labor in an organization is used ordinarily as the basis for dividing an organization problem into subproblems and, furthermore, that the subunits established by such a division of labor will tend to become the organizational guardians of particular subgoals, we can predict a form of local adaptation. Problems that are perceived to arise in one sector of the organization will have solutions sought in the same sector.

In addition, we can predict a kind of free market in alternatives. While some subunits in the organization have problems for which they seek solutions, other subunits have solutions for which they seek problems. Similarly, within a subunit, pet projects will tend to be defined as solutions to conspicuous problems.

Revisions and Elaborations of the Concept of Organizational Learning [7]

"Organizational learning" has the same taint as the concept of organizational goals. To assume that organizations go through the same processes of learning as do individual human beings seems unnecessarily naive. But organizations do exhibit (as do other social institutions) adaptive behavior over time. These adaptations certainly use individual members of the organization as instruments, but the results of the learning process involved seem to be independent of individual characteristics and to proceed substantially uninterrupted through repeated changes in organizational personnel.

Recent work on organizational learning has focused on learning with respect to four different phases in the decision process: learning with respect to decision rules; learning with respect to attention rules; learning with respect to search rules; learning with respect to information coding rules.

In contrast to at least some theories of organizational decision-making, observations of organizations making decisions suggest considerable uncertainty (at least initially) about proper decision rules. Typically this reflects not poor organizational design but some mixture of conflict, uncertainty, and passivity within the organiza-

---

[7] See R. M. Cyert and J. G. March, "Business Operating Procedures," in B. von H. Gilmer, ed., *Industrial Psychology* (New York: McGraw-Hill Book Company, Inc., 1961).

tional coalition. The "details" have to be worked out through a trial
and error process that reminds one of a rat in a maze. A good theory
will include decision-rule learning functions to explain such phenomena.

Similarly, organizations learn what parts of their environment
to attend to. There have been attempts, in recent models of organizational decision-making, to introduce considerations of the
following sort: Let us suppose that an organization subunit has
responsibility for a particular organizational goal. Since this goal
is ordinarily stated in relatively nonoperational terms, the subunit
must develop some observable indices of performance on the goal.
Among the indices objectively available to the subunit, which will
be used? Observation suggests that this is a typical case of learning.
Subunits in the short run do not change indices significantly. But
there are long run shifts toward indices that produce generally
satisfactory results (i.e., in this case, usually show the subunit to
be performing well).

Search rules also change. As has already been pointed out, a
modern theory of organizational choice includes a theory of search.
In such a theory the sequential character of alternative consideration is of prime importance. There now is considerable suggestion
that the order in which alternatives are considered is not fixed but
changes as the organization experiences search success or failure.
Such phenomena need to be reflected in the theory.

Finally, we can observe organizational learning with respect to
information coding rules. Any decision-making system develops
codes for communicating information about the environment. Any
such code partitions all possible states of the world into a relatively
small number of classes of states. Learning consists in changes in
the partitioning. In general, we would want to have a theory that
predicted the gradual development of an efficient code in terms of
the decision rules currently in use. Thus, if a decision rule is designed to choose between two alternatives, the information code
will tend to reduce all possible states of the world to two classes.
If the decision rules changes, the theory should predict a change
in the information code, but only after a time lag reflecting the rate
of learning. The short-run consequences of incompatibilities between the coding rules and the decision rules form some of the
more interesting dynamic features of an organizational, decision-
making model.

General Implications of These Substantive Changes in the Theory

The implications of these substantive results for the development of models of organizational decision-making are reasonably clear:

(1) We require models that, in contrast with classical models, assume multiple, changing, acceptable-level goals.

(2) We require models that, in contrast with classical models, deal explicitly with the problem of internal conflict.

(3) We require models that, in contrast with classical models, include a theory of search and information handling.

(4) We require models that, in contrast with classical models, permit adaptation and change through organizational learning.

This is no small order. Empirical studies of organizational behavior have persistently posed large problems for theory construction. To a limited extent, the problems have been straightforward, and certain aspects of organizational decision-making have been amenable to conventional mathematical approaches. In particular, we can cite productive work, drawing on mathematical economics,[8] game theory,[9] and servo-mechanism theory.[10]

But classical mathematics is not designed to deal effectively with the kind of theory outlined earlier in this paper. Consequently, it is no accident that the relatively complicated, branching models developed in the past few years and explorations in the potential utility of electronic computer programs to represent such models have reinforced each other. The major methodological advance of the past decade has been the development of the computer as an instrument of theory construction. This is, of course, a development that organization theory has shared with a large number of social science fields.

COMPUTERS AND MODEL CONSTRUCTION

Five years ago, computers were virtually unknown to the literature of social science except for some use on data-processing

---

[8] J. Marschak, "Efficient and Viabile Organizational Forms," in Haire, ed., *op. cit.*

[9] M. Shubik, *Strategy and Market Structure* (New York: John Wiley & Sons, Inc., 1959).

[10] C. J. Haberstroh, *Processes of Internal Control in Firms* (unpublished Ph.D. thesis, University of Minnesota, 1957).

chores. They have now become commonplace, as much a standard part of the repertoire of the research worker in the field as statistical test procedures and mathematical models. Whatever hesitation one may have in accepting the extreme forecasts of enthusiasts, it must be recognized that the computer will be a major factor in the development of organization theory in the coming decade.

Computer Simulation and the Description of Organization Decision-Making [11]

The language of computer programs is a natural language in which to describe an organization making decisions. There exist already (although mostly in unpublished form) a number of rather detailed simulations of specific organizations making specific decisions. Hoggatt and Balderston have constructed a model of a part of the lumber industry. Cohen has developed a computer model of the hide, shoe and leather industries. Shubik has constructed some partial models of decision-making by an electrical equipment manufacturer. Cyert and March have specified models of pricing decisions in a large department store. Howard has simulated the pricing decisions in a major American wholesale market.[12] Although these various models vary substantially in the level of aggregation and the precision with which they describe the decision process involved, each of them is built on intensive empirical observation and attempts to specify, in the formal language of the computer, the basic dynamic characteristics of the organization.

The availability of computer programming as a descriptive and analytic tool has permitted two interrelated but highly important advances. First, it has permitted us to discuss intelligently the decision-making properties of relatively complex decision systems. However much confidence we might have had in the propositions of organization theory found in the literature of sociology, social psychology, anthropology, and political science, precise pre-

---

[11] See R. M. Cyert and J. G. March, "Research on a Behavioral Theory of the Firm," in G. W. Brown, ed., *Contributions to Scientific Research in Management* (Los Angeles: Western Data Processing Center, University of California at Los Angeles, 1960); K. J. Cohen and R. M. Cyert, "Computer Models in Dynamic Economics," *Quarterly Journal of Economics*, Vol. 75 (1961), pp. 112-27.

[12] Most of these studies are still unpublished. An exception is K. Cohen, *Computer Models of the Shoe, Leather, Hide Sequence* (Englewood Cliffs, N.J.: Prentice-Hall, 1960).

dictions from the propositions were almost always made awkward by the host of *ceteris paribus* conditions imposed on the proposition. Multiple-proposition systems have been rare—at least in part because there existed no very effective way to deal with them formally.

Second, programming has provided a structure for field observation. The use of field studies seems inescapable for the study of organizations. Yet field studies are expensive to conduct, extremely so if we impose a return on investment criterion. Programming (and the implication that the end result of a field study is to be a simulation of a decision process on the computer) imposes an output standard on a field study that affects significantly the character of the study. In particular, it implies a precise specification of such factors as the decision rules used, the information-handling rules, the search rules, and the pattern of learning.

Consider, for example, a study of the decisions in the United States government with respect to the U-2 incident. Unquestionably, this will be the subject of a number of detailed verbal studies by American political scientists. I think it is even possible to predict with reasonable confidence the nature of the results that will be obtained:

At 2 P.M. Mr. X called a meeting of his principal advisers concerned with espionage activities. Representatives of the State Department, the White House staff, and the Department of Defense were present. Mr. Y emphasized at some length the importance of the information being obtained by the flights. He and some others felt that we should completely ignore the Russian charges and deny any knowledge of the flight, but since they felt a contrary decision had been made, they did not press the point. Some discussion of the space agency position followed. A suggestion was made for delaying any definite decision overnight. Then Mr. Z. indicated that the British had expressed considerable concern over the incident. He stated his conviction that they would probably express public incredulity at a simple denial. After some random discussion a sense of the meeting emerged. It was that the pre-planned cover story should be released to the press through the space agency, along with a complete denial of espionage intent. . . .

One conspicuous feature of such a report is the illusion of specificity it provides. Like the well-written news story that it takes as its model, the usual field report provides us with two things: (1) a "feel" for the decision process used; and (2) a specification of many specific events that occurred. Curiously enough, the first usually turns out to be more valuable than the second. This is because the specific information provided is almost always misplaced specificity. We learn the time at which the meeting was held, the names of the participants, the list of arguments made, and the decision arrived at. But the heart of the study is wrapped up in such expressions as "finally a decision was reached to . . ." or "after some discussion a sense of the meeting emerged." We are left largely uninformed of the specific decision rules used.

With all due respect for the important knowledge we have gained from an assortment of field studies in organizations, the abilities and techniques required to make theoretically relevant observations in the field have frequently exceeded the abilities and techniques available to the reporters of field observations. As a result, many field studies of organizational decisions have about as much relevance to the theory of organization decision-making as the memoirs of a Peeping Tom have to the theory of genetics. The use of simulation contributes to the solution on the technique side. As a result, the ability side becomes less pressing. Specifically, a number of research workers have discovered that, once the training costs are incurred, the use of the computer considerably simplifies the data gathering problem in studying organizational decisions.

Computers and the Development of General Models [13]

The use of simulation as a technique for organizing field study observations is now rather widely accepted. The use of a computer program to develop a more general model of organizational decision-making is increasing. Such use reflects a conviction that the natural language for a theory of organizational decision-making is a computer program and that, if there is to be a general model, it will have to be in computer form. By a general model is meant a model the structure of which is substantially invariant over the class of organizations for which it is designed. Unfortunately for the precise use of terms, the distinction between what is "structure" and what is not "structure" in a computer model is sometimes rather hazy. The objective, however, is clear enough. We wish to develop a model that can be adapted to a number of different organizations with relatively small number of parameter changes. One approximate way to describe the "structure" of a

---

[13] See R. M. Cyert, E. A. Feigenbaum, and J. G. March, "Models in a Behavioral Theory of the Firm," *Behavioral Science*, Vol. 4 (1959), pp. 81-95.

computer program is by specifying a flow chart for it, the implication being that the branching hierarchy defined in a flow diagram is more stable than the values on which the branches occur.

Any such "general" model has two chief uses. First, it forms a framework within which to consider the specific organization simulations discussed above. There is, after all, rather little theoretical interest in Mr. X, Mr. Y, and Mr. Z or in being able to simulate a specific organization making a specific decision or class of decisions. Thus, although it would be useful to the National Security Council to have a good simulation of the decision system of the Soviet military establishment, the uses of such a model to organization theory would depend on how much and in what ways it might be generalized to other organizations. A general model is an attempt to specify such generalizations.

The second use of a general model is implicit in the first. The output of specific models is a set of predictions of how specific organizations will behave. The model is tested by comparing its output with the output of the system it is alleged to simulate. A general model makes somewhat different predictions. Specifically, it makes predictions of the following sort: Given certain values in initial conditions and parameters, an organization of this type making decisions will make these types of decision. An organization of this type will make decisions that are sensitive to changes in these parameters over these ranges. A system of organizations of this type (e.g., firms in a market, armies in a battle, foreign offices in diplomacy, political parties in electoral competition) will exhibit the following characteristics. And so on.

Without the computer it is clear that we could develop few, if any, reasonable general models of organizational decision-making. Since the results are not yet in, it is not certain that we can do so even with the aid of the computer. One conspicuous problem remaining to be solved, for example, is the problem of testing computer models. Conventional statistical techniques seem to offer only modest help in dealing with very large systems having multiple interrelated inputs and multiple interrelated outputs. At the moment, standard computer alchemy calls for an interesting mixture of rough statistical tests, rules of thumb and scientific common sense to determine the adequacy of a complex model. Ultimately, we will have to develop a set of somewhat better rationalized procedures.

EXPERIMENTS ON ORGANIZATIONS

As we have developed both the substantive theory of organizations and computer programs for dealing formally with that theory, we have also started to use experimental methods effectively in testing propositions from the theory. This is to be expected. One of the consequences of attempts at model building is the identification of areas in which laboratory experiments can contribute useful results. At the same time, the general technique of simulation has introduced some new experimental procedures of particular potential utility to the study of organizations.

"Nonorganizational" Experiments

The bulk of successful experimentation (successful, that is, in terms of its contribution to the theory of organizations) has not been experimentation on large complex organizations. Rather it has focused on small group and individual behavior of special interest to the theory. As the theory develops, such experimentation becomes increasingly possible.

Without attempting to compile a detailed bibliography, I would suggest four clusters of recent experimental activity as examples.

(1) The study of communication in groups operating under one or more of the following: a division of labor, imperfect knowledge, conflict of interest. The communication network studies of Bavelas and Leavitt and the elaborations on those studies by Christie, Luce, and Macy, on the one hand, and by Guetzkow and Simon and Guetzkow and Dill on the other, are classics of this type. The studies of Lanzetta and Roby on the effects of alternative divisions of labor have been important additions. Rapoport's studies on small, differentiated groups promise similar contributions.[14]

(2) The study of decision-making in small face-to-face groups. Although much of the research on small group decision-making is directed toward kinds of groups (informal, short-lived, egalitarian, low involvement) that have only a limited role in complex organiza-

---

[14] A detailed review of the network studies can be found in M. Glanzer and R. Glaser, "Techniques for the Study of Group Structure and Behavior; Part II, Empirical Studies of the Effects of Structure in Small Groups," *Psychological Bulletin*, Vol. 58 (1961), pp. 1-27; see also J. T. Lanzetta and T. B. Roby, "Group Performance as a Function of Work-Distribution Patterns and Task Load," *Sociometry*, Vol. 19 (1956), pp. 95-104; and A. Rapoport, "A Logical Task as a Research Tool in Organization Theory," in Haire, ed., *op. cit.*

tions, some of the results seem more generally applicable. Specifically, some of the studies by Bales and his associates and Festinger and his colleagues have had considerable impact on the theories outlined earlier. Among a number of attempts to make such experimental groups of greater prima facie relevance to actual organization groups have been the studies by Kelley and by Cohen, in which some rudimentary hierarchies were imposed.[15]

(3) The study of bargaining, coalition formation, and the resolution of conflict. There have been a number of studies arising either from game theory concepts with respect to bargaining or from what could be called variants on the game theory theme. The net result of these studies has been to cast some doubt on game theory as a predictive theory and to suggest the importance of attention factors (e.g., prominence) as possible factors in bargaining.[16]

(4) The study of individual problem-solving and search behavior. It is clear that organization theory depends heavily on a substantial portion of the research on human learning and problem-solving. Of particular relevance in the recent experimental research has been the work of Bruner, Goodnow, and Austin and of Newell, Shaw, and Simon and the variety of recent work on individual search behavior in a general trouble-shooting situation.[17] Some of this work has been specifically stimulated by organization theory. Some of it has been conducted without any thought to its possible implications for such theory. Although the former state of affairs has some classic methodological merits, a well-defined theory of organizations can use either kind of experiment.

Experiments on Relatively Complex Organization Systems

It is not necessary to organization theory that it be possible to conduct controlled experiments on large, complex systems. In

---

[15] For the works cited and other related studies, see A. P. Hare, E. F. Borgatta, and R. F. Bales, eds., *Small Groups* (New York: Alfred A. Knopf, 1955); D. Cartwright and A. Zander, eds., *Group Dynamics* (Evanston, Ill.: Row, Peterson and Co., 1959) 2nd ed.; and J. W. Thibaut and H. H. Kelley, *The Social Psychology of Groups* (New York: John Wiley & Sons, Inc., 1959).

[16] For some empirical studies of bargaining and conflict resolution, see R. M. Thrall, C. H. Coombs, and R. L. Davis, eds., *Decision Processes* (New York: John Wiley & Sons, Inc., 1960). See also the articles published in the *Journal of Conflict Resolution.*

[17] See, for example, J. S. Bruner, J. J. Goodnow, and G. A. Austin, *A Study of Thinking* (New York: John Wiley & Sons, Inc., 1956); and A. Newell, J. C. Shaw, and H. A. Simon, "Elements of a Theory of Human Problem Solving," *Psychological Review,* Vol. 65 (1958), pp. 151-66.

general, it seems probable that the returns will justify the cost more frequently for the more modest experimental ventures on specific parts of a model rather than for a full-blown experiment on an organization.

In large part, this judgment depends on the fact that hothouse organizations are extremely expensive to grow and maintain. The one massive effort in this direction is the RAND study of a simulated air defense warning and command system.[18] It is probably the most expensive experiment ever run in the social sciences. The return on investment is hard to calculate for at least two reasons. First, one of the major objectives of the experiment was to develop training and operating procedures for use in the SAGE system. Most of the data required to evaluate the extent of success on this objective is not readily available. Second, insofar as a contribution to organization theory was an objective, it would be premature to draw a conclusion. Until quite recently only the most scanty results were available from the experiment. A recent release of substantial portions of the experimental results may increase the general utility of the experiment. To date it has not had an impact in any way proportionate to its heroic dimensions.

Pending a firmer, favorable judgment on the RAND experiment and the general availability of funds for similar duplication of large organizations in the laboratory, some interesting attempts to use quasi-organizational experimental situations seem more likely to expand in the coming decade. With the rapid increase in the use of gaming as a decision training technique (e.g., war gaming, business gaming, international relations gaming), various observers have suggested the feasibility of experiments in gaming situations. In most such situations system complexity is partly simulated, partly real, and in any event greater than the usual small group laboratory experiment. For example, the Carnegie Tech business game requires the several firms to make a series of interrelated decisions on price, output, and scheduling, and on advertising, distribution, market research, and research and development expenditures, and on capital budgeting, financing, and dividend policy. The game has been run with teams as small as three members each and with teams as large as nine members plus a three-man board of directors. Al-

---

[18] See R. L. Chapman, "Data for Testing a Model of Organizational Behavior," RAND Research Memorandum RM-1916 (Santa Monica, Calif.: The RAND Corporation, 1960).

though considerably less complex, Guetzkow's international relations game or the IBM business game provide many opportunities
for organizational experimentation.[19]

PROGNOSIS

Three marks of a good theory are that it has something
nontrivial to say, it has a well-defined and powerful language with
which to say it, and it has observational techniques adequate for
comparing what it says with the real world. The theory of organizational decision-making does not rank spectacularly high on any of
these counts. But the trend is up. The models are better. The language of the high speed electronic computer offers real hope for
a feasible theoretical language. Experimentation and more precisely specified field studies portend more relevant observations.
Hopefully, this is progress.

---

[19] The Carnegie Tech game is described in K. J. Cohen, R. M. Cyert, W. R.
Dill, A. A. Kuehn, M. H. Miller, T. A. Van Wormer, and P. R. Winters, "The
Carnegie Tech Management Game," *Journal of Business* (forthcoming). See
also H. Guetzkow, "A Use of Simulation in the Study of Inter-Nation Relations," *Behavioral Science*, Vol. 4 (1959), pp. 183-91.

The Study of Political Behavior in Britain

David E. Butler
NUFFIELD COLLEGE, OXFORD

Those in the United States who use "political behavior" as a term of art, referring to a specialized approach to the observation and analysis of political phenomena, have as yet no following on the other side of the Atlantic. I know of no British student of politics who would describe himself as a political behavior specialist. It is true that if political behavior is taken in its broadest sense— to refer to studies that depend overwhelmingly upon observation of what people actually say and do, especially *en masse*—the approach has not been altogether neglected, but it would be fruitless to deny that its development in Britain has been comparatively slow.

An American critic, Andrew Hacker, has written an entertaining article, "Political Behaviour and Political Behavior," [1] in which he gives seven reasons for this backwardness among British students of politics. Briefly:

(1) They are less industrious than Americans.

(2) They are few in number.

(3) They come from higher in the social scale and so are shy of research that involves contact with the working classes.

(4) They do not have the stimulus of close assocation with the growing disciplines of sociology and social psychology.

(5) They are too much involved with "the Establishment" to be ready to ask awkward questions about the realities of power within it.

---

[1] A. Hacker, "Political Behaviour and Political Behavior," *Political Studies*, Vol. 7 (1959), pp. 32-40.

(6) They have not been much stimulated by the foundations.

(7) They have not been driven into the fact-anchored security of behavioral research by political pressures against the making of value judgments (which most other types of political writing necessitate).

The second, fourth, and sixth of these factors seem to me incontestable, and I would not wish here to open needless controversy by arguing about the first or the seventh; while I would challenge both the premises and the implications of Mr. Hacker's third and fifth factors, my own summary of the situation would not differ much from his.

On the one hand, the structure of British academic life has not produced the men or the money to develop behavioral research on a large scale nor have British students of politics been impelled in this direction by the incursions of those in neighboring disciplines; on the other hand, the social and institutional structure of Britain makes such research both more difficult and less rewarding than in America. The closely guarded traditions of civil service anonymity and cabinet secrecy, the narrowed range of pressure group activity imposed by the strict discipline of the parliamentary whips, and the ethnic and religious homogeneity of the country help to eliminate many of the questions which have provoked such worthwhile research elsewhere or to render them impossible to answer.

I do not wish to be a chauvinist. There is much that could and should have been studied about British political behavior and the exploitation of techniques developed in America has been regrettably slow. The main British contributions to the study of politics have continued to be in the discussion of political philosophy and (to me more important as well as more relevant to our current theme) in the writings of those who have followed the descriptive, historical, reflective tradition of Bagehot and Bryce. In any list of the important British works on politics published in the last ten years, the great majority would fall within this last category—McKenzie, Williams, Harrison, Morrison, even Finer.[2] An increasingly realistic and dynamic tone has permeated such writing, and

---

[2] R. T. McKenzie, *British Political Parties* (New York: St. Martin's Press, Inc., 1955); H. Morrison, *Government and Parliament* (London: Oxford University Press, 1954); P. M. Williams, *Politics in Post-War France* (London: Longmans, Green and Co., 1955); M. Harrison, *Trade Unions and the Labour Party* (London: Allen & Unwin, 1960); and S. E. Finer, *Anonymous Empire* (London: Pall Mall Press, 1958).

there is more and more research being done in the hitherto neglected field of parties and pressure groups. All this work lacks
scientific rigor; however ample the raw material and however exhaustively it is analyzed, the descriptive approach ultimately depends upon the perceptiveness and judgment of the writer. Since
the human and financial resources are limited and since the number of problems demanding study is very large, there is much to be
said for concentrating on an approach which enables the good
scholar, or even the good journalist, to say so large a proportion
of what is worth saying about any political phenomenon, even
though he employs no elaborate "research technique" and offers
no comprehensive proofs for his conclusions.

In many quarters the study of political behavior is taken to
mean the study of mass political behavior. As far as Britain is concerned such study has been concentrated almost entirely upon electoral behavior, since, for the overwhelming majority of people,
voting is their only explicit political action. (The activities of the
few hundred thousand citizens directly involved in intraparty democracy have been discussed in such general works as McKenzie's
and Harrison's as well as in a number of studies of individual trade
unions, but detailed and quantified accounts of the personnel and
the doings of constituency parties or union branches are few and
far between.) But it is only during the last fifteen years in Britain
that serious academic attention has been given to what happens
during an election.

Psephologists tend to be divided into two classes by whether
their primary interest is in electioneering or in electors. Students
of the latter are peculiarly handicapped in Britain. Work of the
sort done by Professors Siegfried and Goguel in France and by
Professor Gosnell and Mr. Lubell in the United States has been
impossible, partly because of the homogeneity of the British people and the shortage of local social and economic statistics and
partly because of the provisions of the Ballot Act of 1872, which
decreed that voting papers should be shuffled together and only
counted on a constituency-wide basis. Therefore, virtually nothing
has been done to use official election returns to answer the first
question about voting "Who votes how?" which has to be solved
before turning to the really central problem "Why do they do so?"

It cannot be said that very much has been done to use the obvious alternative, sample surveys, to remedy this omission. The

Gallup Poll, it is true, was quick to cross the Atlantic, and since 1938 the British Institute of Public Opinion, now known as Social Surveys (Gallup Poll), Ltd., has provided a rich, though rather neglected, mine of information. Mr. John Bonham is the only scholar really to have explored its possibilities; in his book, *The Middle Class Vote*,[3] he provides a valuable summary of where the parties drew their support in the 1945, 1950, and 1951 elections, in terms of sex, age, and socio-economic status.

The other attempts to gather data about the allegiance and behavior of voters have been on a local level. Manchester University sponsored two useful, though limited, studies: in the Stretford[4] constituency in 1950 and in Droylsden[5] in 1951, Mr. Birch, Mr. Campbell and their collaborators made a single interview survey, trying to find out as much as possible about the background and the past voting of a small cross-section of the electorate. Their findings confirmed, and in one or two respects amplified, the evidence of the Gallup polls.[6] A much more elaborate survey was made in 1950 in Greenwich by the London School of Economics.[7] There Mr. Benney and a large team of assistants set out to imitate Professor Lazarsfeld's pioneer American study, *The People's Choice*.[8] A carefully selected sample of nearly a thousand electors were interviewed before the contest began and again after the poll. The main object of the inquiry was to assess the impact of the campaign on the ordinary voters: Who approach an election with a closed mind, and who waver? What propaganda are they exposed to, and what difference does it make? How far are they aware of the issues of the campaign or in agreement with the party they support? The Greenwich findings suggested no very startling answers to these questions; but, as far as they went, they were con-

---

[3] J. Bonham, *The Middle Class Vote* (London: Faber and Faber, 1954).

[4] A. H. Birch and P. Campbell, "Voting Behaviour in a Lancashire Constituency," *British Journal of Sociology*, Vol. 1 (1950), pp. 197-208.

[5] P. Campbell, D. Donnison, and A. Potter, "Voting Behaviour in Droylsden, October 1951," *Manchester School of Economic and Social Studies*, Vol. 20 (1952), pp. 57-65.

[6] See also F. M. Martin, "Social Status and Electoral Choice," *British Journal of Sociology*, Vol. 3 (1952), pp. 231-41.

[7] M. Benney, A. P. Gray, and R. H. Pear, *How People Vote* (London: Routledge and Kegan Paul, 1956).

[8] P. F. Lazarsfeld, B. Berelson, and H. Gaudet, *The People's Choice* (New York: Columbia University Press, 1944). See also its successor: B. R. Berelson, P. F. Lazarsfeld, and W. N. McPhee, *Voting* (Chicago: University of Chicago Press, 1954).

firmed by the two other studies of this type. In 1951 Messrs. Milne and Mackenzie conducted a somewhat less elaborate investigation in northeast Bristol; [9] they repeated the experiment on a fuller scale in 1955.[10]

The general conclusions that emerge from all these sample surveys of the British electorate are familiar enough. Class seems to be much the strongest determinant of party loyalty; women seem to be more conservative than men, and old people more so than young people; the campaign does not seem to have much influence on the outcome, nor do local issues and the quality of the candidates; [11] those who waver are most frequently those whose party preference differs from that of their family or their workmates; voters often disagree greatly with the line of the party they support and are, on the whole, more conservative in their opinions than their votes. There is no doubt that there is considerable scope for further inquiries along these lines, both on a national and a local level.

The value of all this work is not at all impaired by the fact that it is largely derivative, an attempt to translate research techniques developed in America to the British scene. But it is certainly true that the most distinctively British contribution to the study of elections lies in the analysis of electioneering, not electors. *The British General Election of 1945*, by Mr. McCallum and Miss Readman,[12] set a pattern which has had far-reaching influence. That book and its successors in the Nuffield series [13] have shown how far it is possible without great expense, or even special expertise, to collect the basic facts about an electoral contest.

The purpose of these books has been manifold. In part, they have been written for the benefit of future historians and seek to

[9] R. S. Milne and H. C. Mackenzie, *Straight Fight* (London: The Hansard Society, 1954).

[10] R. S. Milne and H. C. Mackenzie, *Marginal Seat* (London: The Hansard Society, 1958).

[11] See H. Pollins, "The Significance of the Campaign in General Elections," *Political Studies*, Vol. 1 (1953), pp. 207-15.

[12] R. B. McCallum and A. Readman, *The British General Election of 1945* (London: Oxford University Press, 1947).

[13] H. G. Nicholas, *The British General Election of 1950* (London: Macmillan and Co., 1951); D. E. Butler, *The British General Election of 1951* (London: Macmillan and Co., 1952); D. E. Butler, *The British General Election of 1955* (London: Macmillan and Co., 1955); and D. E. Butler and R. Rose, *The British General Election of 1959* (London: Macmillan and Co., 1960).

provide a convenient and reasonably dispassionate summary of the events of an election, together with some assessment of its outcome and of the strategy and propaganda used. In part, they have been designed to make contemporary practitioners and observers of politics more aware of the nature of elections, to set in a better perspective the traditional ritual that is performed whenever a Parliament is dissolved. In part they have been experiments in political research, attempts to devise new techniques or adapt old ones to the analysis of these national convulsions. Each of the five Nuffield surveys, while preserving the central purpose of trying to record current history, has made limited innovations in methodology. The 1945 study showed how a detailed study of the election addresses of each candidate could reveal the difference between the themes most stressed in the national headquarters of the parties and those thought by the local contestants to have most appeal; it also incorporated some new statistical ideas on the relation between seats and votes and, in many other directions, marked out lines of inquiry which have been followed and developed in the succeeding volumes. The 1950 study incorporated more exhaustive analyses of the contents of the press and of the background of the candidates. The 1951 study attempted a more detailed and vivid exploration of the local appearance of an election by introducing surveys of individual constituencies. The 1955 study included a pioneer examination of the role of trade unions in the contest. The 1959 study broke new ground with chapters on the impact of social change on the electorate, on the projection of party images, and on the role of private enterprise advertising.

The Nuffield studies have of course no monopoly in these techniques. There are many other studies of the conduct of the press in relation to a particular historical event.[14] The analysis of the social background of candidates only parallels the work done by Mr. J. A. Thomas[15] and Mr. J. F. S. Ross[16] on members of Parliament. The examination of campaigns on a local level has been done in

[14] See especially A. H. Birch, P. Campbell, and P. G. Lucas, "The Popular Press in the British General Election of 1955," *Political Studies*, Vol. 4 (1956), pp. 297-306.

[15] J. A. Thomas, *The House of Commons, 1832-1901* (Cardiff: University of Wales Press Board, 1939).

[16] J. F. S. Ross, *Parliamentary Representation*, 2nd ed. (London: Eyre and Spottiswoode, 1948).

Glasgow [17] and as an incidental part of the Greenwich and northeast Bristol surveys; on a national level it was attempted by some American scholars in 1950.[18] The statistical dissection of election results has been widely taken up in the press and elsewhere—though with more enthusiasm than illumination.[19]

The fact that the footnotes to this paper constitute an almost complete bibliography of academic work on British elections [20] is revealing. The moral, I believe, is two-edged. It is that the subject has been unduly neglected and that it constitutes, of its nature, a very limited field. Every general election will always be an important enough event to merit description, and students of political behavior and social psychology will benefit by many more detailed investigations of the individual voter. But there is no special science of psephology; no overwhelming discoveries about electioneering lie, like sleeping beauties, awaiting only a research foundation's kiss. The study of elections must never be separated from the study of the political process as a whole. The study of voting behavior is only a part of the study of public opinion: the study of election literature is only a part of the study of propaganda; the study of campaigning is only a part of the study of party organization and sociology. At least as far as Britain is concerned, I believe that the understanding of the nature and significance of an election is more likely to be advanced by developments in these broader studies than by investigations which are narrowly concerned with the specific events and changes of mind that take place during a campaign.

---

[17] S. B. Chrimes, ed., *The General Election in Glasgow, 1950* (Glasgow: Jackson, 1950).

[18] J. K. Pollock, ed., *British Election Studies, 1950* (Ann Arbor, Mich.: G. Wahr Publishing Co., 1951). See also D. E. Butler *et al.*, "Les élections générales brittanniques de 1951," *Revue Française de Science Politique*, Vol. 2 (1952), pp. 213-311.

[19] But for serious studies see, e.g., M. G. Kendall and A. Stuart, "Cubic Proportion in Election Results," *British Journal of Sociology*, Vol. 1 (1950), pp. 183-96; and E. J. Cleary and H. Pollins, "Liberal Voting at the General Election of 1951," *Sociological Review*, Vol. 1, n.s. (1953), pp. 27-41.

[20] Perhaps, for the sake of comprehensiveness, four articles on the study of elections should be added: R. S. Milne, "The Study of Parliamentary Elections," *Cambridge Journal* (August, 1952), p. 174; D. E. Butler, "Voting Behaviour and Its Study in Britain," *British Journal of Sociology*, Vol. 6 (1955), pp. 93-103; W. Pickles, "Psephological Dyspepsia," *Twentieth Century*, Vol. 158 (1955), pp. 30-34; and J. Plamenatz, "Electoral Studies and Democratic Theory," *Political Studies*, Vol. 6 (1958), pp. 1-9.

I wish I could end by recording evidence of dramatic new advances. But the 1959 election saw no constituency studies on the model set by Milne and Mackenzie in academic research. The most encouraging development was a study of the impact of television in two northern constituencies, conducted by an expert whose interest lay in communications rather than in politics.[21] Otherwise, the most hopeful recent signs lie in the growth in newspaper and commercial polling; in the increase of interest in their findings; in the greater public and party awareness of the process of image-building; and in the attention given to the political importance of social change.[22] The affluent society is arriving in Britain, too. Recognition of this fact and curiosity about its implications, together with the current (and, in part, consequent) disintegration of the Labour party, is giving a powerful stimulus to new research into British political behavior. So perhaps I can still end on a note of hope.

---

[21] J. Trenaman and D. McQuade, *Television and the Political Image* (London: Methuen, 1961).

[22] See the articles by Mark Abrams in *Encounter*, Vol. 14 (1960), pp. 57-59 and in *Socialist Commentary* (May and June, 1960), largely reproduced in the Penguin Special, *Must Labour Lose?* (1960). See also the recent Fabian pamphlets by C. A. R. Crosland, *Can Labour Win?* and by R. H. S. Crossman, *Labour and the Affluent Society*.

Studies on Finnish Political Behavior

Pertti Pesonen
UNIVERSITY OF TURKU, FINLAND

In a lecture upon his installment as professor at the University of Helsinki, Jussi Teljo mentioned that "modern political scientists attempt to explain how individuals and groups strive for political power, achieve it and make use of it. Their aim is to find invariances. . . . The final purpose of the new political science is to uncover the regularities which are prevailing in the political activity and in the political attitudes of human individuals and human groups." [1] These ideas were quite new in the traditional Finnish political science of a decade ago. Referring, also, to the necessity of quantitative methods and the importance of building an empirical theory, Teljo actually presented the focal principles now stressed by the practitioners of the so-called behavioral approach to the study of politics.

Although the basic ideas of the behavioral approach are new in Finland, they are no newer than in most other countries. The first Finnish behavioral studies, however, are more recent than actual thinking along such lines. Obviously the approach in general has mainly been inspired by an increasing interest in elections and voting behavior and by the contributions made by scientists who have sociological training. Such is true for Finland, also. The first actual research was performed by sociologists and concerned participation in elections. Even today, voting behavior, or more generally electoral behavior, is the main and almost only field of politics that has been studied via the behavioral approach. This fact in-

---

[1] J. Teljo, "Valtio-opin tehtävät ja menetelmät" (The tasks and methods of political science), *Suomalainen Suomi* (1950), pp. 14-18.

evitably determines the contents of this paper, too, so that it mainly concentrates only on studies of electoral behavior.

The term *voting behavior* has generally been used to cover electorate behavior during the actual campaign period and polling day. Here the words *electorate behavior* not only include voting behavior and other related electoral behavior, but have a wider, more comprehensive meaning. Of course, voting decision and the act of voting cannot be understood separately from the electorate's experiences between campaign periods nor from the citizens' socialization long before they reach voting age. It is a well-known finding that changes in voting decisions are less numerous during the election campaigns than between them. The interest shown in elections also seems to be only one aspect of an interest in politics in general which has many other forms in times of no campaigning and also seems to become socialized at an early age. Although voting behavior, either mainly limited to the act of voting or, as in this paper, more widely defined and therefore better called electoral behavior, has mainly stimulated behavioral research in this field, it should not be separated from its natural, more general context of the political behavior of the electorate. The latter is present every day, the former only in the periodical highlights of political life.

In this connection it might be appropriate to point to certain aspects of the political and electoral system of Finland. The 200 members of the country's unicameral Parliament are elected (in the usual case of no dissolution by the President) every fourth year, in July. Within the fifteen electoral areas the seats are divided proportionally, according to d'Hondt's method. Aland is the only single-member constituency. The multiple party system follows basically the Scandinavian three-party pattern of a socialist, a liberal, and a conservative party, but the left is divided among the Communists (23.2 per cent of the popular vote in 1958), a Social Democratic opposition group (1.7 per cent) and the Social Democrats (23.2 per cent). Peculiar to Finland is a strong Agrarian party (23.1 per cent), and in addition to the Center (5.9 per cent) and the Conservatives (15.3 per cent), the Swedish minority has a nonsocialist party of their own (6.7 per cent).

Another national election takes place once every six years when the 300 members of the electoral college are elected in January to elect the President of the Republic in February. Municipal elections occur in October of every fourth year simultaneously throughout the whole country. There are two succeeding polling days in every election, and the register of voters is automatically kept by the authorities. The possibilities of absentee voting (since 1956 even in hospitals and in certain cities abroad) are provided for. The voting age was lowered in 1945 from twenty-four to twenty-one years, and the electorate now comprises 2.6 million citizens. Campaigning tends to be concentrated in the weeks immediately preceding the election. A rational voting decision may be troublesome due to the difficulty of discerning who the politically responsible really are, as the Finnish party system usually has led to short-lived coalition cabinets. Only the Communists have been kept in a continuous opposition since 1948.

The first major studies on electoral behavior were published in 1956, and even now their quantity is meager. One possible way of classifying the research is according to the method that has been used in gathering data. A classification on the basis of whether the material collected concerns geographical areas or individual persons would seem a convenient way of grouping the work already done as well as the untouched possibilities.

AREA

(1) It is possible to compare the communes as to respective turnout at an election. The task is an easy one, since information on turnout by commune and by sex is readily available from the official election statistics. The only technical difficulty is caused by the rare changes in border lines and combinations, or divisions, of communes. After this basic classification the turnout by commune can be cross-tabulated with all the information that is available on the communes and meaningful for the purposes of the study at hand. This has been done by Erik Allardt.[2] Collecting data on the turnout of the four postwar parliamentary elections of 1945, 1948, 1951, and 1954, Allardt then classified the communes deviating no more than six percentage units from the respective election's average turnout as "normal," thus getting smaller classes of communes with a "low" or a "high" participation in each election. Such classification was followed by an extensive cross tabula-

[2] E. Allardt, *Social struktur och politisk activitet* (Social structure and political activity), (Helsingfors: Söderström, 1956).

tion against data of various political, socio-economic and cultural variables. The method proved very useful, although the commune is an administrative and not a meaningful social unit. Another hindrance is the enormous difference in size between a small rural commune and a big city.

It would also be possible to obtain from the primary material of the official statistics information about smaller geographical units, the voting districts (in 1958, there were 549 communes, divided into 4,983 voting districts). However, for the country as a whole no other useful information is available about the small voting districts in addition to turnout and the division of popular vote among the parties.

(2) One might, of course, as well classify the communes according to their support of the parties or even of individual candidates who compete in an election. The former information is directly given in the official statistics. Here there are more numerous possibilities of classification than in the study of turnout. Such a technique leads to an ecological analysis of the mutual correlations of the "political color" of the areas and of the other variables than can be obtained to describe the inhabitants. The ecological method in the Andre Siegfried tradition has been used by Jaakko Nousiainen, who analyzed ecologically the support of the communist movement in two neighboring electoral areas, a total of fifty-three communes.[3] His main work was not of the cross tabulation type. Emphasis was on the description of one commune at a time, taking historical material into consideration. Evidently the ecological method provides political history and the behavioral approach to political science with a new common ground. Thus, Hannu Soikkanen has included in his study of the arrival of socialism in Finland statistical anaylses of how the popular backing of socialism in the election of 1907 correlated with the economic and social conditions of the communes.[4] The ecology of the vote has also been treated within single cities.[5] It might be interesting

---

[3] J. Nousiainen, *Kommunismi Kuopion läänissä* (Communism in the province of Kuopio), (Helsinki: Joensuu, 1956).

[4] H. Soikkanen, *Sosialismin tulo Suomeen* (The arrival of socialism in Finland), (Turku, 1961).

[5] P. Burman, *Helsinki poliittisena käyttäytymisalueena* (Helsinki as a political behavioral area), (unpublished Master's thesis, University of Helsinki, 1957); and O. Lehto, *Oulun kaupunki poliittisena käyttäytymisalueena* (The city of Oulu as a political behavioral area), (unpublished Master's thesis, University of Helsinki, 1959).

to develop this technique, for instance, by leaving the nonvoters out of the analysis of how the area's political affiliation correlates with demography, since the register of voters, including an after-election check as to who voted, could be used by the scholar.

Moreover, developments in analytical techniques offer increased possibilities for comparing areal units. Allardt is presently engaged in a factor analysis of Finnish communes, mainly to find explanations for the support given to the different leftist parties. His study is based upon a total of forty-one variables about the political, historical, economic, and other social background of the communes. The matrices of the analysis have been run on the University of Illinois' electronic digital computer.[6]

INDIVIDUALS

(1) If one wishes to study further the participation in elections, one does not have to be content with using the turnout of geographical areas as units of analysis. Even without performing an interview, it is possible to know whether or not a particular Finnish citizen voted, simply because the election board makes note of such in the register of voters. The method has been made well known by Herbert Tingsten of Sweden. A minor inaccuracy in Finland is caused by the fact that it is not possible to check whether the "extracts" from the register, duly taken in advance for absentee voting purposes, really have been used or not. Therefore, all the persons who have prepared for absentee voting have to be considered *a priori* participants in the election. The sex, age, marital status, address, occupation, and even the native language spoken are additional variables readily available from the register. Helsinki's Office of Statistics has made some use of this kind of material, which has also been further analyzed by Allardt and Kettil Bruun.[7] It is possible to add data from other official and private records to this basic information as, for instance, the taxable income, the length of residence in the commune, membership in some associations, etc., of each person; and with the additional trouble of searching the records of previous elections, as far they

---

[6] E. Allardt, "Social Factors Affecting Left Voting in Developed and Backward Areas," (a paper delivered at the Fifth World Congress of the International Political Science Association, Paris, 1961).

[7] E. Allardt and K. Bruun, "Characteristics of the Finnish Non-Voter," *Transactions of the Westermarck Society*, Vol. 3 (1956), pp. 13-25.

are preserved, the constant and occasional nonvoters could be traced. Moreover, as this application of the law of the publicity of documents is hardly known at all, it provides the interviewer with a reliable way of checking whether the interviewees have given correct answers regarding their participation. The present writer has, for instance, studied how the data that was obtained from the formal register of associations and from the lists of candidates of an election correlated with information about the respective person's participation, and he has further experimented with a note after every name made by the election board in the register as to what time the voters selected for going to the polls. So far, the possibilities that the use of official documents might offer for the analysis of voting participation have been used only to a very slight extent.

(2) Evidently the political participation and activity of an individual refers to such a wide range of behavior that it can be more fully understood only by means of interview data. This is, of course, also the only way of getting information about the party affiliation of individual persons. Unfortunately, the costs of performing interviews have often been a prohibiting factor. The correlation of political attitudes with other variables has sometimes been made possible by including in the questionnaire a question about the party affiliation, even when the survey was mainly interested in other social problems. However, more often this question has been eliminated because of the fear that inquiring about the interviewees' political views might be dangerous to the study, since political beliefs are thought to be extremely private in Finland and they are seldom discussed with other persons. Using some national samples, the Finnish Gallup Poll has collected valuable data, but very little of it has been published or even further analyzed for the purposes of political science. Political opinions were included in the research material which was collected by the Institute of Social Policy of the University of Helsinki in 1960, when 1,900 interviews were conducted in twenty-five communes with different levels of urbanization in order to study the presently occurring changes in levels of aspirations and the Christian culture of Finnish society.[8]

---

[8] Cf. O. Riihinen, "The Levels of Achievement and Aspirations in a Rapidly Growing Economy" (in preparation); and P. Seppänen, "The Changing Patterns of Christian Culture in Finnish Society" (in preparation).

Also, political affiliation has been one variable in some research on industrial sociology,[9] and the behavior and ideology of the members of the Conservative party have been analyzed through interviews by Onni Rantala.[10] Numerous surveys have thrown light on different aspects of social participation and also on its relationship to interest shown in politics.

(3) The only way of achieving valid information about the dynamics of political decision-making among the electorate seems to be repetition of interviews of the same sample. The present writer has conducted a panel interview of the Finnish students of voting age.[11] A sample of 430 were interviewed in the beginning of December, 1955, and 410 were reinterviewed immediately after the election of the college of presidential electors, which took place on January 16 and 17, 1956. A new project dealing with the parliamentary election of 1958 is in progress. The new material was collected by interviewing cross-sectional samples of 501 and 97 of the city of Tampere and the rural commune of Korpilahti respectively, both in May and after the election of July 6 and 7.

If the effect of the campaign is to be studied in Finland and only two waves of interviews are to be used, the first interview need not be more than two months before the election. The nominated candidates to the Parliament are allowed to be announced to the election authorities as late as forty days before the first polling day, and often the final spurt of campaigning lasts no more than a couple of weeks. A technical difficulty in the interview is caused by the fact that a great deal of the inhabitants of Finnish cities are vacationing in July, the regular month of the parliamentary election. Thus far in Finland there is no experience with panel surveys of electoral behavior which have lasted for a longer period or consisted of more than two interviews of the same sample.

---

[9] P. Koli, *Ennakkoluuloista teollisessa organisaatiossa* (On prejudices in industrial organization), (Helsinki: WSOY, 1955); and V. Laakkonen, *Työntekijä ja teknillinen uudistus* (The worker and technical change), (Helsinki: WSOY, 1958).

[10] O. Rantala, *Konservatismi ja sen kannattajat* (Conservatism and its supporters), (Helsinki: Tammi, 1960), and *Konservatiivinen puolueyhteisö* (The Conservative party community), (Vammala, 1956).

[11] P. Pesonen, *Valitsijamiesvaalien ylioppilasäänestäjät* (Student voters in the election of the College of Presidential Electors), (Helsinki: Tammi, 1958), and "The Voting Behavior of Finnish Students," *Democracy in Finland* (the Finnish Political Science Association, 1960), pp. 93-104.

PROBLEMS AND FINDINGS

A description of the techniques of data collection still gives no idea of the special problems that have been touched upon by the Finnish research on electorate behavior. The following glance at the problems and areas of inquiry is by no means a complete or a systematic inventory of Finnish research; but the twelve points may give some idea of what has been dealt with by contemporary work in this field.

(a) The first Finnish research on voting behavior was inspired by the hypothesis regarding how cross pressures, as compared to uniform social pressures, affect the election turnout (first presented by Paul F. Lazarsfeld in connection with electoral studies). A comparison of communes led Allardt to the findings that the turnout is higher in communes where (1) one party clearly dominates, (2) the political traditions are strong, (3) farms are equal in size, (4) the economy is either predominantly rural or very industrialized, (5) no deep social stratification exists, and (6) the strongest political and religious movements work in harmony.[12] The starting proposition was that a high degree of social, cultural or political uniformity within a community would make for a high turnout, while the heterogeneous communes would have a lower voting frequency. This was confirmed by findings. However, the proposition, which is not called an empirical hypothesis, only holds where the parties, as usually under proportional representation, have reason to make an effort to get out the vote. The Swedish-speaking inhabitants of Aland or the Southerners in the United States do not have ample motivation to get to the polls.

The cross-pressure hypothesis has also guided the analysis of material collected from the voting register.[13] The fact that the Swedish-speaking women vote in all age groups more frequently than do the Finnish men, has been explained through the Swedish women's social segregation which protects them against cross pressures. The turnout of women in sales and other service jobs was strikingly low, but they also are exceptionally cross pressured. Similar explanations have been given to the findings that workers turn out highest in Helsinke's working class or leftist voting districts, while the upper class and white collar are most active in the nonleftist and with few workers populated districts.

---

[12] Allardt, *Social struktur och politisk activitet.*
[13] *Ibid.*; and Allardt and Bruun, *op. cit.*

(b) The correlation of political participation with geographical and social mobility has also been interpreted in the light of the cross-pressure hypothesis: the mobile have shown a lower turnout, and they may be considered as subject to more conflicting pressures than the stable persons. Helsinki's Office of Statistics noticed in a survey of the twenty-one- to twenty-five-year-old residents of the city that the turnout of the youth born in Helsinki or remainng in their father's occupational class was higher than that of the residentially or socially mobile persons.[14] Among the students the children of working-class parents voted less frequently and, when voting, tended to postpone their voting decision or to change the intention more often than the rest of the student population.[15] Their exceptionally uncertain decision-making was explained as a result of their intention to rise socially and of their minority position in the student community where the students born to upper and middle class families formed a great majority, both of which can be seen as causes of conflicting social pressure.

(c) Another fruitful set of hypotheses has concerned the *cumulative character of participant activities*. A survey among a national probability sample of youth aged ten to twenty-nine showed a positive intercorrelation of high participation in most activities in the community, with the exception of religious activity.[16] Also, different forms of political participation are of a cumulative character. Of the students, those who in the first interview judged themselves as interested in politics were the most likely to score high in a scale that measured their later behavioral interest in the election.[17] Among the other intercorrelating variables were the intensity of party affiliation, the exposure to campaign propaganda, the exposure to political, noncampaign mass communication, the turnout, keen participation in political discussions, and the number of po-

---

[14] K. Bruun, "Nuorisotutkimus vuonna, 1951" (Youth survey of 1951), *Tilastollisia kuukausitietoja Helsingistä*, Vol. 3 (1952), pp. 193-264. See also Allardt and Bruun, *op. cit.*

[15] Pesonen, *Valitsijamiesvaalien ylioppilasäänestäjät*, pp. 192-94; and Pesonen, "The Voting Behavior of Finnish Students."

[16] E. Allardt, P. Jartti, F. Jyrkilä, and Y. Littunen, *Työläisnuorison harrastustoiminta* (The leisure activities of working class youth), (Helsinki: Tammi, 1956); Allardt *et al.*, "On the Cumulative Nature of Leisure Activities," *Acta Sociologica*, Vol. 3 (1957), pp. 165-72; and Allardt *et al.*, *Nuorison harrastukset ja yhteisön rakenne* (The leisure activities of youth and social structure), (Helsinki: WSOY, 1958).

[17] Pesonen, *Valitsijamiesvaalien ylioppilasäänestäjät*, pp. 146-47.

litical opinions offered. Among the variables added to the Tampere survey are knowledge of politics, the feeling of the election's importance, and different forms of active campaigning.[18] As might be expected, the interest in politics in general is significantly related to keen participation and exposure during the campaign and the polling days.

(d) Fruitful as the general cumulativeness hypothesis may be, one has reason to fear that it might also lead to overly broad generalizations. Therefore, a detailed study of deviant types of interest and of *different factors of political participation* now seems to be in order. Finnish data have not been specifically analyzed to distinguish purely spectator interests from citizen activation by involvement and affiliation, but enough is known to state that the interested, yet nonparticipating spectators are a rare exception. The division of political activity into expressive and instrumental action, so termed by Talcott Parsons, has made possible fruitful interpretations,[19] and it will no doubt breed additional useful hypotheses.

(e) The study of the role of *opinion leaders* has linked the analysis of participation with that of the "two-step flow of communication." The most recent work was performed by Paavo Piepponen.[20] He interviewed in the spring of 1957 a random sample (394) of the inhabitants of Tampere and went on to interview later the 373 persons who were named by the first sample as their opinion leaders. In cultural activities, he distinguished the influentials in the selection of book reading, theater production, and motion pictures. The influential persons were well exposed to the mass communication of their field. In the second interview political opinion leaders were traced; they were likely to be influential in the selection of reading material, but not in the selection of theater and even less of motion pictures. The very significant cumulativeness found in opinion leadership in book, theater, and movie selection, partly even in politics, contradicts the findings of Katz and

---

[18] E. Allardt and P. Pesonen, "Finland," in "Citizen Participation in Political Life," *International Social Science Journal*, Vol. 12 (1960).

[19] Cf. E. Allardt, "Social Factors Affecting Left Voting in Developed and Backward Areas"; A. Eskola, "Mielipiteiden määrä sosiologisena muuttujana" (The number of opinions as a variable in sociology), (mimeo., 1961); and Y. Littunen, "Aktiivisuus ja radikalismi" (Radicalism and activity), *Politiikka*, Vol. 4 (1960), pp. 151-85.

[20] P. Piepponen, *Harrastusten valinta* (The selection of leisure activities), (Helsinki: WSOY, 1960).

Lazarsfeld (in *Personal Influence*, 1955) on the specialization of influentials in their respective fields. Of the students in Helsinki, the political opinion leader tended to be the most interested in politics and the most exposed to propaganda.[21]

(f) *The time of voting decision* is a problem basic to the understanding of voting behavior or the effect of election campaigning. The percentage distribution of the electorate among the constants in intent, the conveyors, the crystallizers, and the nonvoters in the student sample was $67 + 16 + 6 + 11 = 100$ (n $= 410$); the corresponding figures during the campaign of 1958 in Tampere were $62 + 11 + 10 + 17 = 100$ (n $= 466$) and in Korpilahti commune $54 + 10 + 13 + 23 = 100$ (n $= 94$). According to both panel surveys, the persons who tended to make an early voting decision also were especially inclined to cast their ballot on the first polling day. By means of another method, it has been shown in Tampere that married couples were likely to vote together, but if they did not, the husbands usually voted first while the wives tended to vote later or not at all. Not only does the time of final voting decision correlate with the time of actual participation, but the early deciding and the early voting persons are likely to be more active and better informed; the delayers would be most in need but are the least likely to get information through propaganda. Contrary to some American findings, it seems that the voters who become converted during the campaign are not as a rule the passive ones; for example, opinion leaders of the students changed their position as frequently as the others.[22] Apparently it is the tendency to delay decision-making, correlating it with late or no balloting, that is typical of the passive section of the Finnish electorate.

(g) A simultaneous focus on the flow of communication and the time of voting decision leads further to evaluations of *the effect of campaign propaganda*. Because most persons do not change their voting intention during an electoral campaign, the over-all converting effect of propaganda appears to be smaller than the party headquarters hopes for. Moreover, in Finland as well as in other countries which have been studied, propaganda reaches mainly those who are the least likely to be converted. A majority of the population of Tampere, however, considered newspapers to be the

---

[21] P. Pesonen, *Valitsijamiesvaalien ylioppilasäänestäjät*, pp. 131-35.

[22] *Ibid.*, p. 188.

most important source of campaign information. Radio ranked second and private discussions only third in importance. But the later a person reached his final decision, the more likely he was to consider discussions as the most important source of information; and the persons who considered discussions important were also likely to be on the passive side in discussions. In addition, they were often accompanied by a friend to the polling place. Consequently, evaluations of the actual effect of mass propaganda have to wait in Finland until more is known about the personal influence that the most exposed persons are exerting within their small groups.

(h) Of the determinants of party affiliation those connected with *communism* may be of special interest due to the relatively strong backing of the communist movement by the Finnish electorate. Nousiainen came to the conclusion that economic factors have an effect on the division of electors between socialists and nonsocialists, but not on the division of the electors between Social Democrats and Communists. The support of communism could be connected with a social or cultural isolation from the rest of the community and with the local political traditions of which the experiences of civil war and the critical period after World War II are most important. Unemployment measures a state of economic insecurity, but, more than that, it measures in Finland an alienation from the ordinary ways of living. Even a memory of it has been found to work effectively in favor of communism.[23] According to the new factor analysis,[24] Communists are relatively strong in both poor and wealthy communes, while their backing is smaller in areas of medium income level. One may speak of southwestern industrial communism and northeastern woodland communism. Only the former is explainable in terms of social background factors and socialist traditions, both of which are shared by the Social Democrats. But the latter kind of Finnish communism seems to be a result of a sudden rise in the aspiration level, accompanied by structural restraints on social participation.

(i) The research conducted on *industrial sociology* has further helped us to trace some psychological components of party affilia-

---

[23] Cf. Allardt, *Social struktur och politisk aktivitet,* p. 84; Allardt, "Social Factors Affecting Left Voting in Developed and Backward Areas"; Nousiainen, *op. cit.;* and S. M. Lipset, *Political Man* (Garden City, N.Y.: Doubleday and Co., 1960), p. 123n.

[24] Allardt, "Social Factors Affecting Left Voting in Developed and Backward Areas."

tion among the workers. In three industrial plants, the backers of the Social Democratic party were slightly inclined to be free from prejudice; none of the nonsocialist workers were prejudiced towards their superiors, while almost every backer of the Communists was prejudiced.[25] Vesa Laakkonen classified as "insecure" the workers of a steel foundry, who thought that some one person or a group of persons would suffer because of the technical changes. The insecure workers apparently were more communistic than were the secure ones.[26] In a factoral study of some social attitudes Paavo Koli used socialist orientation and political resignation as two of his eleven attitude dimensions for testing workers, foremen, and managers; his final four factors were interpreted as prejudice, tenderminded-ness, authoritarianism, and social insecurity.[27] In this connection one should also remember that the growing interest of scholars in democratic procedures within the unions gives promise for fruitful mutual comparison of electoral and organizational behavior. An example is given by a finding on the Social Democratic locals' rela-tively passive and the Communist dominated locals' active partici-pation in the elections of the Union of Railroad Workers,[28] which has its counterpart in studies on behavior in national elections.

(j) The *party organizations* and their members hold a focal position in the electorate's behavior. Both the organizations them-selves and their role within the electorate are worthy objects of inquiry. The members of the Conservative party participated vaguely in the party machine's work. The approaching election increased their activity greatly but, surprisingly enough, even some members did not care about getting to the polls.[29] Yet, the most active part of the electorate is to be found among the partisan ones.[30] Within the party organization itself great differences exist in both participation and opinions held. The members who held positions of trust identified themselves most strongly with the party's ideology.[31] This finding is in line with the proposition of

---

[25] P. Koli, *op. cit.*, pp. 83-87.

[26] V. Laakkonen, *op. cit.*, pp. 208-10.

[27] P. Koli, "Ideology Patterns and Ideology Cleavages," *Transactions of the Westermarck Society*, Vol. 4 (1959), pp. 22-31.

[28] A. Heikkilä, *Ammattiosasto ja jäsenten aktiivisuus* (A union and the ac-tivity of its members), (unpublished Master's thesis, University of Helsinki, 1960).

[29] Rantala, *Konservatiivinen puolueyhteisö*, pp. 180, 190.

[30] Allardt and Pesonen, *op. cit.*

[31] Rantala, *Konservatismi ja sen kannattajat*, p. 139.

George G. Homans [32] that the high ranking in an organization identify themselves best with the norms of the organization. A survey of the male students' attitudes towards the defensive forces points in the same direction: the highest-ranking ex-servicemen agreed most with the army's ideology and also demanded most student pressure-group activity for increases in the defense budget. In addition, not only did a high position call for a favorable attitude, but a favorable attitude towards the organization prior to joining it seemed to be a precondition for success in it.[33] Comparative behavioral studies of party members and members of other organizations and of the loose social organization that consists of the voters of a party might prove an interesting endeavor.

(k) The understanding of the "life history" of the electorate calls for research on *political socialization*. Apparently, the family of origin is an important instrument of socializing people into an interest in politics.[34] Apparently, too, the family is the most important channel to party affiliation; 64 per cent of the students supported the same party as did their parents, although a leftist position (which was a minority among the students) was less inherited.[35] The influence of the childhood home also explains why, among the workers in 1948, the left was supported by 80 per cent of the descendants of workers but only by 42 per cent of the descendants of middle class fathers, and also, why among the middle-class a leftist party was chosen more often by the sons of workers than by the sons of nonmanual fathers.[36] Of the members of the Conservative party those with conservative parents more enthusiastically identified themselves with the party ideology and more actively participated in the activities of the party; among the supporters of different parties about 90 per cent had always been true to their present party.[37] It is the consistency of nonvoting of some persons and the generally high persistence of party selection that make the early socialization process crucial to the understand-

---

[32] G. C. Homans, *The Human Group* (New York: Harcourt, Brace and Company, 1950).

[33] P. Pesonen, "Ylioppilaat ja maanpuolustus" (Students and national defense), *Politiikka*, Vol. 4 (1960), pp. 20-43.

[34] Allardt and Pesonen, *op. cit.*, p. 37.

[35] Pesonen, *Valitsijamiesvaalien ylioppilasäänestäjät*, p. 98.

[36] S. M. Lipset and R. Bendix, *Social Mobility in Industrial Society* (Berkeley: University of California Press, 1959), pp. 67, 70.

[37] Rantala, *Konservatismi ja sen kannattajat*, pp. 135, 165.

ing of electorate behavior. Obviously, increased efforts by scientists to analyze the first voting decision thoroughly are now in order. In addition to the family of origin, other socializing factors may also have been effective prior to the first voting decision. Among such life experience variables are those connected with geographical and social mobility which are of considerable importance in the rapidly changing Finnish society.

(1) The validity of making *international comparisons* should be neither underestimated nor overestimated. A general political theory can only emerge if based on and retested by data from a variety of countries. The first Finnish panel study of voting behavior aimed at making comparisons with findings from the American and British applications of the method. The comparisons led to the conclusion that, on the whole, the correlations and the generalizations made concurred with those of earlier findings. Obviously too, the inconsistencies declined as the comparison was freed from that of demographic factors and transferred to the psychological variables and explanations. One simple reminder of the dangers of relying too much on the most apparent demographic classifications was the finding of Allardt and Bruun that the lower turnout of women, well-known everywhere, was in Helsinki due almost completely to the greater number of women in the older age groups and in the group of unmarried people.[38] At the moment there seems to be a growing number of presentations of political sociology which point out striking similarities within the Western political cultures. In Finland, studies on electoral behavior are still few but the approach is by now recognized and rooted well enough to promise increasing contributions to the growing general knowledge in this field.

OTHER BEHAVIORAL APPROACH

In other areas of political science the behavioral approach has also made its appearance, although one is yet by no means justified in calling it rooted. In the first *quantitative study of the legislature*, the monetary units served as a means of measuring. Thus, Teljo [39] pointed out the over-all tendency of the Parliament to increase the budget's social expenditures (such as education,

---

[38] Allardt and Bruun, *op. cit.*, p. 65.

[39] J. Teljo, *Eduskunta ja valtion tulo- ja menoarvio* (The Parliament and the state budget), (Helsinki-Jyväskylä: Gummerus, 1938).

social welfare, and vocational improvements) but to decrease the
general, more "distant" expenditures (police, justice and national
defense) from the amounts that were proposed by the cabinet.
Only about two decades later has the behavior of *individual members* been subjected to quantitative analysis. P. G. Nyholm [40] has
made use of the tabulated votes, in which the stand of every
member has been recorded. He has sought to determine how cohesive the different parliamentary groups have been, for what general reasons they have divided, and how consistent the individual
members have been. In the Parliament, three major voting blocs
existed, the "right-left," the "rural-urban," and the "Communist-
non-Communist." Of the groups, the Communist group was the most
and the Swedish People's party the least cohesive. In general, however, the members within the various groups were far from being
as unanimous as might be expected in a multi-party system, which
points to the efforts of the different parties to broaden the social
bases of their electoral support.

The *social background* of Finnish legislators has been analyzed
by Martti Noponen.[41] In addition to the various demographic factors he has placed emphasis on the occupational and educational
background and the class structure of the members of Parliament,
their parents' social structure, and their own social and geographic
mobility. The usual pattern of the citizens' tendency to support
candidates who are above their own social level, as well as the
townspeople's better chances of getting elected, holds true in
Finland, too. The average age of the members of the unicameral
Parliament showed a continuous tendency to rise (from forty in
1907 to fifty in 1939), and re-elections of the members were numerous. These are signs of the oligarchic tendencies in the Parliament.
Of special interest appear to be the findings of the members' active
participation in decision-making within the sphere of local self-
government and their leadership in both party organizations and

---

[40] P. G. Nyholm, "Havaintoja eduskuntaryhmien koheesiosta vaalikaudella
1948-51" (Observations on the cohesion of parliamentary groups during the
term 1948-51), *Politiikka*, Vol. 3 (1959), pp. 42-52; and Nyholm, *Suomen
eduskuntaryhmien koheesio* (in preparation).

[41] M. Noponen, "Piirteitä kansanedustajien sosiaalisesta taustasta" (Some aspects of the social background of the members of the Finnish Diet), *Politiikka*,
Vol. 3 (1959), pp. 95-112; and Noponen, *Kansanedustajien sosiaalinen tausta
Suomessa vuosina 1907-39* (The social background of members of Paraliament
in 1907-39), (unpublished Licentiate thesis, University of Helsinki, 1961).

various economic and voluntary organizations prior to their election to the Parliament, which points to a high level of cumulation of social activity and leadership in the hands of the country's political élite.

Noponen has based his work on bibliographical and recorded data. Two Parliaments have also been subjected to interviews. Lolo Krusius-Ahrenberg interviewed the members who were elected in 1951; only one-half of the Communist members then refused to cooperate.[42] Her purpose was to find out how close and what kind of personal connection the parliamentry groups had with the major interest groups. Most members declared that they represented at least one economic interest; especially well represented were the two co-operative movements. Organized labor was represented by only Social Democratic and Communist members, while the employers, private enterprise, and the "white collar" organizations had only nonsocialist representatives. The preliminary material contains additional information about the members' social background, their participation in communal politics and in the activity of voluntary organizations, and also the relationship of their constituency support and their stands taken in Parliament.

Karen Erickson [43] interviewed in 1959-60 all except two of the 200 members of Parliament and a total of 63 other political leaders of the country for a study of *leadership opinion* in Finnish politics. The average length of each interview was one hour and fifty minutes. The questions concerned the activities of the state as well as institutions, groups, and forces which influence political decision-making. By April, 1961, the preliminary findings included: (1) reliance on law is the most important integrating factor in the Finnish political system; (2) party alignments are temporary and provisional; (3) political leadership opinion is moderate rather than conservative or radical; and (4) the political leadership perceives an image of the national interest which cuts through group lines; here the degree of consensus on the nature of the image is undetermined. The respondents were notably interested in the kinds of questions posed by the interview—the proper functions of government, relationship between groups and the government,

---

[42] L. Krusius-Ahrenberg, "Kring intresserepresentationen i vår riksdag" (Concerning the representation of interests in our Parliament), *Ekonomi och kultur* (Helsingfors, 1955).

[43] K. Erickson, "Leadership Opinion in Finnish Politics" (in preparation).

and the position of the individual in the state are not settled issues, although usually subordinated in considerations of quantity and degree in the political arena.

Public administration has barely been studied via the behavioral approach in Finland. One study of administrative decision-making is due to be published shortly.[44] It deals with the work that has been performed by the government's advisory body for science, the commission for the natural and the humanistic sciences. The Ministry of Education each year appropriates public funds for research and other scientific activities, for which purpose the revenue from money lotteries and betting is partly reserved. Its own personnel includes no official with scientific training other than a law degree. Yet, a considerable proportion of these decisions are made in the department without asking for the expert bodies' advice, thus also supporting purposes which the commissions do not consider scientific at all. The study reveals the department's special tendency to make its decisions alone, if the application is made by a representative of the humanistic sciences, while relying more on the expert bodies' advice when the natural sciences are concerned.

In general, the new behavioral approach is inspiring especially the younger generation of Finnish political scientists. But political science is also making simultaneous progress along other, often more traditional, lines. Even here the studies on Finnish political behavior may be contributing by drawing the attention of political scientists to new, untouched areas for investigation.

---

[44] P. Pesonen, *Tiede ja opetusministeriö* (Science and the Ministry of Education), (in preparation).

Elections and Voting Behavior in Poland*

Jerzy J. Wiatr
UNIVERSITY OF KRAKOW

The present paper deals with the main lines of electoral research in Poland after World War II and their contribution to the
empirical analysis of political behavior in that country. It is necessary, however, to discuss some features of the Polish elections which
make them different from elections in many other countries and
which explain the general orientation and character of Polish electoral studies. This will be done in the first section of the paper
while the next two sections will deal respectively with the electoral
studies and main research problems in the field of voting behavior.

POLISH ELECTIONS AFTER WORLD WAR II

The elections in postwar Poland were mainly determined
by the changing internal situation of a country undergoing rapid
socialist transformation in the framework of the proletarian dictatorship, and partly determined by the various factors of international
situation. The electoral system in Poland can hardly be treated as
a stable one, since during three parliamentary elections [1] after the

* This paper was prepared during the writer's stay at the Department of
Sociology, University of Michigan (1960), arranged by the Ford Foundation
and the Institute of International Education. It has benefited from many suggestions of Professor Morris Janowitz, Dr. Warren Miller, and Dr. Donald Stokes.

[1] After the war there were three parliamentary elections in Poland (1947,
1952, and 1957) as well as two elections to so-called "national councils"
(1954 and 1958). National councils are the local government bodies acting
on several levels (voivodships, counties or towns, districts, and villages). Elections to all councils are direct, and they are organized simultaneously.

war there existed three different electoral laws. The changes in the political situation were even more important than the changes of the electoral law.

From the point of view of the meaning and character of these elections we can divide them into three main types: "semi-Civil War elections," "safe elections," and "consent elections."

Semi-Civil War elections of January 19, 1947, were characterized by a very unstable political situation in the country, the existence of the illegal rightist organizations and the guerrillas supported by them, the real elements of the limited civil war which started with the rightist armed opposition to the creation of the people's government. The elections were won by the "Bloc of the Democratic Parties and Organizations" running against the Polish Peasant Party (PSL) and the few smaller parties.[2] The governmental bloc of democratic parties, created in September, 1946, was composed of four parties: Polish Workers' Party, Polish Socialist Party, Peasant Party, and Democratic Party. These parties formed a political alliance during the German occupation and organized the first provisional government on the areas liberated by the Soviet Army in 1944. In 1945 the representatives of the Polish Peasant Party (S. Mikolajczyk and others) joined the government, which was reorganized as the provisional government of the national unity. Nevertheless, during the political campaign preceding the elections of 1947, a factual break occurred between the PSL and the other parties of the government coalition, the PSL being directly or indirectly supported by the rightist underground. Under these conditions, the election of January, 1947, was only a part of the political struggle between the democratic alliance and the rightist forces, as was openly stated by the ruling bloc's speakers on the eve of these elections.[3] It is impossible to analyze them in terms

---

[2] The voting turnout was 89.9 per cent. The bloc of democratic parties obtained, according to official sources, 80.1 per cent of all valid votes, the Polish Peasant Party 10.3 per cent, with the remaining votes being cast for two smaller parties running independently and for independents. Of the 444 parliamentary seats, the government bloc obtained 384, the PSL 28, and other groups 22.

[3] For example, Roman Zambrowski in a pre-election article published in the main theoretical paper of the Polish Workers' Party wrote: "Democracy cannot mean freedom for the enemies of freedom. While powerful centers of political banditry are still alive, while these centers conduct open penetration of legal organizations like the state apparatus, there can be no privileges of democratic freedoms for some persons": partia przed wyborami, *Nowe Drogi,*

of the theory of voting behavior in normal, stable conditions. However, these elections have an important meaning for the understanding of some elements of the Polish revolution.

Safe elections are those elections which are organized in a very stable political situation, in which the power of the ruling forces is not challenged from any side and which are conducted on the basis of the electoral law permitting virtually no choice between the candidates. This characterization of safe elections can be applied to the parliamentary elections of 1952 and—but only to some extent—to the local elections of 1954.

The new electoral law, passed in 1952, abolished the proportional voting existing in the 1947 elections. The country was divided into sixty-seven constituencies, each of them having the number of parliamentary seats proportional to the number of eligible voters. Candidates could be presented only by political parties and various social organizations jointly. This was done by the formation of the National Front composed of three existing political parties,[4] youth unions, trade unions, peasants' organizations, and other mass organizations; the lists of candidates presented by the National Front had the same number of candidates as the number of seats in constituencies. The campaign was a very intense one; various forms of propaganda were employed including the massive individual agitation by the "activists" of the parties and nonparty organizations.[5] The National Front won the election with the overwhelming majority of 99.8 per cent of all votes cast for its candidates and 95.03 per cent voting turnout.

In theory the possibilities of the voters' choice were limited only to two questions: (1) to vote or to abstain, and (2) to vote for the candidates of the National Front or against them (by striking all or some of them off the list).[6] Actually, however, even those

---

No. 1 (1947), p. 25; translation quoted from R. F. Staar, "Elections in Communist Poland," *Midwest Journal of Political Science*, Vol. 2 (1958), pp. 204-05.

[4] There were (and still are) the following parties: Polish United Workers' Party (created in December, 1948, by the fusion of the Polish Workers' Party and the Polish Socialist Party), United Peasant Party (created by the fusion of all existing peasant parties), and Democratic Party.

[5] For the description of this electoral campaign, see Staar, *op. cit.;* and also J. J. Wiatr, *Niektore zagadnienia opinii publicznej w swietle wyborow 1957 i 1958 roku* (Warsaw: PWN, 1959), pp. 67-69 (which contains summaries in Russian and English).

[6] Since a majority of more than 50 per cent of all valid votes was necessary for being elected, this could eventually lead to the by-elections.

possibilities were limited because there existed a strong pressure toward mass electoral participation and toward plain, manifestation-like voting for the proposed candidates. Under these conditions nonvoters were almost exclusively people who really could not vote, and the scant number of negative votes represented only the most defiant part of resistant voters.

Two years after the election of 1952, the first elections to the national councils were organized. Before this date national councils were composed of the designated representatives of the political and social organizations. The question whether these elections could be called "safe elections" is an open one. The elections of December 5, 1954, were held on the basis of laws essentially similar to those of the parliamentary elections of 1952. But there existed at least one quite important difference. The electoral law provided that the elections had to be secret, and the electoral commissions in fact sought to enforce the secrecy of voting. Therefore, the voter was free to strike off as many candidates as he wanted, though no possibility of voting for anybody else existed. Since, in this period, important changes were made in the functioning and organization of the police apparatus (tending toward the increase of the socialist legality), it is reasonable to believe that the voters could feel themselves more free in deciding whether to take part in the voting.

Under these conditions the National Front obtained once more a full electoral victory with 96 per cent voting turnout and 98 per cent voting for the Front's candidates (note the increase of voting turnout and the decrease of the percentage of those voting for the Front's candidates, as compared with the 1952 returns). However, there existed a negative selection of candidates in some (mostly rural) constituencies: 473 candidates failed to get necessary 50 per cent of all valid votes and were not elected. This makes only 0.2 per cent of the total number of candidates, but the political importance of the phenomenon needs not to be underestimated. One can imagine that in the case of a more widespread negative selection, the by-elections could become a nation-scale political event. There is evidence [7] that the government and the leadership of the Polish United Workers' Party paid great attention to these electoral

---

[7] Especially important from this point of view were the report and discussions at the third plenary session of the Central Committee of the PUWP in January, 1955.

results; they influenced some changes in the political life of the country being treated as a proof of the growing possibilities of step-by-step democratization.[8] Moreover, in contrast with the 1952 elections, the elections to the national councils in 1954 had some importance because of the pre-electoral selection of candidates; 27,000 candidates to village councils had been disapproved by the voters' meetings during the campaign (it made 18.4 per cent of all candidates to these councils) and 72 per cent of all these protestations were finally followed by the changes of candidates.[9] It is my opinion that the elections of 1954 were a transitory form from *safe elections* to *consent* ones.

The very concept of *consent elections* as it is being used in this paper demands some discussion and clarification. We distinguish here between competitive elections and consent elections. The concept of competitive elections and the criteria for such elections are proposed in the study by M. Janowitz and D. Marvick.[10] Consent elections, by contrast, are those elections in which the voter does not make any choice between parties competing for power, but: (1) he is personally free to express his acceptance or disapproval of the governmental policy with the assumption that his vote would have some meaning for the future policy; (2) he can influence the selection of the members of representative bodies both in negative and positive way (by voting against some and/or for some other candidates). The consent elections do not decide who will rule the country, but they influence the way in which the country will be ruled.[11]

---

[8] "The political meaning of these elections," reads the report presented by Boleslaw Bierut at the third plenary session of the Central Committee of the PUWP, "is especially important from the point of view of the further strengthening of the liaison between the state and the widest masses of the people, of the further growth of their participation in the rule of the people's state": *Zadania partii w walce o umacnianie codziennej wiezi z masami pracujacymi* (Warsaw, 1955), p. 11.

[9] For fuller discussion of this problem, see Wiatr, *op. cit.*

[10] M. Janowitz and D. Marvick, *Competitive Pressure and Democratic Consent: An Interpretation of the 1952 Presidential Election* (Ann Arbor: University of Michigan Press, 1956), pp. 5-6.

[11] This was frankly declared before the 1957 elections by Wladyslaw Gomulka in a speech at a pre-electoral meeting in Warsaw on January 14, 1957:

"What is at stake in the elections is not whether the people's government and our Party, together with other parties of the Front of national unity, will go on keeping power. A revolutionary party of the working class . . . will never surrender power to reaction and to restorers of capitalism in Poland. We will not surrender it because any other power could be a tragic misfortune for Poland

Two of the Polish postwar elections belong to this type: the parliamentary election of January 20, 1957, and the local elections of February 2, 1958. Both took place after the political changes of 1956, and the former one was greatly influenced by the immediate results of these changes.

In the fall of 1956 the term of the *Sejm* (Parliament) elected in 1952 expired.[12] New elections were to have taken place not later than in January, 1957. In October, 1956, the *Sejm* passed the new electoral law, reflecting to some extent the wave of democratization so strong in the country and in the party itself. Two provisions of the electoral law had a special importance for the character of the third postwar parliamentary elections in Poland. Article 33 declared that "the right of nominating candidates for deputies belongs to political, trade and co-operative organizations . . . and other mass organizations of working people," which right could be exercised by the organizations concerned either jointly or separately (Article 35). Article 39 declared that the number of candidates permissible for each list in a given constituency had to be greater than the number of seats in the constituency, but the total number of additional candidates were not to be higher than two-thirds of the number of seats. Since the number of seats in constituencies varied from three to seven, the lists of candidates could have from five to eleven names. This provision of the electoral law made possible not only the negative selection of candidates but also the positive one.[13]

---

and for the working class, for all toiling people in towns and villages it would be many times worse than the worst people's power. . . . What is at stake is whether the people's power will have the conditions necessary for the realization of its new program. What is at stake is whether we shall be able to go on widening the democratization of our life or whether we shall be forced to restrict it": *Przemowienia, pazdziernik 1956-wrzesien 1957*, p. 193.

[12] For reasons of limitations of space, it is not possible to describe in this paper the political situation in which the electoral campaign and elections of 1957 took place. There exist, however, comprehensive accounts in both English and Polish describing these events: see Z. A. Pelczynski, "Poland, 1957" in D. E. Butler, ed., *Elections Abroad* (London: Macmillan and Co., 1959), pp. 119-66; Staar, *op. cit.*; and Wiatr, *op. cit.*

[13] According to the electoral law votes cast without any deleting were counted as cast for the first candidatee in the order of the list (three, four, etc., corresponding to the number of seats in the constituency). To achieve the consolidation of votes and to avoid the massive deleting of some (especially Communist) candidates, the leaderships of the political parties issued an appeal to voters asking them to cast unaltered ballots. The appeal was followed by the majority of voters. All but one of these candidates (called "seat place"

However, the main innovation of the election of 1957 lay more in the nonformal conditions of the campaign and of the balloting itself than in any particular article of the law. In the political conditions created by the events of 1956, the election became the real political campaign, in which the governmental coalition sought for the popular consent by fair means, by persuasion and not by coercion. The elections were won by the Front, with the total turn-out of 94.14 per cent, voting for the lists of the FNU of 98.05 per cent and the average percentage of valid votes polled by the "seat place" candidates of 89.37. The meaning of the elections was defined by a Western scholar as follows: "A basically Communist government thus sought, and obtained, a genuine mandate to govern the country—at least for the time being." [14]

The elections to the national councils in February, 1958, were based on the electoral law essentially similar to that of the 1957 elections. More candidates than seats were proposed on the lists (but not more than 50 per cent additional candidates). The main difference between the electoral law of 1958 and that of 1957 lay in three articles: (1) Article 39 declared the right of all organizations to nominate their candidates either jointly or separately, but stated, at the same time, that once the decision of proposing the joint lists of candidates had been taken by the national authorities of the organizations concerned, the separate lists proposed by their local authorities would be automatically invalid; (2) Article 67 declared that those candidates are elected who polled the greatest number of valid votes without the necessity of polling the absolute majority of more than 50 per cent; (3) Article 15 introduced in the elections to the national councils special "industrial" constituencies in big factories (voters from these constituencies could not vote in their territorial ones).

The basic difference between the 1958 elections and those in 1957 lies, however, in the political atmosphere and in the popular interest. With the situation being much more stabilized and the elections to local councils less politically important than the parliamentary elections, the level of popular interest was rather low.

---

candidates) were elected. The percentage of votes polled by the "seat place" candidates (ranging from 45.8 per cent in the case of the only non-elected top candidate to 99.4 per cent in the case of Wladyslaw Gomulka) was in these conditions one of the indices of the popular support gained by the Front of National Unity.

[14] Pelczynski, *op. cit.*

The overwhelming majority of voters supported the Front, but the degree of this support was slightly lower than in 1957.[15] This trend seems to support the proposition expressed above, that the elections in Poland after 1954 became the *consent elections* in which the governmental coalition has sought for a democratic consent of the population and in which the extent of this consent has varied from time to time.

THE ELECTORAL STUDIES

No Polish electoral studies were conducted before World War II and in the first decade of the postwar period. On the elections of 1947 and 1952, as well as on the elections to the national councils of 1954, one can find almost no scientific literature at all.[16] Electoral studies were begun when the elections of 1957 were studied in Poland and abroad. The first publication concerned with these elections appeared in Poland; it was based on the "historical" description of the electoral campaign.[17] In 1959 another historical analysis of the 1957 elections was published in the volume *Elections Abroad* edited by David E. Butler.[18] This study shows that the historical method makes it possible to find very interesting evidences and to make meaningful generalizations even when the study is being done by the scholar working independently.

The elections of 1958 were studied in Poland in three main ways: (1) historical analysis of the campaign and the modified ecological analysis of the election results, compared with the similar analysis of the 1957 elections; [19] (2) pre- and post-electoral polls in one of

---

[15] Since the voting was for the councils of several levels, the results split according to the level of councils as follows:

Type of Councils	Total number of eligible voters	% of the voting turnout	% of votes cast for FNU
Voivodships and big cities	18,116,428	85.7	96.9
Counties	12,270,692	85.3	97.6
Towns	5,986,289	88.8	98.4
Districts in the cities	2,693,394	84.4	97.3
Villages	9,550,268	83.9	98.4

[16] For the elections of 1947 and 1952, see Staar, *op. cit.*; for the election of 1954, see Wiatr, *op. cit.*

[17] J. J. Wiatr, "Wybory sejmowe 1957 roku w swietle wstepnej analizy," *Studia Socjologiczno Polityczne*, Vol. 1 (1958). This article was later enlarged and included in the book cited above.

[18] Pelczynski, *op. cit.*

[19] Wiatr, *Niektore zagadnienia opinii publicznej w swietle wyborow 1957 i 1958 roku.*

the big towns (Lodz), dealing mainly with problems of the popular interest in elections and of the impact of the mass media on voters' interests; [20] (3) several monographic studies of the elections to district councils in selected districts of Warsaw prepared by the group of students (as their M.A. theses); these monographs were based on observations of several aspects of the campaign and on the statistical analysis of the results.[21]

Although all existing approaches to the study of electoral behavior are to be applied and modified in the future Polish electoral studies, one of them has a special importance, namely, the *historical approach* as developed in the British electoral studies.[22] There are two main reasons of the special importance of this approach for Polish studies. First, historical analysis of the elections can be done with very limited apparatus; since the sociological centers dealing with these problems are not specialized institutes but university chairs, this consideration is a very important one. Second, the changing role of the elections and the changing social and political structure of the society undergoing socialist transformations indicate this approach as the best way of analyzing electoral behavior and the electoral system in transition. It does not mean, however, that the other approaches may be neglected. Especially, some monographic studies (based both on the sample surveys and on other techniques) can make an important contribution to the understanding of the "grass-roots" politics.

SOME THEORETICAL PROBLEMS IN ELECTORAL RESEARCH

The problems arising in the electoral study vary in relation to the type of elections. In the case of Polish consent elections only some traditional questions of electoral research can be analyzed, because some others do not apply to the actual political

[20] Z. Gostkowski, "Popular Interest in the Municipal Election in Lodz, Poland," *Public Opinion Quarterly*, Vol. 23 (1959), pp. 371-81. This article is also printed in French in *Sondages*, Vol. 1 (1959), pp. 13-25.

[21] One of these monographs was published: S. Bereza, "Wybory do Dzielnicowej Rady Narodowej Warszawa Ochota w roku 1958," *Studia Socjologiczno Polityczne*, Vol. 2 (1959), pp. 159-94; this article contains summaries in Russian and English.

[22] For the presentation of the theoretical framework of this method, see D. E. Butler, *The British General Election of 1951* (London: Macmillan and Co., 1952); and Butler, "Voting Behavior and Its Study in Britain," *British Journal of Sociology*, Vol. 6 (1955), pp. 93-103.

and electoral system. It would, for example, hardly be possible to find, by the electoral studies, how the electorate is divided in its attitudes and opinions on problems of the national preferences. Moreover, since the electoral system is still a very fluid one, it is practically impossible to discover any continuous trends in electoral behavior of various groups or strata. (This, however, does not mean that no such trends exist; their discovery will be possible in the future, provided there is no major change in the electoral system.)

There are, it seems to me, three main questions arising when we try to analyze the consent elections in Poland:

(1) What is the actual political acceptance of the governmental policy, as expressed by the voting? The number of votes cast for the Front of National Unity is only one index of this acceptance, because some voters express their disapproval in ways other than voting against the FNU—either by electoral absenteeism or by the selection of candidates directed against the Front, mainly against the candidates belonging to the Polish United Workers' Party.

(2) How much popular interest is there in the elections? How is it created, and what factors influence its fluctuations?

(3) What is the meaning of the electoral campaign, and what is the meaning of the elections themselves? What is their role in the political life of the country?

Measurement of the Political Acceptance of the Governmental Policy as Expressed by the Electoral Results

The extent to which the voter expresses his acceptance or disapproval of the governmental policy can vary, and the election gives him some opportunity to express his attitudes toward this policy.

From the standpoint that elections reflect a degree of voter acceptance of governmental policy, all eligible voters may be grouped into the following categories:

(1) *nonvoters* (a part of them, perhaps, abstained from voting for some political reasons);

(2) *voters casting invalid votes* (in some cases invalidation is caused by writing slogans on the ballot and then could be related to the political attitudes; in others, it is caused by confusion—for example, by writing the names of persons who are not candidates);

(3) *voters voting against the lists of the FNU* (according to the electoral law, those voters who deleted all candidates of the FNU);

(4) *voters voting for the lists of the FNU* (for at least one candidate from the list of the FNU); these voters may be divided into the following subgroups:

(a) those who voted for the lists of the FNU but deleted some "seat place" candidates, especially candidates belonging to the Polish United Workers' Party;

(b) those who voted for the lists of the FNU, deleting some "seat place" candidates but not especially candidates belonging to the PUWP;

(c) those who voted for the lists of the FNU without deleting any of the "seat place" candidates; these voters followed the appeal of the parties' leaderships and may be treated as the strongest followers of the governmental coalition.

On the basis of the electoral results it is impossible to calculate the percentage of the voters belonging to the categories (a), (b), and (c) respectively, but the average percentage of votes polled by the "seat place" candidates indicates the extent to which the voters selected among these candidates and the direction of the selection.

In the statistical analysis of the results of the 1957 and 1958 elections we introduced four main *indices of the political acceptance.* Under the conditions prevailing in Poland, these indices are:

(1) *the index of the electoral participation* (I_1) calculated as the ratio of the number of actual voters to the number of all eligible voters;

(2) *the index of the support for the lists of the FNU* (I_2) calculated as the ratio of all votes cast for the lists of the FNU (with or without deleting) to all valid votes.

(3) *the index of the extent of the selection of the "seat place" candidates* (I_3) calculated as the average percentage of votes polled by the "seat place" candidates.

(4) *the index of the direction of the selection of the "seat place" candidates* (I_4) calculated as the average percentage of votes polled by the "seat place" candidates belonging to the various political groupings (three political parties and nonparty candidates). Since the extent to which the selection was directed against the Communist candidates was the most important indication of the political

acceptance, the average percentage of votes polled by the "seat place" candidates—members of the PUWP—was treated as the index of the direction of the selection of candidates.

The indices of the political acceptance have been calculated for the whole provinces (voivodships), as they are basically social units; alas, the differences inside the voivodships between various subregions and constituencies were not studied sufficiently. In the elections of 1957 the average indices of political acceptance varied in the voivodships as follows:

I_1 (index of the electoral participation) varied from 96.2 per cent (Koszalin voivodship in the northwest) to 91.7 per cent (Lublin voivodship in the east). The differences in the electoral participation between the voivodships were not very great, with, generally speaking, higher turnout in the recovered territories (western and northern) than in the central ones and higher in the more urbanized than in the predominantly rural ones.

I_2 (index of the support for the lists of the FNU) varied from 99.6 per cent (Warsaw city) to 90.3 per cent (Opole voivodship in the southwest). However, the case of the Opole voivodship can hardly be treated as a typical one, because in the Bialystok voivodship, which was second to it, this percentage was 97. If the Opole voivodship is excluded, all differences in index 2 between the voivodships are only in the limits of 2.3 per cent. Their pattern is basically similar to that of index 1.

I_3 (index of the extent of the selection of candidates) varied from 96 per cent (Warsaw city) to 83.4 per cent (Lodz voivodship). This index shows important differences between the voivodships. The appeal for unaltered ballots was strongly followed in the western territories (but also in Opole and the northern voivodship Olsztyn, belonging also to the recovered territories) and in two city-voivodships (Warsaw and Lodz). The selection was stronger in the predominantly rural provinces of central and eastern Poland.

I_4 (index of the direction of the selection of candidates) from 95.6 per cent (Warsaw city) to 80.2 per cent (Lodz voivodship). In almost all voivodships the candidates belonging to the PUWP polled the lowest percentage of votes, but there existed significant differences between the voivodships in the extent of this phenomenon. The negative selection of these candidates was lower in the Western voivodships and big cities than in the central-eastern and rural areas. The regional differences had greater influence than the degree of urbanization. The Opole and Olsztyn voivodships voted less favorably than other viovodships of the recovered territories.

The negative selection directed against the members of the PUWP was reflected in the national-scale average percentages of votes polled by "seat place" candidates according to their partisan affiliation as follows: members of the PUWP—87.9 per cent; members of the Peasant party—89.2 per cent; members of the Democratic Party—90.8 per cent; nonparty candidates—94.3 per cent. It can be explained by two factors: (1) the strongest followers of the PUWP and also of the other parties of the coalition voted without any deleting; their votes were not cast especially for members of their own parties; (2) the negative selection done by the "resistant" voters was directed mainly against the members of the strongest and most important party and what reflected the position of this party in the political system of the country.

More significant differences in voting can be discovered on the basis of the *cumulative index of political acceptance*, calculated as the total of the average percentage variations of indices 1, 2, 3, 4, taken separately. This index shows the continuum of the political acceptation as expressed by the electoral results in the voivodships (Table 1).

The main hypotheses interpreting these indices are: (1) with the high absolute level of political acceptance expressed by the indices 1-4, the difference between western and other territories and between more urban and more rural shows that the support for the FNU was especially strong among two groups of population: inhabitants of western (recovered) territories and the population of big cities; (2) when these two factors worked in the opposite direction, the influence of the regional differences was stronger than that of the urban-rural pattern of voting; (3) in one voivodship (Opole) a group of voters of strong antigovernmental attitudes changed the general pattern of voting, making this province an exception to the trends dominant in the region to which it belongs. The results of 1958 elections seem to support these hypotheses, although the absolute differences of voting were smaller in these elections than in 1957.

The main theoretical question in the measurement of the electoral consent seems to be: can we or can we not say whether the consent was high or low? My indices lead only to the construction

TABLE 1. POLITICAL ACCEPTANCE AS MEASURED FOR THE VOIVODSHIPS BY THE CUMULATIVE
INDEX OF POLITICAL ACCEPTANCE; ELECTIONS OF 1957

| Voivodship | Cumulative Index | The direction of the variation of indices 1, 2, 3, 4: | | | |
		I_1	I_2	I_3	I_4
Warsaw city	+17.12	+	+	+	+
Szczecin	+13.75	+	+	+	+
Katowice	+11.35	+	−	+	+
Koszalin	+10.14	+	+	+	+
Gdansk	+ 7.93	+	+	+	+
Lodz-city	+ 7.73	+	+	+	+
Zielonogora	+ 7.01	+	+	+	+
Wroclaw	+ 6.78	+	+	+	+
Warsaw	+ 2.75	−	−	+	+
Bydgoszcz	+ 1.18	+	+	+	−
Poznan	− 0.75	+	−	−	−
Kielce	− 3.15	−	+	−	−
Olsztyn	− 3.54	+	−	−	−
Rzeszow	− 5.32	+	+	−	−
Lublin	− 7.31	−	−	−	−
Bialystok	− 7.36	+	−	−	−
Krakow	−11.50	−	+	−	−
Lodz	−15.49	−	−	−	−
Opole	−21.05	−	−	−	−

of the continuum of voivodships (the same could be done for constituencies). In the case of the 1957 election, five groups of voivodships could be distinguished according to the cumulative indices
for these voivodships (the horizontal lines in Table 1). But the
question of the measurement of the absolute level of acceptance
still seems to be open. Only after several elections shall we be able
to discover the critical difference of acceptance—the limits in which
the consent is actually wavering. Then some criteria for the evaluation of electoral consent in terms of measurable indices may be
elaborated.

Measurement of the Popular Interest in the Elections

The measurement of popular interest in the elections has
a special importance in the case of the consent elections, which are,

more or less, a kind of referendum. The electoral turnout is one, but not the only one, of the indices of this interest. As a matter of fact, the conclusions about the relation between electoral participation and interest in the elections seem to be inconsistent. Only very weak correlation existed between this participation and the popular interest as measured by the course of the verification of the electors' lists in various voivodships.[23] The monographic analysis showed some correlations between the frequency of voting and the participation in pre-electoral meetings.[24] The results of the pre- and post-electoral pollings in Lodz show that the popular interest in the elections was much lower than the actual voting turnout.

These considerations lead to the conclusion that only a part of voters vote because of any real interest in the voting. This issue is open to interpretations, but only a small percentage of them are as yet verifiable by our electoral studies.

The results of the electoral polls in Lodz explain, at least to some extent, the causes of the lack of popular interest in the 1958 elections. The majority of respondents was very critical toward the records of the former national councils in the city, especially in various fields of social and community administration. Two kinds of negativism were distinguished: active negativism and passive negativism. The former leads to the relatively strong interest in the elections, because the voters still hope that something can be improved. The latter is expressed by the lack of any interest in elections. In the population of Lodz, 1958, the passive negativism was much stronger than the active one.[25]

It is impossible to make any generalizations concerning the trends of popular interest in Polish elections. High interest in the 1957 elections could be explained either by the extraordinary political situation in which the elections took place or by the greater interest of voters in the parliamentary elections as compared with the interest of local ones; perhaps, both factors worked together. There is, however, some evidence of the strong correlation between

---

[23] Wiatr, *Niektore zagadnienia opinii publicznej w swietle wyborow 1957 i 1958 roku*, pp. 148-51.

[24] Bereza, *op. cit.*, pp. 180-87. In this study Bereza employed the indices of selection to discover that for the selecting voters nonpolitical factors were of the greatest importance (e.g., whether they knew the candidate or not, and the place on the list occupied by the candidate).

[25] Gostkowski, *op. cit.*, pp. 378-79.

the lack of interest in elections and the insufficient information about candidates and issues.[26]

The Course and Meaning of Electoral Campaigns

A historical analysis of electoral campaigns is especially important in the case of elections which, as in Poland, do not represent any well-stabilized pattern of political behavior but are in the stage of continuous transformations both of their type and of their meaning. We do not know very much about the importance of the campaign in the formation of voters' opinions and decisions. The historical analysis of the 1957 elections seems to lead to the conclusion that in these elections the entire decision of the voters was formed during the campaign itself, mainly in its final stage. Gostkowski supposes that in the 1958 elections, the interest in voting was created only by the campaign.[27] Further studies of the electoral campaign will make generalizations concerning the meaning of the campaigns in the Polish elections more explicit.

Other aspects of the historical analysis of the elections are important for the understanding of the Polish electoral system as well as of Polish voting behavior. One of the main limitations of our studies stems from the lack of any study of the nominating process. This process is an extremely meaningful part of the elections, because on this level the first selection of candidates is made from a large number of names suggested by various organizations and by voters' meetings. Who makes the final decision? How? How are the vested interests expressed in the nominating process? How is the political compromise achieved? These and other questions could be answered mainly by the historical analysis of the nominating process in several elections.[28]

Whether and in what ways the electoral studies can contribute to the theory of the socialist democracy is an open question. It is difficult, or perhaps even impossible, to make any generalizations on the similarities or dissimilarities of voting behavior in the socialist political system and in the systems of a multi-party democracy.

---

[26] *Ibid.;* Bereza, *op. cit.;* Wiatr, *Niektore zagadnienia opinii publicznej w swietle wyborow 1957 i 1958 roku.*

[27] Gostkowski, *op. cit.*, p. 381.

[28] Pelczynski, *op. cit.*, pp. 141-48, makes some interesting remarks about the nominating process in the 1957 elections, but his analysis is also limited only to secondary sources, mainly information from the press.

Some comparisons, however, are possible in the functioning of the electoral system and in the role of some elements of this system.

The most important problem in the theoretical discussion of the implications of the empirical electoral studies seems to be: how do the elections express the social and political "articulations" of the society, the balance of various groups and interests, and how do they enable those groups to influence the political decision-making process?

Even the most homogeneous society is composed of some social groups of differing interests. These interests are more or less openly expressed in the political behavior of the social groups. The analysis of the political behavior, and especially the analysis of the voting behavior, tends to discover some trends in the interdependence between the social structure and the political behavior. However, there is also another problem. How far can the tendencies existing in the society express themselves in the recognized and politically relevant forms? The "articulation" of the society is the process of transformation of social groupings into politically oriented forces (but not necessarily political parties, nor even pressure groups). The elections belong to the category of political institutions which enable the "articulated" social and political groups to participate in ruling the country.

By the nature of the consent elections this is not done through any competition of rival political parties or coalitions seeking political power. When the existing power is not at stake in the election, other forms of voters' influence on the decision-makers are elaborated. The consent elections give the voters an opportunity to criticize the governmental policy by lowering the electoral acceptance of this policy. This is a new phenomenon in the functioning of the proletarian dictatorship, and it seems to have some important consequences. The role of popular consent, expressed by elections, in the functioning of this political system is one of the major problems of the theory of socialist democracy. The empirical study of elections and voting behavior could contribute to the evaluation of this element of the political system of socialist society. This could be interesting from the point of view of political theory and also useful for the development of practical policy.